Same-Sex Marriage in Latin America

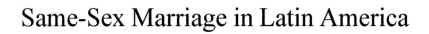

Same-Sex Marriage in Latin America

Promise and Resistance

Edited by Jason Pierceson, Adriana Piatti-Crocker,
and Shawn Schulenberg

LEXINGTON BOOKS
Lanham • Boulder • New York • Toronto • Plymouth, UK

Published by Lexington Books
A wholly owned subsidary of The Rowman & Littlefield Publishing Group, Inc.
4501 Forbes Boulevard, Suite 200, Lanham, Maryland 20706
www.rowman.com

10 Thornbury Road, Plymouth PL6 7PP, United Kingdom

British Library Cataloguing in Publication Information Available

Library of Congress Cataloging-in-Publication Data

Same-sex marriage in Latin America : promise and resistance / edited by Jason Pierceson, Adriana
Piatti-Crocker, and Shawn Schulenberg.
p. cm.
Includes index.
ISBN 978-0-7391-6702-1 (cloth : alk. paper) — ISBN 978-0-7391-6703-8 (pbk. : alk. paper) —
ISBN 978-0-7391-6704-5 (electronic)
1. Same-sex marriage—Law and legislation—Latin America. 2. Civil unions—Law and legislation—
Latin America. I. Pierceson, Jason, 1972– II. Piatti-Crocker, Adriana, 1963– III. Schulenberg,
Shawn, 1979–
KG147.S26 2013
346.801'68—dc23
2012041675

☉™ The paper used in this publication meets the minimum requirements of American
National Standard for Information Sciences Permanence of Paper for Printed Library
Materials, ANSI/NISO Z39.48-1992.

Printed in the United States of America

Contents

Preface

This book is a follow-up volume to our book *Same-Sex Marriage in the Americas: Policy Innovation for Same-Sex Relationships*, published by Lexington Books in 2010. That book chronicled and analyzed developments surrounding the movements for relationship equality in South America, North America, Central America, and the Caribbean. After the book's publication, we realized that the story of the rise of relationship equality policies in Latin America, and resistance to them, continued to rapidly evolve. Consequently, we conceived of a volume focused exclusively on Latin America, particularly given the generally surprising and unexpected creation of same-sex policies. The first section of the book explores general political science themes relating to these developments, while the second section examines development in individual countries or regions.

Chapter one, by Adriana Piatti-Crocker, examines the diffusion of same-sex policy innovations in Latin America. It analyzes the spread of same-sex policies throughout the region at both national and sub-national levels and employs both external and domestic factors to interpret diffusion. Starting in the city of Buenos Aires a decade ago, other Latin American countries, including Brazil, Colombia, Ecuador, Mexico (at sub-national levels) and Uruguay, have approved civil unions, same-sex marriage, or other similar policies for same-sex couples. These policies have been introduced either by constitutional reforms, new legislation, or judicial decisions. Diffusion of policy for same-sex couples in the region was modeled after Western European legislation and, more particularly, the Spanish same-sex marriage law, shaped by international norms and organizations, and the adoption of same-sex friendly policies in other countries within the region. Internally, several similar patterns of policy adoption have been experienced in Latin America, including the significant influence of grassroots organizations, judicial decisions, and the key role of political leaders, such as members in the executive branch and influential legislators.

Chapter two, by Shawn Schulenberg, analyzes the impact of the Latin American left in policies that affect LGBT peoples in Latin America, and it includes both individual country-cases and general common patterns in the region to explore this issue. According to the author, whereas LGBT peoples had trouble finding political supporters in any Latin American country just ten years ago, since then, there have been some dramatic and positive changes in how the left treats issues of sexuality, particularly in countries led by the moderate left. In addition, Schulenberg argues that while countries led by right-wing leaders have seen less progress for gay rights, support for same-sex rights has not emerged along partisan lines in Latin America. LGBT groups in Latin America have found allies among elites in political parties of both left and right ideologies. Overall, when LGBT groups use their connections with political parties and the party infrastructures themselves, important advancements for LGBT rights have been made in the region.

Chapter three, by Germán Lodola and Margarita Corral, explores public opinion concerning same-sex marriage in the Americas. The authors analyze the levels of support for same-sex marriage employing both individual and national-level determinants, and using the 2010 round of the American Public Opinion Project (LAPOP) survey to examine these issues. The findings lead the authors to conclude that whereas citizens in the Latin American and Caribbean region, on average, express relatively low levels of support for same-sex marriage, there is significant cross-national variation in the region. At the individual-level of analysis, strong religious values and more conservative ideologies have a significant negative impact on individual support for same-sex marriage, while higher levels of support are found among wealthier people, individuals living in larger cities, and women. At national-levels, both economic development and education increase support for same-sex rights.

Chapter four, by Jason Pierceson, analyzes patterns of judicialization of LBGT rights and equality in the Americas. According to the author, judicialization of politics (court decisions on policy traditionally reserved to the legislative and executive branches of government), has occurred in many North and South American countries. However, the record of judicialization in the Americas has not been clear and uniform, particularly in matters concerning same-sex relationships. Indeed, while many Latin American countries may be moving away from judicial deference and restraint, which has traditionally characterized civil law regimes, policy advances on same-sex relationships in most countries in the region—with the exception of Brazil, Colombia, and recently Mexico—have been led by non-judicial actors, including legislatures, parties, interest groups, and executives. This chapter explores whether courts may be unwilling to act more aggressively because of cultural biases in some jurisdictions.

Chapter five, also by Schulenberg, examines the progress (or lack thereof) of LGBT issues in the understudied region of Central America. The chapter analyzes the slow development in the advancement of policies for same-sex couples in Central America, and more specifically in Panama, and compares and contrasts these policies to other parts of the Americas. For this research, the author includes approaches on social movements and public policy and finds that the central issue for the lack of progress on same-sex policies in Panama is the nascent and weak nature of LGBT groups in the country. The author claims that LGBT groups are ill-equipped to challenge powerful cultural biases in the region, owing to lack of experience and resources at their disposal. LGBT groups should improve their organizational capacity and build stronger ties with international allies. These two strategies may allow the LGBT movement to win rights, including the legal recognition of same-sex relationships in the region.

Chapter six, by Diego Sempol, examines the adoption of the 2007 Civil Partnership Law, *Unión Concubinaria*, in Uruguay for both same-sex and opposite-sex couples, the first country in Latin America to adopt this type of legislation nationwide. The adoption of this law was due to two major factors: the electoral victory of the progressive *Frente Amplio* Party (FA) in the country's national legislature, and the significant role of Uruguay's LGBTQ movement in favor of the law. The final wording of the law and its legislative process demanded negotiations among various sectors of the FA party and LGBTQ organizations and fell short of original LGBTQ expectations. In its final version, Uruguay's Civil Partnership Law excludes adoption rights for same-sex couples, though a new 2009 law granted these rights, and requires five years of cohabitation for the union to be legally recognized.

Chapter seven, by Daniel Bonilla, explores constitutional court decisions on the legal status and rights of same-sex couples in Colombia. Colombia's Constitutional Court has made several significant decisions on sexual minority rights and provided a complex set of arguments to evaluate what legal and political status should be granted to members of the LGBT community in a liberal democracy like Colombia. Through jurisprudence on same-sex relationships, the chapter analyzes the constitutional court decisions intended to eliminate discrimination against the LGBT community in Colombia. These rulings recognized the legal existence of same-sex couples for the first time in the history of the country and gave them an important set of legal and constitutional rights and obligations. These rights and obligations cover topics as varied as human dignity, equality, health, pensions, and the nationality of members of same-sex couples.

Chapter eight, by Maria Gracia Andía, explores the legal activism of the LGBT movement in Argentina leading eventually to the adoption of same-sex marriage legislation. The chapter analyzes the factors that led the LGBT movement to choose the courts as a political strategy; discusses the influential role of the country's courts on the National Congress as well as on media coverage; and explores whether social mobilization—or the support structure—had an influential role on policy innovation and adoption. LGBT groups are prominent examples of how grassroots organizations in Latin America have been able to press for change and attain some significant political achievements over the past decade or so. Normative and societal developments, as well as other variables, have contributed to Latin American LGBT groups' ability to accomplish several political achievements in the 2000s. The Argentine Egalitarian Marriage Law of 2010 is a major development and an example of this trend.

Chapter nine, by Genaro Lozano, examines the adoption of civil unions in Coahuila State and both civil unions and same-sex marriage in Mexico City, and compares and contrasts the factors producing similar outcomes in both jurisdictions. The chapter explores how Mexican LGBT activists were able to advance the legal recognition of same-sex couples in Mexico City first in the form of civil unions through formal institutions and then through a same-sex marriage law with full parenting rights in 2009. It also analyzes the adoption of a civil union law in the Northern State of Cohauila, despite its very weak LGBT movement. The adoption of policy-innovations in Mexico was due to several social, economic, and political changes in the country within the past two decades. More particularly, these policy innovations were the result of Mexico's democratization process, where LGBT issues traditionally discussed within the "small inner circle of debate" (LGBT and feminist activists) reached a "larger outside circle" (formal and traditional political actors, such as presidential candidates, other political leaders, political parties, and mass media, among other actors).

We would like to thank the editors at Lexington Books: Joseph Parry for seeing promise in this project, and Lenore Lautigar and Alison Northridge for their patience and support throughout the process. We also would like to thank Nathan Franklin for assistance in editing the manuscript. Chapter three is reprinted with permission from *Americas Quarterly* and Vanderbilt University's Latin American Public Opinion Project.

Part I

Themes

ONE

Diffusion of Same-Sex Policies in Latin America

Adriana Piatti-Crocker

Despite a political culture traditionally characterized by machismo and religious conservatism, within the last three decades and since the return of democracy to Latin America, the region has made major progress in the adoption of new social legislation. As a result, and despite strong opposition, many Latin American countries have adopted some of the world's most extensive policies for same-sex couples, including civil unions and same-sex marriage laws at national and sub-national levels. These policies are intended to remedy persistent inequalities in civil law for same-sex couples in the region.

Buenos Aires, the capital city of Argentina, was the first locality in Latin America to adopt a civil union law in 2002, and in 2010, Argentina was the first country in the region and one of only ten countries in the world to adopt a national level same-sex marriage law. Within the last decade, many other Latin American countries including Brazil, Colombia, Ecuador, Mexico (at sub-national levels) and Uruguay have approved civil unions, same-sex marriage or other similar policies for same-sex couples, and they have been introduced either by constitutional reforms, new legislation, or judicial decisions. These recent phenomena may be interpreted as a process of regional diffusion, shaped by both external and internal developments. In the first case, the role of Western European models and, more particularly, that of Spain, the influence of international norms and organizations, and the adoption of same-sex friendly policies in other countries within the region, helped shape domestic policies. Internally, several similar patterns of policy adoption

3

have been experienced in Latin America, including the significant influence of grassroots organizations, judicial decisions, and the key role of political leaders, including members in the executive branch and influential legislators. Finally, the processes leading to the adoption of same-sex union policies and particularly same-sex marriage laws have been relatively cumbersome, due to the strong opposition of the Catholic Church, other religious groups, and conservative forces.

This chapter will study the diffusion of same-sex policy innovations in Latin America. It will examine the spread of same-sex policies throughout the region at both national and sub-national levels, and will employ an integrative methodology, including both external and domestic factors to interpret diffusion. Overall, this chapter provides fresh insights concerning the internal and external dimensions of policy diffusion and illustrates how the local and the global interact in politically significant ways.[1]

DIFFUSION OF SAME-SEX POLICIES IN LATIN AMERICA

Most of the scholarship concerned with the study of diffusion has applied the approach to interpret the evolution of past events in a time-space context. Yet, the purpose of explaining diffusion is not merely to introduce a historically descriptive analysis, but also to analyze some aspects of the process by which new phenomena are communicated. A number of scholars identify this process as "socialization."[2]

In broad terms, diffusion "refers to the process by which institutions, practices, behaviors, or norms are transmitted between individuals and/ or between social systems."[3] The process "involves a set of assumptions about the nature of systems, how they interact, and how the environmental context will affect the units studied."[4] However, the nature, forms, and consequences of the diffusion of policy and behavior are complex subjects because they can be studied at several levels of analysis and may refer to distinctive processes. In all cases, Emanuel Adler observes that "there is a dynamic relationship between historical and structural forces that helps explain the nature of the diffusion of values." Adler identifies this dynamic process as "cognitive evolution." The author suggests that because "our ideas, beliefs, and behaviors are learned from other people," collective learning will be closely related to the ability of groups to convey their experiences to other groups.[5] Yet, a given institutional framework will help shape how these beliefs are translated into action, how they are implemented, and what makes some ideas possible or impossible to enforce. Adler claims that just as science progresses, social processes also evolve through what he calls an "inter-subjective consensus," or the unconscious agreement between relevant actors within a specific institutional framework.

Everett Rogers suggests that an innovation can be communicated in a number of ways; however, socialization plays a critical role in facilitating its diffusion. In Rogers' view, socialization arises "within a web of places, people, physical, and communications links in which information, people, and goods flow play a key role in the diffusion of policy innovation."[6] Thus, through socialization, members of a diffusion network are exposed to new ideas or policies. Michael Mintrom and Sara Vergari claim that communication channels, including interpersonal exchanges or organizational networks increase significantly the chances of diffusion.[7] In other words, diffusion may be contingent to the "social networks" or the socialization stage of the process and the extent to which such networks have the capacity to influence others to adopt innovations. Harvey Starr posits that one of the key factors in the study of innovation-diffusion is "where the stimulus for emulation comes from, or the existence of a model or a prototype." The prototype "exhibits certain behavior and the observer," he adds, "matches that behavior."[8] John Kingdon calls this process the "bandwagon effect," by which people or groups of people first "speak of a growing realization, an increasing feeling, a lot of talk in the air, and coming to a conclusion," and then, after a certain degree of general acceptance there seems to be what Kingdon refers to as the "the take-off point," when many people begin to discuss the proposal or idea.[9]

This consensus seems to be connected also to new frameworks on regionalism.[10] New literature on regionalism no longer conceptualizes regions in terms of mere geographical contiguity, but rather in terms of purposeful social, political, cultural, and economic interaction among states.[11] Theorists on regionalism argue that regional interactions can lead to the creation of a regional political culture and a regional "identity" that may have important political implications.[12] This regional context with frequent interactions of NGOs and intergovernmental agencies in Latin America has helped shape the process of diffusion of policy for same-sex couples both sub-nationally and cross-nationally, as it will be explained in the next subsection.

EXTERNAL DETERMINANTS: THE EUROPEAN MODEL

Legislation concerning registered partnerships or civil unions and same-sex marriage in Latin America was rooted primarily on Western European models. Activists and policy-makers viewed European same-sex friendly legislation and the discourse that accompanied its support as an important source of legislative innovations in Latin America.

In 1989, Denmark became the first country to institute legislation granting rights to registered same-sex partners with similar legal effects to those of marriage. However, the law originally restricted the rights of couples to adopt children jointly, but since 2009 the law on same-sex partnerships was modified to allow also adoption. [13] In 1996, other Northern European countries, including Norway, Sweden, and Iceland, enacted similar legislation and Finland introduced legislation for same-sex couples six years later. [14]

In 1999, France adopted the Civil Compact of Solidarity, *Pact Civile de Solidarité*, (PACS) or the equivalent to civil unions for both same-sex and opposite-sex partnerships. France's civil unions "confer most of the tax benefits and legal protections of marriage" and has become a popular mechanism not only for same-sex couples, but has been favored over marriage also by opposite-sex couples. Yet, marriage is still restricted to opposite-sex couples in France. [15] The adoption of a civil union law in Buenos Aires and other sub-national and local districts in Argentina and elsewhere in Latin America reflect this Western European trend. Marcelo Suntheim, a leading activist in Argentina, claimed that "without the European precedents, civil unions would have not likely gained support in Argentina." [16]

Fewer countries have adopted same-sex marriage laws due to the strong opposition of religious and conservative forces, and most same-sex marriage policies have been adopted in Western Europe, though with recent same-sex marriage laws enforced in South Africa, Canada, and some Latin American countries, this regional trend is expanding to other areas of the world.

The Netherlands became the first country to grant full civil marriage rights to same-sex couples in 2001. The bill was introduced in 1997 because Christian Democrats, who had positioned themselves against same-sex marriage, were not part of the country's ruling coalition. In September 2000, the final draft of the legislation was debated in parliament and passed a year later. [17] Belgium was the second country in the world to legally recognize same-sex marriages in 2003. The policy was originally restricted to nationals or to foreign same-sex couples, only if their country of origin also allowed these unions. Legislation enacted in October 2004, however, allows any couple to marry in Belgium, if at least one of the spouses has lived in the country for a minimum of three months. [18]

Expanding on the 1996 same-sex partnership law, Iceland introduced a "single-marriage act" in 2009, which is now inclusive of both opposite-sex and same-sex couples. The law was sponsored by the coalition platform of the Social Democratic Alliance and Left-Green Movement. The bill received overwhelming support and was made effective in 2010. More significantly, Icelandic Prime Minister Johanna Sigurdardottir—the world's first openly-lesbian head of government—married her female partner under Iceland's new marriage equality law. [19]

Spain adopted a same-sex marriage law in June 2005 under the auspices of the Socialist Party (PSOE), despite opposition by the Roman

Catholic Church and national bureaucracies. The bill submitted by the government in 2004 was disputed by the General Council of the Judiciary (GCJ), an organization that, among other functions, studies the constitutionality of bills introduced by the government. In its findings, the GCJ claimed that marriage between same-sex couples was not required by the Spanish Constitution and that civil unions should be sufficient to remedy discrimination for same-sex couples. Despite these arguments, the government introduced a same-sex marriage proposal to congress, which required amending article forty-four of the Spanish civil code by which only partners of different sex were allowed to marry. The bill that passed in the chamber of deputies was rejected in the senate, but deputies were able to override the senate's opposition and the bill became law. Before the final vote, Prime Minister José Luis Rodríguez Zapatero of the PSOE claimed, "We are expanding the opportunities for happiness of our neighbors, our colleagues, our friends and our relatives. At the same time, we are building a more decent society."[20] Finally, Portugal became the sixth country in Europe to legalize same-sex marriage in 2010. Sponsored by the government of Prime Minister José Sócrates, the bill passed in the Assembly of the Republic early in 2010 and was declared legally valid by the Portuguese Constitutional Court a few months later.[21]

Latin America gay and lesbian NGOs, governmental agencies, and legislators sponsoring civil unions and same-sex marriage legislation have modeled their bills after Western European policies. For example, before submitting a same-sex marriage bill in the Argentine legislature activists held several informal meetings with members of the Spanish PSOE.[22] In addition, Uruguayan and Paraguayan lesbian and gay activists have sponsored same-sex marriage legislation using the same wording and discourse of the Spanish precedent and the Argentine law of 2010.

INTERNATIONAL NORMS AND ORGANIZATIONS

International norms and organizations have been a major legal source of human rights in Latin America. Based on the principles of equality before the law and non-discrimination, both the United Nations through its agreements, declarations, and specialized organizations and the Organization of American States—mainly through its Inter-American Commission of Human Rights—have served as the normative basis for grassroots organizations sponsoring policy innovations for same-sex couples.

The Universal Declaration of Human Rights, adopted by the UN General Assembly in 1948, is one of the most widespread examples of human rights protection. Although not a legally enforceable instrument as such, questions arise as to whether the Declaration had subsequently become binding either by way of custom or by general principles of law, or indeed by virtue of interpretation of the UN Charter itself and by its subsequent practices.[23] In addition, the Universal Declaration of Human Rights has been influential in the development of human rights found in the constitutions of many countries. The Declaration's thirty articles cover a wide variety of rights, but pertinent to this case are article one, which affirms that "all human beings are born free and equal in dignity and rights"; article two, which claims that every person is "entitled to the rights and freedoms set forth in the Declaration without distinction of any kind, including sex"; and article sixteen, which proclaims the principle of "equality before the law."[24]

Within the UN system, the UN Human Rights Council has made some attempts in promoting LGBT rights, because, according to Hillary Clinton, the UN system recognizes that "everyone is entitled to all rights and freedoms without distinction of any kind." But this position has not been echoed uniformly.[25] Other mechanisms, such as the Universal Periodic Review, was established by the UNHRC to review every four years the human rights situation in member states. Argentina was among the countries surveyed in the first round of reviews, and CHA (*Comunidad Homosexual Argentina*) participated actively in this process, together with the International Association of Lesbians and Gays (ILGA) and ARC International. The evaluation was based on a formal report, prepared by the government of each country to the High Commissioner for Human Rights of the UN. CHA submitted two reports along with the Argentine Secretariat for Human Rights, the United Nations Program for Development (UNDP) and the United Nations High Commissioner Organization for Human Rights (UNHCHR) aimed at strengthening the promotion of rights and freedoms for gays and lesbians in Argentina. In addition, CHA along with other international NGOs conducted a survey among Argentine political leaders. One of the questions in the survey dealt with civil unions and same-sex marriage and the respondents' role in support of the national bills.[26]

Progressive legal innovations in Latin America should be complemented with the expanding role and legitimacy of the Inter-American Human Rights System. The American Convention of Human Rights is one of the major regional human rights agreements. The Convention also known as the Pact of San José of Costa Rica was first signed in 1969 and came into force in 1978. The agreement includes a chapter on individual civil and political rights. More particularly, article twenty-four states that "all persons are equal before the law. Consequently, they are entitled, without discrimination, to equal protection of the law."[27] As it will be discussed in the next subsection, the 1948 Declaration, the Pact of San José and other human rights treaties have been granted constitutional ranking in many Latin American countries since the wave of democratization in the region, and domestic judicial decisions in favor of same-sex marriage have been justified on these accounts.

The relationship between domestic constitutional law and international human rights law has been influenced by the expanding inter-American system of human rights. Nearly all Latin American countries in the region (with the exception of Cuba) are parties to the American Convention on Human Rights. Accordingly, member-states must abide by the decisions of the Inter-American Commission of Human Rights, and the majority recognizes the judicial competence of the Inter-American Court of Human Rights. The Commission hears individual petitions against any of the OAS member-states for human rights violations, may hear individual complaints when the procedure before the Commission has not produced compliance by member-states (complemetarity clause), but limits its jurisdiction to those countries that have accepted it explicitly. Even though equality issues (including sexual discrimination) are almost absent from the doctrine of the Court, recent decisions may "signal a positive shift toward gender justice."[28]

Finally, international nongovernmental organizations (INGOs) including International Gay and Lesbian Human Rights Commission (IGLHRC), the International Association of Lesbians and Gays (ILGA), and ARC International to mention a few, have played an influential role in promoting gay and lesbian rights throughout Latin America. ILGA has helped enforce the Universal Periodic Review (UPR) on issues regarding LGBTI rights and with other bodies within the UN system, such as the Commission of Women (CSW) and ECOSOC. The International Human Rights Law Group and the International Gay and Lesbian Human Rights Commission (IGLHRC) have worked along with the Center for Justice and International Law to press for the adoption of legislation that would deal more directly with several of the articles of the American Human Rights Convention. More particularly, these organizations have played a critical role in helping prevent and remedy social and legal discrimination against same-sex partners.[29] International norms and organizations help shape collective learning. With the normative and legal influence of organizations within the UN framework, INGOs, and international and regional agreements, policy innovations regarding same-sex couples were introduced successfully in Latin America.

INTERNATIONAL HUMAN RIGHTS LAW IN THE DOMESTIC REALM

Whereas international norms and organizations lack the necessary mechanisms to directly enforce legislation in the domestic realm, they have been influential in shaping the domestic legal system. Indeed, recent constitutional reforms in Latin America have given prevalence to international agreements, particularly regarding human rights law. Apart from a predominant monist view in Latin America—or the view that ratified international treaties are automatically incorporated to domestic law—within the last few decades (perhaps to avert future human rights violations), many Latin American countries have granted a privileged legal status to human rights treaties in three broadly defined ways. Some countries have granted constitutional rank to specific human rights treaties; others have incorporated human rights treaties into the so-called "constitutional block"; and yet in other cases, human rights treaties have been ranked below the constitution but above ordinary legislation.[30] The relationship between international agreements and their interpretation in domestic Latin American courts is important because, as seen in the next subsection, arguments against the constitutionality of domestic laws that allow marriage exclusively between a man and a woman have been based not only on national constitutional principles but on human rights principles of several international conventions.

Among the Latin American countries granting constitutional rank to specified human rights treaties are Argentina and Venezuela. In Argentina, the constitutional reform of 1994 provides constitutional rank to ten international human rights treaties explicitly listed in the constitution (article 72, subsection 22). In addition, Congress was granted the power to raise other treaties to constitutional status, by means of a supermajority vote. In Venezuela, the most recent "Constitution of the Bolivarian Republic of Venezuela" assigns constitutional rank to all human rights treaties, although in practice so far, the courts have been less inclined to incorporate these treaties into judicial decisions.[31]

On the other hand, Bolivia and Colombia have assigned a ranking similar to their constitutions to some human rights treaties using the "constitutional block" concept. According to this concept, incorporation of international human rights treaties into domestic law requires a combined interpretation of constitutional rights with the human rights contained in international treaties. Both groups of rights must be interpreted in a complementary and mutually reinforcing manner. Furthermore, in case of conflict between domestic and international law, priority is granted to the source that recognizes a broader scope of rights (pro-homine interpretation). As it will be discussed on the next subsection, recent decisions by Colombian courts regarding legislation for same-sex couples have relied on this combined interpretation of human rights treaties along with other fundamental rights found in the country's constitution.[32] Finally, Mexican and Brazilian courts have generally (but not exclusively) followed the tendency of ranking international treaties above regular laws but below the Constitution.[33]

In any case, courts of law in Latin America have been more inclined to incorporate international human rights treaties to interpret domestic laws.[34] Moreover, gay activists in Argentina, Brazil, Colombia, and Mexico have based their judicial claims against the constitutionality of laws that allow marriage exclusively between opposite-sex couples on both constitutional and human rights treaties, including the Declaration of Human Rights, the Pact of San José de Costa Rica, and the International Convention on Political and Civil Rights. Perhaps it was for this reason that Ecuador's constitutional reform of 2008 included a ban against same-sex marriage despite allowing same-sex civil unions in another article of the reformed constitution.

In sum, international models, particularly European countries, inter-national organizations, and human rights agreements, have played an important role in shaping the Latin American domestic environment, leading eventually to the adoption of policy innovations in Latin America. Based on the recognized human rights principles of equality before the law and non-discrimination, Latin American legislatures in some cases, or courts of law in others, introduced civil unions and same-sex marriage policies in the region.

THE INTERNAL PROCESSES: ARGENTINA AND BEYOND

Whereas external determinants, including international norms and or-ganizations and European models had a significant influence in the de-velopment of policy innovations for same-sex couples in Latin America, the adoption of same-sex friendly legislation involved internal forces that included national governmental mechanisms, legislators, or other mem-bers of government, NGOs, and court decisions. This chapter first exam-ined the "external factors," which helped shape ideas within the Latin American legal context. In this subsection, this chapter will analyze the "internal factors" of policy adoption, or how some Latin American coun-tries translated ideas into action.

The Case of Argentina

The process leading to the adoption of civil unions and same-sex mar-riage legislation in Argentina has been slow and cumbersome for several reasons. First, the mobilization in favor of civil unions began at the sub-national level in the capital city of Buenos Aires, instead of a nationwide movement that may have been more expedient and effective. Second, and precisely because of this bottom-up process, the legislation diffused very modestly due to cultural and institutional barriers. Only the south-ern province of Rio Negro in 2002 and the cities of Villa Carlos Paz and Rio Cuarto in the Province of Córdoba adopted similar legal mechanisms. Third, despite the fact that Western European countries conveyed a strong and positive model for emulation, domestic NGOs and political parties did not form a cohesive group with a uniform agenda. Indeed, the Argentine gay and lesbian organizations initially followed two broad paths: the recognition of civil unions by national law pursued primarily by CHA and some legislators; and the adoption of a national same-sex marriage law, led primarily by *Federación Argentina de Lesbianas, Gays, Bisexuales y Trans* (FALGBT); *Instituto en Contra de la Discriminación* (IN-ADI); and a few legislators. Finally, the Catholic Church with the support of some politicians led a strong opposition against the adoption of legislation for same-sex couples. Yet, in 2010 and due to the efforts of INADI, FALGBT, the gay community, and Argentina's president Cristina Kirchner, a same-sex marriage law was adopted, making Argentina the second country in the Americas to adopt national-level legislation.

From Sub-national Civil Unions to a National Same-sex Marriage Law

The collapse of the military dictatorship and the return of democracy to Argentina in 1983 provided a new, more open, institutional framework for the organization and mobilization of gay and lesbian NGOs in Argentina. More particularly, since the 1990s cultural changes in the Argentine society have tended to endorse gay and lesbian issues. According to Suntheim, in recent years it has been politically correct to support gay and lesbian issues in Argentina, and activist Maria Rachid claims that one of the reasons for these changes is the more recent emergence and diffusion of leftist ideology in Argentina as well as in many other Latin American countries.[35]

CHA has been one of the most influential organizations for lesbian and gay rights in Argentina. Founded in Buenos Aires in 1984 with less than two hundred militants, it spread quickly to other areas of the country and the number of supporters increased dramatically. By the late 1990s, CHA had become the most influential gay and lesbian grassroots organization in the country. Regarding legislation for same-sex couples, CHA led the drive for a civil union bill that was adopted in the capital city of Buenos Aires in 2002 (law 1004), making Buenos Aires the first city in Latin America to adopt a law of this kind. Law 1004 allows both same-sex and opposite-sex couples who have been partners for at least two years to benefit from their partners' health insurance, hospital visitation rights, and subsidies that are explicitly provided by the city.[36] The law was supported by the city's major parties, but there was also opposition led by legislators with ties to the Catholic Church. Apart from other religious arguments, the opposition claimed that the city was not competent to legislate in matters related to family rights because they were under the exclusive jurisdiction of the national government.

As in France, civil unions in Buenos Aires have become a common feature for both same-sex and opposite-sex couples. According to data from the Civil Registry of Buenos Aires, between 2004 and 2007, there was an increase of unions of more than 400 percent, whereas legal marriages in the Capital City decreased by more than four-fifths during the same time-period.[37] Following Buenos Aires, the Province of Rio Negro, and the cities of Villa Carlos Paz and Rio Cuarto, in the Province of Córdoba also adopted civil unions for same-sex and opposite-sex couples. Even with some variations, for example, registration is not required for civil unions in Rio Negro and there is a minimum of five years residency required in Villa Carlos Paz to apply for civil unions, the scope and effects of these sub-national laws are similar. Finally, civil union bills were also introduced at provincial levels in Chaco, Santa Fe, Córdoba, Corrientes, and Mendoza.[38]

Whereas CHA has been more supportive of same-sex civil unions for philosophical and practical reasons, Rachid (FALGBT) claims that the problem with provincial and local-level civil unions is that they cannot legislate in matters regarding family law, such as adoption or inheritance rights, because such matters fall under the exclusive jurisdiction of the national civil code of law. On these grounds, CHA along with Senator Diana Conti (FREPASO) submitted a national civil union bill to the Senate in December of 2005. The bill strengthened and expanded the rights offered by the existing Buenos Aires law. The bill included inheritance and adoption and pension rights. During the 2010 debate of the same-sex marriage law in the senate (see next subsection), several senators were ready to debate the same-sex civil union proposal if the same-sex marriage bill failed to pass.

Argentina and Same-Sex Marriage

Same-sex marriage was first sponsored by FALGBT in Argentina. This domestic NGO was founded in 2006 at the LGBT (Tenth) *Annual Encuentro*. It is an umbrella organization composed of a network of fifteen LGBT organizations, and it is led by long-time LGBT rights activist María Rachid. FALGBT pressed for the adoption of same-sex marriage using the Spanish law as model. The organization's same-sex marriage proposal advocated "same rights with same names" and based its discourse on the principles of legal equality and non-discrimination for same-sex couples. Before the law was adopted in 2010, petitions of *recursos de amparo* (writs of amparo), sponsored by FALGBT, were filed by same-sex couples in courts of law on the basis that marriage, as legislated in the Argentine civil code, violated the constitutional right of equal legal treatment and individual and collective rights evinced in international human rights agreements.[39]

In 2007, an *amparo* was introduced by Rachid and her long-time partner Claudia Castro after a marriage license at one of the National Registries was denied to the couple. The argument made by petitioners was rooted on the unconstitutionality of articles 172 and 188 of the National Civil Code which allows marriage only between individuals of different sexes. They justified their petition on the American Convention of Human Rights and the United Nations Universal Declaration of Human

Rights.[40] By 2009, a few *amparos* were granted by courts. For example, a court in Buenos Aires approved a same-sex marriage, ruling that articles 172 and 188 of the Civil Code were unconstitutional, but whereas the city's executive did not appeal the ruling, the wedding was blocked by another court. Later in 2009, the governor of the Province of Tierra del Fuego ordered the civil registry office to perform and register a same-sex marriage. Seven other same-sex couples appealed to courts for marriage licenses. Yet, court decisions remained inconsistent.

Along with FALGBT, INADI was very influential in both appealing to courts—authorities from both organizations helped prepare the court cases and provided counseling—and in promoting same-sex marriage via legislation. Created in 1995, by executive order, the purpose of this organization is to protect people on the basis of nationality, ethnicity, political and religious beliefs, and gender and sexual orientation. INADI denounces institutions or groups that actively promote discrimination, and it sponsors educational campaigns to deal with discrimination. The organization also works in conjunction with lesbian and gay NGOs and, more particularly, with FALGBT. INADI's most recent vice president was Maria Rachid (also former president of FALGTB). Both same-sex marriage bills, one submitted in the Chamber of Deputies in 2007 and the other one in the Senate early in 2008 were sponsored by INADI through FALGBT. In March 2008, INADI sent a letter to the members of the Chamber of Deputies urging them to debate and pass the bills sponsored by the organizations. More importantly, in May 2008, INADI submitted a third same-sex marriage bill to Deputies, this time seeking the support of Argentina's president, Cristina Kirchner.[41] The campaign in favor of same-sex marriage was endorsed by numerous politicians and organizations who signed petitions. Though members of CHA favored civil unions over marriage, they also argued that by only allowing opposite-sex couples to marry, the legislation was discriminatory and on such basis CHA supported a same-sex marriage law.[42]

Similar to the Spanish model, the bill did not create a new legal figure but instead amended around thirty articles of the Argentine National Civil Code. The law replaced the terms "women and men" or "husband and wife" for contrayentes (covenants), esposos (spouses), or cónyuges (conjugal unions). After the passage of the law in 2010, Rachid claimed that "Argentina was now a more just country." She asserted that the law not only recognized "the right to form a family," but also provided for access to a partner's healthcare, pension, and inheritance rights and to adopt children.[43] However, the final vote in the Senate was not reached without contention. Indeed, a campaign by the Roman Catholic Church and evangelical groups to oppose the bill raised some doubts about the likelihood of its passage in the Senate. There were those sponsoring a civil union law for both same-sex and opposite-sex couples ready to debate the bill if the same-sex marriage proposal failed to pass. In the end, parliamentary maneuvers kept the Senate from voting on civil unions and the government pressed for the more politically difficult option of marriage. "I'm proud that we never tried for civil unions, always for complete equality," said Esteban Paulon, the LGBT federation's general secretary. He credits "an enormous conviction that equality means the same rights with the same names."[44] Hence, the support of several NGOs and legislators was important, but the role of President Kirchner and INADI was crucial for the passage of the law.

BEYOND ARGENTINA: POLICY INNOVATIONS IN LATIN AMERICA

Same-sex civil unions or similar policies for same-sex couples have been legalized in Brazil, Ecuador, the Mexican State of Coahuila, Mexico City, and Uruguay, and they are being considered by Chilean politicians. Apart from civil unions, Mexico City has adopted recently a same-sex marriage law. In Colombia, its Constitutional Court recognized same-sex partnerships and a Brazilian court decided that same-sex couples had a constitutional right to marry. In addition, Paraguayan activists are pressing for same-sex friendly policies. Overall, Latin American countries have introduced significant policy innovations for same-sex couples, as a result of increased activism and significant political support. However, the process has been relatively slow and cumbersome, due to religious and political opposition.

In Brazil, recognition of cohabitation rights was legalized in 2004 in Rio Grande do Sul. This legal arrangement grants rights to partners similar to those of marriage, including adoption, pension and inheritance rights, social security, and other health benefits. In addition, in 2011, Brazil's Supreme Court ruled that same-sex couples were legally entitled to civil unions, and a Brazilian judge from the state of São Paulo allowed two gay petitioners to convert their civil union into full marriage. Luiz Mott, founder of Grupo Gay da Bahia, the oldest LGBT rights organization in Brazil, called the court's decision a "huge step for LGBT rights in the country." He said that "now any couple can ask for the same thing. It's a great advance."[45]

Colombia has yet to pass legislation for same-sex couples; a bill intended to recognize same-sex marriage was proposed and defeated six times in the Colombian Congress, due to opposition by political and religious organizations. However, court decisions have been critical in asserting the rights and promoting the adoption of legislation for same-sex couples. Indeed, in 2009 a decision by Colombia's constitutional court allowed same-sex couples to form *uniones de hecho* (de facto unions). According to the 1991 Constitution, *uniones de hecho* are legally equal to marriage and may be recognized after a couple has lived together for at least two years. Unions may be registered or unregistered and both have the same legal status, but registered unions may provide greater legal efficacy. The 2009 Court decision granted "same-sex partners all of the guarantees and benefits offered" to *uniones de hecho* for opposite-sex couples, except the right of adoption.[46] More recently, the court instructed Congress to pass a remedy for same-sex couples who do not enjoy the same rights afforded to opposite-sex couples and should include a "comprehensive, systematic, and orderly legislation." The court also demanded that congress should approve a law to address these imbalances quickly and ruled that if there is no legislation by 2013, a notary or a court should legally register same-sex marriages.[47]

Ecuador adopted a new constitution after a popular referendum overwhelmingly supported the reforms. Ecuador's president, Rafael Correa, had openly stated that he wanted the document to allow same-sex unions. He asserted that "the profoundly humanistic position of this [Ecuadorean] government is to respect the intrinsic dignity of everyone, of every human being, independently of their creed, race, and sexual preference." Article 68 of the reformed constitution grants full rights to same-sex civil unions. However, under the new constitution same-sex marriage and adoptions by same-sex couples are not recognized.[48] According to the reformed constitution, "marriage is the union between a man and a woman and is based on the free consent of the parties and their equal rights, obligations and legal capacity" (article 67). Thus, whereas in Ecuador same-sex couples have been granted a constitutional right to form civil unions, there are also constitutional bans to marriage and adoption by same-sex couples under these reforms.

In 2008, Uruguay became the first Latin American country to adopt a national civil union law (Ley de Unión Concubinaria). The bill was proposed by Senator Margarita Percovich from the ruling party *Frente Amplio* (FA). As the Buenos Aires law did before, civil unions in Uruguay are intended to legalize the status of both same-sex and opposite-sex couples, as long as the couples demonstrate shared residency for at least five years. Under this legal figure, couples are entitled to social security benefits, inheritance rights, and joint ownership of goods and property, but the law denies joint adoption rights.[49] In addition, a separate government-backed bill allowing same-sex couples to adopt children was approved by both houses in 2009.[50]

Given the secular and federal nature of Mexico's 1917 constitution, only civil marriages are recognized by the law and all its proceedings fall under state or local legal systems. Therefore, legislation for same-sex couples in Mexico has been introduced at sub-national levels. A same-sex civil union law was adopted in Mexico City despite strong opposition by conservatives from National Action Party (PAN) in 2006, and similar legislation in the northern state of Coahuila (Civil Pact of Solidarity, PSC) was also implemented. Three years later, the Party of the Democratic Revolution (PRD), the ruling party in Mexico City, announced its intention to amend the Civil Code and legalize same-sex marriages. Despite, strong opposition by PAN and the Roman Catholic Church, the bill was endorsed by the local head of government, Marcelo Ebrard, and over 600 nongovernmental organizations.[51] The law was adopted at the end of 2009 and came to force in March 2010, making Mexico City the first Latin American jurisdiction to legalize same-sex marriage. This law was later challenged before the National Supreme Court, but the court upheld the constitutionality of Mexico City's same-sex marriage law and later ruled that Mexico City's same-sex marriages were valid throughout the country.[52]

Both the Mexican and Argentine models may have helped initiate a trend in Latin America. Gay activists in Chile hoped that Argentina's gay-marriage law may influence the Chilean congress to debate a similar bill. There was some significant political support in Chile for a same-sex marriage bill introduced in the country's legislature less than a month after the Argentine same-sex marriage law was approved. However, the bill sponsored by Senator Fulvio Rossi of the Chilean Socialist Party met the strong opposition of conservatives and members of the Evangelical Church in Chile. A recent bill of *Acuerdo de Convivencia no-Matrimonial* (Non-marital Cohabitation Agreement) would legalize civil unions for same-sex couples and has the support of President Sebastian Piñera. He asserted that he was willing to "protect and safeguard the dignity of those couples, whether of the opposite or same sex," but at the same time, he rejected the legalization of same-sex marriage.[53]

In addition, activists in Paraguay planned to propose a same-sex marriage law similar to the one in Argentina, but the current vice-president of Paraguay, Federico Franco, is opposed to the new law. In addition, the Catholic Church has organized a campaign to prevent "the law of marriage between people of the same-sex that was approved in Argentina from coming to Paraguay." On the other hand, a same-sex marriage law in Uruguay seems more attainable. Indeed, Uruguayan gay activists unsatisfied with the civil-union law are preparing legislation that would allow same-sex marriage by reforming the civil law code as Spain and Argentina had done before, and, in this case, the Uruguayan president much like his counterpart in Argentina is in favor of the proposed law.[54]

In sum, Latin America has experienced an unprecedented number of policy innovations for same-sex couples in recent years. The more dominant tendency has been to adopt civil unions rather than same-sex marriage because of the strong opposition of political and religious forces. Yet it seems that with the exception of Argentina, most same-sex civil unions have served as a springboard to the more overarching yet traditional legal figure of marriage. Based on principles of equality and non-discrimination evinced in constitutions and international and regional human rights agreements, activists, politicians, and court decisions have pressed for same-sex policies in the region.

CONCLUSION

Diffusion may be seen logically both as an international process where external factors influence the domestic affairs of a state, and also as one subfield of linkage politics, where both internal and external events interact within a state.[55] Thus, an appropriate explanation of diffusion should be given in terms both of the unit of analysis (for example, states, individuals, or groups of individuals) and the social structures in which these units are embedded (for example, world or regional systems). This chapter dealt with both dimensions by emphasizing processes of international diffusion through global and regional socialization, and it briefly described the internal factors that led some countries to adopt legislation for same-sex couples successfully.

This chapter argued that international trends and, more particularly, European civil unions and same-sex marriage laws were the "take-off point" for the sort of "bandwagon effect" in Latin America.[56] The external process was also influenced by transnational organizations and international human rights agreements. In addition, various domestic factors, including the demands of grassroots organizations, legislators, governmental organizations, and the role of the executive (the presidents of Ecuador and Argentina and the Mayor of Mexico City) and judicial decisions, have been critical in shaping the internal processes and in leading to policy adoption. Moreover, future developments in other Latin America countries, including Chile, Paraguay, and Colombia, seem to be linked to regional diffusion.

Overall, the integrative approach employed in this chapter helped to overcome significantly the analytical dichotomy between what occurs within a state (the domestic realm) and what occurs outside of it (the international realm). Certainly, such an integrative methodology has helped analyze more adequately the factors that led to same-sex policies in Latin America.

NOTES

1. Jaqui True and Michael Mintrom, "Transnational Networks and Policy Diffusion: The Case of Gender Mainstreaming," *International Studies Quarterly* 45 (2001): 27–57.

2. See, for example, Adriana Piatti-Crocker, "Constructing Policy Innovation in Argentina: From Gender Quotas to Same-Sex Marriage," in *Same-Sex Marriage in the Americas: Policy Innovation for Same-Sex Relationships*, eds. Jason Pierceson, Adriana Piatti-Crocker, and Shawn Schulenberg (Boulder: Lexington Books, 2010). See also, Adriana Piatti-Crocker, ed., *Diffusion of Gender Quota Laws in Latin America and beyond: Advances and Setbacks in the Last Two Decades* (New York: Peter Lang Publishing, 2011), 6–8; Ann Florini, "The Evolution of International Norms," *International Studies Quarterly* 40: 371; Michael Mintrom, *Policy Entrepreneurs and Social Change* (Washington, D.C.: Georgetown University Press, 2000).

3. Benjamin Most, "Diffusion, Reinforcement, Geopolitics and the Spread of War," *American Political Science Review* 7 (1980): 940.

4. Harvey Starr, "Democratic Dominoes: Diffusion Approaches and the Spread of Democracy in the International System," *The Journal of Conflict Resolution* (June 1990): 358.

5. Emmanuel Adler, "Cognitive Evolution: A Dynamic Approach for the Study of International Relations and their Progress," in *Progress in Postwar International Relations*, eds. Emmanuel Adler and Ben Crawford (New York: Columbia University Press, 1991): 43.

6. Everett Rogers, "Diffusion of Innovations," 5th ed. (New York: Free Press, 2003): 2-3.

7. Michael Mintrom and Sara Vergari, "Policy Networks and Innovation Diffusion: The Case of State Education Reforms," *Journal of Politics* 60 (1998): 126–148.

8. Ibid., 6.

9. John Kingdon, *Agendas, Alternatives, and Public Policies*, 2nd ed. (Boston: Little Brown, 1995): 140.

10. Jeffrey Checkel, "The Constructivist Turn in International Relations," *World Politics* 50 (1) (1998): 324–48; Peter Katzenstein, "Regionalism in Comparative Perspective," *Cooperation and Conflict* 31 (2) (1996): 123–59.

11. Stephen Calleya, "Post-Cold War Regional Dynamics in the Mediterranean Area," *Mediterranean Quarterly* 3 (7) (1996): 42–54.

12. See Emmanuel Adler and Beverly Crawford, *Constructing a Mediterranean Region: A Cultural Approach.* Paper presented at "The Convergence of Civilizations? Constructing a Mediterranean Region," Arrábida Monastery, Fundação Oriente, Lisboa, Portugal, June 6–9, 2002; and Young Jong Choi and James Caporaso, "Comparative Regional Integration," in *Handbook of International Relations*, eds. Walter Carlsnaes, Thomas Risse, and Beth A. Simmons (London: Sage, 2002): 480–99.

13. Linda Nielsen, "Family Rights and the Registered Partnership in Denmark," *International Journal of Law and the Family* 4 (1990): 298.

14. Robert Wintemute, and Andenæs Mads, eds., *Legal Recognition of Same-Sex Partnerships: A Study of National, European and International Law* (Oxford: Hart Publishing, 2001); Turid Noack, "Cohabitation in Norway: An accepted and gradually more regulated way of living," *International Journal of Law, Policy and the Family* 15 (2001): 108.

15. Scott Sayare and Maia De La Baume, "In France, Civil Unions Gain Favor over Marriage," *New York Times.* http://www.nytimes.com/2010/12/16/world/europe/16france.html. Accessed August 8, 2011.

16. Marcelo Suntheim. Interview by author. Tape recording. Buenos Aires, Argentina. June 13, 2008.

17. International Gay and Lesbian Human Rights Commission. *EU Network of Independent Experts, 2002.*

18. ILGA Europe. http://www.ilga-europe.org/home/guide/country_by_country/belgium/belgian_same_sex_marriage_law. Accessed August 27, 2011.

19. Peter Lloyd, "Iceland's Prime Minister marries long-term partner," *Pink News.* http://news.pinkpaper.com/NewsStory.aspx?id=3298. Accessed June 28, 2011.

20. Jennifer Green, "Spain Legalizes Same-Sex Marriages," *Washington Post.* http://www.washingtonpost.com/wp-dyn/content/article/2005/06/30/AR2005063000245.html. Accessed August 28, 2011.

21. Law 9/XI (May 2010). http://portugalgay.pt/politica/parlamento07x.asp. Accessed August 15, 2011.

22. Maria Rachid. Interview by author. Tape recording. Buenos Aires, Argentina. June 18, 2008.

23. See Malcom Shaw, *International Law*, 5th ed. (New York: Cambridge University Press, 2003) and Piatti-Crocker, ibid., 2.

24. UN Declaration of Human Rights. http://www.un.org/en/documents/udhr/. Accessed October 13, 2011.

25. United States Department of State, "Free And Equal In Dignity And Rights." http://www.unhcr.org/refworld/docid/4ee1bba22.html. Accessed December 31, 2011.

26. Piatti-Crocker, ibid., 2

27. American Convention of Human Rights (Pact of San José de Costa Rica). http://www.oas.org/juridico/english/treaties/b-32.html. Accessed November 8, 2011.

28. Patricia Palacios Zuloaga, "The Path to Gender Justice in the Inter-American Court of Human Rights," *Texas Journal of Women and the Law* 17:2 (2008): 227–96. http://www.utexas.edu/law/centers/humanrights/get_involved/writing-prize07-zuloaga.pdf. Accessed June 10, 2011.

29. http://www.arc-international.net. Accessed May 25, 2011.

30. See, for example, AA.VV. "Transición democrática y reforma constitucional en Centroamérica," Fundación para la Paz y la Democracia (San José, 2001); Roberto Gargarella, "Recientes Reformas Constitucionales en America Latina: Una Primera Aproximación," in *Desarrollo Económico* 36, 144 (Jan–Mar 1997): 971–990; José María Serna de la Garza, "La Reforma del Estado en América Latina: los casos de Argentina, Brasil y México," UNAM, Mexico, 1998; Rodrigo Uprimny y Mauricio García Villegas, "Corte constitucional y emancipación social en Colombia," in Boaventura de Sousa Santos and Mauricio García Villegas, eds., *Emancipación social y violencia en Colombia* (Bogota: Norma, 2004). See also, Application of Convention No. 169 by domestic and international courts in Latin America. http://www.ilo.org/wcmsp5/groups/public/---ed_norm/---normes/documents/publication/wcms_123946.pdf, International Labour Organization, Geneva: 2009. Accessed June 10, 2011.

31. See Constitution of Argentina; Article 72, subsection 22, paragraph 3 and Article 75, subsection 22, paragraph 1 of the Constitution of Argentina: "Treaties and conventions have a higher ranking than laws." For the Constitution of the Bolivarian Republic of Venezuela, see article 23.

32. See Carlos Ayala Corao, "La Jerarquía Constitucional de los Tratados Relativos a Derechos Humanos y sus Consecuencias" (FUNDAP, Querétaro, 2003); Rodrigo Uprimny, "El bloque de constitucionalidad en Colombia: un Análisis Jurisprudencial y un Ensayo de Sistematización Doctrinal," in *Compilación de jurisprudencia y doctrina nacional e Internacional* (United Nations Office of the High Commissioner for Human Rights, 2001).

33. For Brazil, see Inter-American Commission of Human Rights (OAS), *Report on the Situation of Human Rights in Brazil*, 2011. http://www.cidh.oas.org/countryrep/brazil-eng/chaper%201.htm. Accessed September 10, 2011. George Galindo, "'That Is a Step on Which I Must Fall Down . . .' Brazilian Judiciary Reform As a Backslide in Terms of International Protection of Human Rights in Brazil," *Global Jurist Topics* 6:3, Article 2 (2006). For Colombia, see Cristof Heyns and Frans Viljoen, "The Impact of the United Nations Human Rights Treaties on the Domestic Level," *Human Rights Law Quarterly 23*, 3 (2001): 483–535.

34. For Mexico, see International Labour Organization, "Application of Convention No. 169 by domestic and international courts in Latin America." http://pro169.org/res/materials/en/general_resources/Application%20of%20convention%20no.%20169%20-%20Casebook.pdf. Accessed December 2, 2012.

35. Suntheim, ibid., 16 and Rachid, ibid., 22.

36. Ibid., 16.

37. Piatti-Crocker, ibid., 2.

38. "Córdoba: aprueban la unión civil entre homosexuales en Villa Carlos Paz," *Diario Clarín*, http://edant.clarin.com/diario/2007/11/23/um/m-01547228.htm (accessed September 1, 2011); "Río Cuarto: Aprueban la Unión Civil de Parejas Gays," *Diario La Voz*. http://archivo.lavoz.com.ar/09/05/07/Rio-Cuarto-aprueban-union-civil-parejas-gays.html. Accessed March 13, 2011.

39. An "amparo," is a proceeding analogous to a habeas corpus. However, rather than restricting physical liberties, an amparo is petitioned when other basic freedoms are allegedly violated.

40. "Argentina: Un Recurso de Amparo se debate por el Matrimonio Gay en la Corte Suprema," Pagina 12 (October 18, 2007); see also, "Una Pareja Gay irá a la Justicia si no le dan Turno para Casarse por Civil," Diario Clarín. http://www.clarin.com/diario/2007/06/13/sociedad/s-03902.htm. Accessed May 20, 2008.

41. Ibid., 22.

42. Ibid., 16.

43. "Argentine Senate backs bill legalizing gay marriage," BBC. http://www.bbc.co.uk/news/10630683. Accessed June 10, 2011.

44. Alexei Barrionuevo, "Argentina Approves Same-sex Marriage, First, for Region," *New York Times*. http://www.nytimes.com/2010/07/16/world/americas/16argentina.html. Accessed April 15, 2001.

45. "Brazil's supreme court recognizes gay partnerships," *Reuters.* http://www.reuters.com/article/2011/05/06/us-brazil-gayrights-idUSTRE74503V20110506. Accessed June 11, 2011.

46. Helda Martinez, "Equal Rights for Same-Sex Partners." http://ipsnews.net/news.asp?idnews=45944. Accessed May 27, 2011.

47. "Court Gives Colombia Congress Two years to Pass Gay Marriage Bill." *Colombia Reports.* http://colombiareports.com/colombia-news/news/17896-colombian-supreme-court-calls-on-congress-to-pass-gay-marriage-bill-in-two-years.html. Accessed August 15, 2011.

48. Piatti-Crocker, ibid., 2.

49. "Uruguay President Grants Legal Rights to Gay Couples," *Pink News*. http://www.pinknews.co.uk/news/articles/2005-6419.html. Accessed March 2, 2011.

50. "Lawmakers in Uruguay Vote to Allow Gay Couples to Adopt." http://www.nytimes.com/2009/09/10/world/americas/10uruguay.html. Accessed December 12, 2010.

51. Cecilia Barría, "México DF: Aprueban Matrimonio Gay." http://www.bbc.co.uk/mundo/america_latina/2009/12/091221_2340_mexico_gay_gm.shtml. Accessed October 25, 2011.

52. David Agren, "Mexican States Ordered to Honor Gay Marriages," *New York Times*. http://www.nytimes.com/2010/08/11/world/americas/11mexico.html. Accessed June 12, 2011.

53. "Chile President Sebastian Piñera Proposes Civil Unions," BBC. http://www.bbc.co.uk/news/world-latin-america-14469625. Accessed August 9, 2011.

54. Carlos Santoscoy, "Argentine Neighbors, Uruguay and Paraguay, to Debate Gay Law." http://www.ontopmag.com/article.aspx?id=6072&MediaType=1&Category=24. Accessed July 13, 2011.

55. Jaqui True and Michael Mintrom, ibid., 1; Harvey Starr, ibid., 4; Frances Berry and William Berry, "State Lottery Adoptions as Policy Innovations: An Event History Analysis," *The American Political Science Review*, 84, 2 (1990): 389–401.

56. Ibid., 9.

TWO

The Lavender Tide? LGBT Rights and the Latin American Left Today

Shawn Schulenberg

Over the past decade, the Latin American Left has swept back into power in what many scholars today refer to as the "pink tide." Unlike earlier periods of leftist resurgence, the United States has remained more hands off this time as terrorism has replaced socialism (and the associated Cold War) as its greatest threat, and its resources are also bogged down in other conflicts across the globe (for example, Afghanistan and Iraq). The result is that leftist parties in Latin America have had less foreign hegemonic interference and more freedom to be judged for the first time on their own merits and results.

Meanwhile, there has also been a noticeable gay rights revolution in the region.[1] In this part of the world, typically characterized by its machismo and adherence to Catholic traditions, many countries have moved rapidly forward recognizing the rights of LGBT peoples. Argentina and parts of Mexico today recognize same-sex marriage; civil unions are accepted nationwide in Brazil, Ecuador, and Uruguay; and other countries—such as Chile, Colombia, and Cuba, among others—are currently considering legislation granting partnership rights.[2] Indeed, this change has been rapid, as all of these changes have happened within just one decade.

A number of recently published articles and edited volumes study various aspects of the pink tide;[3] however, most of these works focus specifically on the economic consequences, while only two look at some of the social policy implications.[4] No essay yet looks at the region as a whole to ask what impact this resurgence of the Left has had on LGBT rights in Latin America.

This chapter is an attempt to come up with some preliminary observations about the impact of this swing to the left on policies that affect LGBT peoples in Latin America today.[5] More specifically, is there a relationship between the pink tide and what I call this "lavender tide"? A few case studies are now beginning to emerge to explain the Left's policies on gender/sexuality within a single country—each of which is very important because the Left in each country has its own individual unique characteristics. However, it is also important to look at whether we can make some general observations about the Left as a whole. As a result, this study aims to complement those rich emerging works that look at the individual cases in more detail.

This chapter will begin by providing some background on the how the Left in the region has historically treated issues of (homo)sexuality and consider whether it is any more supportive today. Is the Left more supportive of LGBT issues than it was in the past? Next, it will look at this issue in terms of parties and partisanship: does this issue cause cleavage between the Left and Right in Latin America like it does in the United States? Is the Right the same, better, or worse in its support for LGBT communities? How well does the rise of the Left help explain recent gains by for same-sex couples on the issue of partnership recognition? Finally, what do these conclusions mean when we take public opinion into account? Do political parties (and their ideologies) matter more than public opinion? This chapter will try to tackle all of these questions.

LITERATURE REVIEW

As the conquistadors overran the Americas, so too did their social understandings of sexuality from the Iberian Peninsula, mostly usurping indigenous norms. Mediterranean gender roles and Catholic teachings on lust inform this perspective, both of which reach the same general conclusion: homosexuality is wrong because it violates not only social custom but also God's natural law. However, Napoleonic Code eventually served as the main influence when modern legal codes were written, and most Latin American countries removed explicit prohibitions against homosexuality in the 1800s. This led to a framework in the Americas for more than a century where homosexuality was legal yet socially unacceptable and taboo. Within this context, it was heavily stigmatized both within the public (wider society) and the private (family) spheres. In the former, although homosexuality and sodomy were technically legal, police often used other "public decency" laws to harass and arrest LGBT peoples.

As more formal LGBT movements began to materialize centuries later in the 1960 and 1970s, they had few-to-no allies: neither the Right nor the

Left wanted anything to do with them. One might expect that the Left would be the first to accept LGBT peoples into their memberships as a means of uniting diverse oppressions under one umbrella. However, international Marxist/socialist movements have a long history of entrenched homophobia, and Latin American leftists were no exception.

James Green and Florence Babb, in their introduction to a special issue of *Latin American Perspectives* on sexuality, chart out this history and identify a number of reasons for the specific nature of the homophobia within the Left in Latin America (beyond just general homophobia).[6] First, those countries that heavily influenced the Latin America Left (and leftism generally in the world) were saturated with homophobia themselves. As socialist ideas disseminated from the USSR to the rest of the world, homophobia also followed. Although the criminal code enacted by the Bolsheviks after they came to power in the Soviet Union in 1917 did not criminalize sodomy, references were inserted into the law after Stalin came to power in 1934. The logic behind this was simple: "[H]omosexuality came to be associated with upper-class men and 'bourgeois decadence.'"[7] Consequently, Marxist movements throughout the world viewed it as a feature unique to capitalism, the system they were trying to dismantle; it was not an issue of importance or related to working class concerns.

Second, homosexuality ran antithetical to the *machista* image of the Left as portrayed by revolutionary leaders such as Che Guevara and Fidel Castro. These leaders appropriated and deployed this imagery of the strong leader to appeal to wider societies used to following a caudillo (strongman leader). The symbol of a macho revolutionary provides no space for homosexuality, which can force people to question basic gender roles and ideas of masculinity/femininity, potentially emasculating the movement. If the movement were to consider questions of (homo)sexuality, it might be taken as a sign of weakness/femininity.

Finally, as a tactical consideration, because the LGBT movement is "multiclass in composition, some Marxists argue that it could, at times, run at cross-purposes to the 'interests' of the working class and its organizations."[8] Because the Marxist struggle is primarily focused on uniting the proletariat against the owners of capital, it may run into organizational problems as LGBT people are born all across the economic spectrum into all classes, making it more difficult to unite as a group with common interests. Therefore, it was easier to focus on issues that would not split apart this working class coalition.

For all three of these reasons, homophobia was pervasive in the Left (above and beyond just society generally). LGBT activists often faced great difficulties as they tried to forge tighter relationships with leftist activist circles in the second half of the twentieth century. In countries like Cuba, Argentina, Brazil, Nicaragua, and Chile, leftist parties often rejected the incorporation of lesbian and gay issues into their platforms and prohibited LGBT people from holding leadership positions within political parties and social movements.[9] Moving into the 1980s and 1990s, resistance from leftist parties to LGBT concerns continued. For example, as Brazil was crafting its new constitution in the 1980s, leftist party members quickly rejected adding sexuality as a protected category from which one could not discriminate, like race and gender. Likewise, in neighboring Argentina, it took several years for Peronist President Carlos Menem to agree in the mid-1990s to legally recognize the primary LGBT organization in the country, *Comunidad Homosexual Argentina* (CHA), as a formal organization.[10] Clearly, at the end of the twentieth century, lesbians and gays were still making little headway in the political arena.

However, over the past decade something has changed. LGBT movements are rising in visibility and have won several important public policy battles. Legal prohibitions against sodomy have been nearly universally repealed (those that emerged in the twentieth century), and activists have pushed for and passed laws banning discrimination, increased penalties for hate crimes, and even partnership recognition (same-sex civil unions/marriage). Indeed, there seems to be a gay rights revolution happening in the region, what I call the "lavender tide."[11]

Meanwhile, the Left has recently surged back to power in elections throughout the region in what scholars frequently refer to as the "pink tide." Leftist parties today now control the executive branch in Argentina, Bolivia, Brazil, Costa Rica, Cuba, Dominican Republic, Ecuador, El Salvador, Guatemala, Nicaragua, Peru, Uruguay, and Venezuela. Only in a handful of countries are rightist parties in power: Chile, Colombia, Honduras, and Paraguay.[12] Clearly, the Left is doing something right.

However, this presents us with a question: What is the relationship between the "pink tide" and the "lavender tide"? Is the advancement of LGBT rights in the region a consequence of the pink tide? How does the Left today treat LGBT issues? Have their positions evolved or do they remain as homophobic as they were in the past?

Before we can answer this, we need to look at a broader question: How might we explain or categorize the Left in power today? The debate over how to classify this pink tide is heavily contested. The authors of the 2006 Latinobarómetro characterize the Left in power today as a single group: "[T]he word 'left' is open to misunderstanding. It does not mean the same as in the 1960s when revolutionaries sought the dictatorship of the proletariat. Today's left is a reformist elite that campaigns on issues like poverty in competitive elections, defends democracy and plays by the rules of the international economy."[13] However, most believe that this pink tide is not a monolithic group. Jorge Castañeda was one of the first try to come up with a classification system of the Left in Latin America. In his 2006 *Foreign Affairs* article, he differentiates a good Left from a bad Left. In the first category, we have the "good, reform-minded" Left: "This left emphasizes social policy—education, antipoverty programs, health care, housing—but within a more or less orthodox market framework. It usually attempts to deepen and broaden democratic institutions."[14] In many ways, this first group is modeled after the Latinobarómetro definition; these leaders are focused on producing good policy through orthodox means. Although they may have been more radical in the past, their leaders today are more centrist. Presidents who fall under this scheme include Tabaré Vásquez in Uruguay, Lula da Silva in Brazil, and Michelle Bachelet in Chile. Castañeda clearly views this group positively and distinguishes them from what he considers the "bad antidemocratic, populist" Left: "For all of these leaders, economic performance, democratic values, programmatic achievements, and good relations with the United States are not imperatives but bothersome constrains that miss the real point. They are more intent on maintaining popularity at any cost, picking fights as much as possible with Washington, and getting as much control as they can over sources of revenue."[15] In other words, these leaders are more concerned with maintaining power through undemocratic means than on actually producing good policy. He places leaders such as Hugo Chavez of Venezuela, Evo Morales of Bolivia, and Daniel Ortega of Nicaragua in this camp.

Many have taken exception to Castañeda's classification system. John D. French, for example, argues that the characterization of good social democratic versus bad populist is too simplistic; the key problem, according to French, is that this new schema lumps together very divergent styles into old categories that do not clearly reflect reality today.[16] More specifically, the confrontational approach to Washington does not necessarily coincide with populist, antidemocratic politics. Likewise, there are important differences in party structures that we might need to consider. In the end, he advocates using an approach that recognizes the "many lefts" that exist throughout the region today. Maxwell Cameron agrees that this Left in Latin America is too diverse to classify by this populist versus social democratic dichotomy.[17]

In *Leftist Governments in Latin America: Successes and Shortcomings*, Kurt Weyland, Raul Madrid, and Wendy Hunter examine the performance of these left-wing governments in power: Now that we have a few years of evidence from these administrations, how well have they fared in producing sound economic policy? [18] In the introductory chapter, Kurt Weyland proposes his own dichotomous classification system—Contestatory versus Moderate Left. While multidimensional schemes may be useful for other purposes, he argues that this model works best to understand policy output. In many ways this classification schema is modeled after the Castañeda model, but without the normative judgment. He explains the difference between these two factions of the Left as follows: "The moderate current tempers its pursuit of leftist goals prudently, respecting economic constraints and political opposition. When encountering problems and resistance, it negotiates rather than trying to impose its own will. By contrast, the more radical wing challenges neoliberalism, defies structures of globalization, and attacks the political opposition."[19]

For the purposes of this chapter, I will follow the classification schema proposed here by Weyland. Since my primary consideration here is policy out on social issues, I am particularly interested in whether the Contestatory Left and Moderate Left vary in terms of both their *position* and their *performance* on LGBT rights. In terms of the first question, is the Contestatory Left more or less sympathetic to lesbian and gay concerns than the Moderate Left? Second, does one variation of this Left actually do a better job passing laws important to LGBT peoples? Finally, taken these two groups together as a whole, how well has the Left performed compared to the Right addressing issues of sexuality?

METHODS AND DATA

To compare how party affiliation influences support for LGBT issues, I have compiled and compared data from a number of sources. First, for my independent variable, I have classified nearly all Latin American countries over the past ten years according to the parties in control of the executive branch. Because I am primarily interested in looking at whether parties (especially those with Marxist roots) have "evolved" on the question of LGBT inclusion, I began by distinguishing parties along three lines: those who come from a traditional Marxist background and/or are aligned with organized labor (the Left), those with a pronounced pro-business, anti-Marxist orientation (the Right), and those that do not fit into either of these categories (the unaffiliated). I then took this one step further to separate the Left into the two camps today recognized by Weyland:[20] the Contestatory Left and the Moderate Left. Taken together, I come up with four types of political parties: 1) Contestatory Left, 2) Moderate Left, 3) unclear affiliation, and 4) Right (see Figure 2.1). This visual representation shows how strongly the Left has conquered the region: the continent has clearly trended from blue to red.

Some difficulties arise when making this chart as some parties and presidents do not always clearly follow the Left versus Right economic dynamic. In those cases where I do not think a party fits perfectly into the Contestatory versus Moderate Left dichotomy, or even Left versus Right in general, I classify them nonetheless but limit my use of these cases for making general observations.[21] However, I still think it is important to bring them into the discussion to see where these "fuzzy" cases fit.

For my dependent variable, I researched both the positions and policy outputs of the executives in these countries with respect to LGBT friendly laws. Have presidents passed major laws advancing LGBT interests? Here, I also classify each of the presidents according to their record on LGBT issues as follows:

	2002	2003	2004	2005	2006	2007	2008	2009	2010	2011	SSM%
Argentina	Duhalde	Nestor Kirchner					Cristina Fernandez de Kirchner				63.9
Uruguay	Jorge Batlle			Tabaré Vázquez					José Mujica		50.5
Brazil	Cardoso	Lula da Silva								Rousseff	39.8
Chile	Ricardo Lagos				Michelle Bachelet				Piñera		39.7
Mexico	Vicente Fox				Felipe Calderón						37.8
Colombia	Alvaro Uribe								Juan Manuel Santos		34.4
Peru	Alejandro Toledo				Alan Garcia				Humala		26.3
Bolivia	Quiroga	chez de Loz	Carlos Mesa	Rodriquez	Evo Morales						24.7
Panama	Mireya Moscoso			Martin Torrijos				Martinelli			22.8
Honduras	Ricardo Maduro		Manuel Zelaya				Mich.	Porfirio Lobo Sosa			22.6
Venezuela	Hugo Chavez										22.5
Costa Rica	Abel Pacheco			Oscar Arias				Laura Chinchilla			20.7
Dominican Republic	Hipólito Mejía		Leonel Fernandez								18.6
Ecuador	Noboa	Lucio Gutiérrez		Alfredo Palacio	Rafael Correa						18.4
Guatemala	Alfonso Portillo		Oscar Berger				Alvaro Colom				16.5
Paraguay	Angel González M.	Nicanor Duarte					Fernando Lugo				16.1
Nicaragua	Enrique Bolaños				Daniel Ortega						15.6
El Salvador	Francisco Flores Pérez		Antonio Saca				Mauricio Funes				10.3
Cuba	Fidel Castro					Raul Castro					No Data

Key: ■ Contestatory Left ■ Moderate Left □ Unclear Affiliation ■ Right

Figure 2.1. Latin American presidents (2002–2011) by political affiliation, sorted by public opinion support for same-sex marriage (2010) Germán Lodola and Margarita Corral, "Support for Same-Sex Marriage in Latin America," AmericasBarometer Insights Series 44 (2010), http://www.vanderbilt.edu/lapop/insights/I0844.enrevised.pdf.

- Extremely Positive: Same-sex marriage proposed or adopted, or constitutional recognition of unions
- Very Positive: Proposals or adoption of partnership rights short of marriage
- Positive: Decriminalization, non-discrimination protections proposed or adopted
- Negative: Proposals or adoptions to rollback gay rights laws

However, the context for these debates can often be quite important, so the paper will also briefly discuss each case.

Finally, I have also included country-by-country data on public opinion data for/against same-sex marriage in Latin American.[22] The column *SSM%* in Figure 2.1 reports the percentage of the population in the country that supports same-sex marriage. I include this data as a means to compare the explanatory power of party affiliation to public opinion. Perhaps public opinion can explain policy outputs in these countries better than the party in power? Finally, I also use this data to compare how each type of party does relative to public opinion. Do some types of parties stand ahead of the public while others fall behind?

"MODERATE" LEFT

A significant amount of progress has come about in Argentina, Brazil, and Uruguay as Moderate Left parties have advanced gay rights on a number of fronts. Before we attribute all of this to party organizations, though, it is important to note that all three of these countries have the highest numbers of public support for same-sex marriage.

LGBT movements in Argentina have seen significant gains working through the Front for Victory (FPV) faction of the Peronist party under the Cristina Fernandez de Kirchner administration. During her presidential campaign in 2007, Fernandez de Kirchner did not stake out a clear position on gay rights. For example, when asked about same-sex marriage, she argued that it was an issue for the legislature to consider. However, in 2009 her tune changed significantly, as various iterations of same-sex marriage bills were making their way through committees in the National Congress. She began to speak out very forcefully in favor of same-sex marriage, and it is clear that there was coordination between the LGBT lobby and various executive branch agencies to steer this bill toward success.[23] Together, the convergence of strong public opinion and strong executive branch support, led to a victory as Argentina became the first country in Latin America to recognize same-sex marriages nationwide.

The first decade of the twentieth century has been a time of remarkable progress for LGBT rights in Uruguay. The leftist administrations of presidents Tabaré Vázquez and José Mujica have brought swift progress in the area of partnership recognition. Uruguay became the first country in all of Latin America to recognize civil unions nationwide (in 2008) and adopt rights for same-sex couples (in 2009), and it is currently debating a bill that would recognize same-sex marriage. The Broad Front Party coalition in this case made all of this possible as they advocated and coordinated their strategies.

Likewise, the Lula da Silva administration from the Workers' Party (PT) in Brazil has also been very pro-gay both in rhetoric and policy as a number of important LGBT initiatives advanced during his tenure. Most of the policy progress that we have seen in Brazil has been the result of executive orders, which include the creation of Brazil without Homophobia (an initiative to cut down violence motivated by homophobia and transphobia), the National Plan to Promote LGBT Citizenship and Human Rights, and the National LGBT Council (a body tasked with combating discrimination). Unfortunately, Lula has been less successful pushing his initiatives through the Congress as opposition leaders have the power to veto anything they oppose.[24] However, this says more about the institutional features of Brazilian democracy that prevent change than about the PT's ability to organize around an issue.

Finally, we have also seen very little progress in a number of countries with Moderate Left leadership in power. One of the most disappointing is that of the center-left government of Michelle Bachelet, which failed to propose any legislation in support of the LGBT movement. Two things make this tragic. First, Chile ranks as one of the most supportive countries in terms of public opinion in support of same-sex marriage. One might expect a leftist president here to propose a bill recognizing same-sex unions, but she did not. Some might argue that this was impossible in a socially conservative country like Chile, but her successor from a center-right coalition proposed a civil union bill soon after coming into office, meaning that she is more conservative on this issue than a president from a center-right party/coalition.

Other countries with Moderate Left presidents have also seen little progress. Costa Rica's President Laura Chinchilla campaigned on an anti-gay marriage platform, but has since endorsed civil unions and even gone so far as to say that she would respect a Supreme Court decision if it were to decide that the state must grant marriage to same-sex couples. However, she has yet to use her presidential power to advance this legislation. Likewise, little to nothing has happened in other Moderate Left countries such as the Dominican Republic, Guatemala, Paraguay, or El Salvador. However, nearly all of these countries have very little public support for same-sex marriage, so public opinion might be a better place for LGBT movements in these countries to start.

"CONTESTATORY" LEFT

How do countries with presidents from Contestatory Left treat this issue? According to Figure 1, six countries today are led by presidents who are far left in their embracing of Marxist/anti-imperialist ideologies and rhetoric: Bolivia (Morales), Cuba (Castro), Ecuador (Correa), Nicaragua (Ortega), Peru (Humala),[25] and Venezuela (Chavez). In every single one of these countries, we see some progress over the past decade for LGBT peoples, but progress here has been much more limited under these leftist administrations: almost all of these countries have extended protections covering LGBT citizens, but all of them are completely opposed to recognizing same-sex marriages. Procedurally, many of these changes have come about not as isolated pieces of legislation but as a tiny piece of broader constitutional reform.

Cuba, the grandfather of socialism in the Western Hemisphere, has lightened up in its punishment of sexuality as Fidel Castro himself has said that the persecution of lesbians and gays was a mistake. Moreover, in the 2000s, the national health system began to provide sexual reassignment surgery for transgender persons free of charge. We cannot make any comparisons here to public opinion because this data is not available.

In Nicaragua, homosexuality was decriminalized as the entire legal code was replaced and references to sodomy were removed in 2007. Likewise, in Bolivia the new 2009 constitution prohibits discrimination on the basis of sexual orientation and gender identity. In Venezuela, the new constitution written by Chavez in 1999 also decriminalized sodomy and banned discrimination in employment, and it allowed lesbians and gays to serve in the armed forces. Hate crime laws were later passed in 2008, and there is chatter today about legalizing civil unions for same-sex couples.

Ecuador presents a unique case for LGBT activists in the region. The new constitution implemented in 2009 after the election of Rafael Correa gives same-sex couples all of the legal rights associated with marriage in the form of civil unions. In some ways, this represents the strongest legal partnership laws in the region as it would take a constitutional amendment (a very large hurdle for opponents) to strip them away. Also, it is very remarkable because public support for same-sex marriage is also extremely low here (just 18.4 percent) putting it as number 15 out of 19 of the countries ranked in this survey. However, this is not all good news for LGBT groups; this same clause in the constitution also legally defines marriage as between one man and one woman. For same-sex marriage advocates, this might be seen as a very large step backwards because it would now also take a constitutional change for same-sex marriage to be realized (more difficult than it was before).

What sense can one make of the Contestatory Left on these issues? First, the Marxist Left has made a great deal of progress shedding its former homophobic values. Although many of these parties are still opposed to equal marriage rights for same-sex couples, they have also rapidly advanced other lesbian and gay priorities, such as decriminalization, hate crime and anti-discriminations protections, and partnership recognition in one case. Finally, these leftist parties have proven quite remarkable as vehicles for advancing gay rights within the context of very negative public opinion. It remains to be seen how these contestatory parties would operate were their societies to have a more favorable opinion of lesbian and gay rights/same-sex marriage.

PARTIES NOT LEFT OR RIGHT?

Panama is the only country in this study that does not easily fit within this left/right paradigm. In this case, we have never seen a strong Marxist/anti-imperialist political movement, nor has a strong labor movement ever developed. The result is that the political parties that exist today do not fall along a left/right divide, neither in history, rhetoric, nor policies. There is no way to clearly characterize the administrations over the past decade in this context. Regardless, it presents an interesting case because of its uniqueness. So what has happened over the past ten years? Very little. No major protections have been advanced in Panama with the exception of the decriminalization of sodomy, which was passed by an executive order in 2008.

RIGHT

Now that we've seen how parties on the left, and those without clear political alignment, deal with issues of sexuality when in power: How do conservative parties treat this topic? For the most part, the three administrations in power today share one characteristic: All govern countries that rank near the top in support for same-sex marriage. However, their reaction to gay rights has varied from homophobic (Mexico), to relatively neutral (Colombia), to somewhat gay friendly (Chile). Almost universally, these right parties do not take strong anti-gay stances nor try to roll back earlier advancements on gay rights (recriminalize sodomy, delete anti-discrimination and/or hate crimes laws, strip partnership recognition, etc.) as all have mentioned needing to respect LGBT people as human beings. In some of these countries, we have seen progress during conservative administrations; however, with the exception of Chile, no progress has been *the result of* these conservative administrations.

Chile represents a unique example here of a conservative government potentially advancing gay rights; in 2010, center-right President Sebastián Piñera proposed legislation to recognize civil unions. Piñera was elected as president in January 2010 and took office just two months later in March as the candidate for the center-right Coalition for Change. His political party, National Renewal, was created in the late 1980s. Many of its members supported keeping Pinochet in power in the 1988 plebiscite. Clearly he comes from a movement that has a strong foundation in conservative economic principles. Moreover, Chile remains as one of the most socially conservative countries in the region, being the last in South America to legalize divorce finally in 2004.[26]

Yet his presidency is unique because his victory represents a rebuttal to the pink tide: he is the first right-wing head of state since Chile's return to democracy in 1990. However, this is also a remarkable case because he is the first president from the Right in Latin America to propose on his own a piece of legislation recognizing same-sex couples in the form of civil unions (in 2011). This is not to say that the Right as a whole has embraced this new position. In fact, many conservative members refused to attend the ceremony where Piñera submitted the legislation and will actively fight against it.

His proposal would create a national civil union registry, open to opposite-sex and same-sex couples alike, which would have all of the rights and responsibilities of marriage (just lacking the name). Within the Chilean context this might appeal to lesbians and gays as well as to many long-term cohabitating heterosexual pairs, many of whom have avoided marriage because of its strict regulations before divorce was legalized. Piñera, like many of those within the Contestatory Left, is adamant that he does not support same-sex marriage rights.

Gay rights have advanced quite swiftly in both Colombia and Mexico, but in neither case did this come about because of support from the conservative administrations. In Colombia, earlier laws from the 1990s protected lesbians and gays from discrimination. However, same-sex couples have won a number of important partnership rights from rulings from the top constitutional court. A 2007 decision granted same-sex couples the right to form civil unions. Ultimately, in 2011, the high court ruled that the President and the Congress had two years to pass a law recognizing same-sex marriage, or these couples would just gain this right automatically by July 20, 2013. Meanwhile, the past two administrations that have ruled for the last decade have represented traditional economic conservatives taken little action to oppose. In this instance then, although they have not been supporters of gay rights, they have not been vehemently anti-gay, either.

Mexico may be the closest to linking conservative themes on both economic and social issues under the banner of a single party. The National Action Party (PAN), under the administrations of Vicente Fox and Filipe Calderón, have publicly blasted legislation and court rulings that have called for the recognition of same-sex partners in the forms of civil union and/or marriage. However, neither of the conservative presidents elected in the 2000s, neither Vicente Fox nor Calderón, went out of their way to roll back the advancement of gay rights/same-sex marriage that was slowly being won at the local level and through pronouncements by the nation's high court.[27]

After this brief overview of the conservative parties—most of which have not been terribly antigay—you may be asking yourself: so where is the opposition? Most of the opposition comes in the form of individual personal opinions that still arise from in the culture codes rooted in machismo and mores of the Catholic (and now in some places evangelical protestant) churches. The actors who continue to oppose gay rights are religious leaders in the churches themselves. While these religious institutions may have great sway over individual attitudes (including political elites) in the country, by most measures they have failed to organize political parties along these lines. This is not to say that anti-gay opposition is weak; it's just that it permeates individual attitudes throughout society regardless of party affiliation.

DISCUSSION

Looking at all of these cases as a whole, we can make a number of observations. First, the Moderate Left and Contestatory Left vary both in terms of their positions and outcomes. This is most evident on the issue of same-sex marriage. Only in Argentina and Uruguay (Moderate Left states) have the heads of state come out in favor of it, while no presidents in Contestatory Left countries are in favor. Moreover, Argentina is also the only state that recognizes same-sex marriages nationwide, while Uruguay is on the verge of doing this. Does this mean we can unequivocally state that that Moderate Left parties are more pro-gay than contestatory parties, everything else being equal?

Not necessarily. Argentina and Uruguay are also the two countries with the highest public opinions supporting same-sex marriage. Once we control for public opinion in all of these cases, we see that contestatory presidents are actually quite progressive on these issues, supporting things like civil unions even when support for marriage is just very small. Many of the leaders from Contestatory Left are actually *more* gay-friendly than their Moderate Left peers with similar approval ratings for same-sex marriage. Within these contexts where public opinion is strongly anti-gay, these contestatory parties have accomplished a lot. In the case of Ecuador, Contestatory Left President Raphael Correa enshrined same-sex unions in the constitution in a country that shows only 18.4 percent of the population is in support of same-sex marriage. While homophobia may linger, leftism appears to be a driving force for support for LGBT rights as Contestatory Left countries are ahead of public opinion on these issues.

Table 2.1. Support for Gay Rights by Party Type and Public Opinion

	Contestatory Left	Moderate Left	Right
Extremely Positive [i]	Ecuador 18.4%	Argentina 63.9% Uruguay 50.5%	—
Very Positive [ii]	Bolivia 24.7% Venezuela 22.5%	Brazil 39.8%	Chile 39.7%
Positive [iii]	Cuba ND Nicaragua 15.6%	Chile 39.7% Costa Rica 20.7%	Colombia 34.3%
Negative [iv]	Ecuador 18.4%	—	Mexico 37.8%

[i] *Same-sex marriage proposed or adopted or constitutional recognition of unions*
[ii] *Proposals or adoption of partnership rights short of marriage*
[iii] *Decriminalization, non-discrimination protections proposed or adopted*
[iv] *Proposals or adoptions to rollback gay rights laws*

Second, we also learn from this study that homosexuality has not become a partisan issue in most Latin American countries, which contrasts greatly with the United States where a wide range of social issues have found cleavages along party lines. Geoffrey Layman explains how this happened historically in the United States.[28] Prior to the middle of the twentieth century, the Republican and Democratic parties in the United States differed little on social issues. This was especially true on the topic of homosexuality, where condemnation spread equally among both parties. However, as issues began to increase in salience, religious movements gradually began to identify with the Republican Party and secularists moved to the Democratic Party.

One danger to this partisanship is that LGBT groups in the United States have become "captured" interest groups, meaning that neither electoral party needs to be especially responsive to their interests.[29] LGBT people will rarely vote for Republican officials because they are so anti-gay, meaning that Democrat representatives also do not necessarily need to perform well to secure the vote of this constituency.

Unlike the United States, issues of homosexuality have not been a major point of cleavage between the Left versus the Right as LGBT issues have not polarized along party lines of secular, pro-labor, pro-gay Left versus religious, economically conservative, anti-gay Right (with perhaps the exception of Mexico). Instead, Left versus Right has kept its tradition-al economic indication, but secular and religious members have joined the ranks of both left-wing and right-wing parties. Christian Democratic parties on the Left attract religious members because their Christian Lib-eration theology equates poverty, inequality, and homosexuality all as sins. Likewise, we also see many situations where economically conser-vative parties stay true to a classical liberal philosophy of "hands off" and believe that government should play a small roll, both in the boardroom and in the bedroom. Candidates from these parties oppose unions but at the same time support gay rights. One upside to this story is that LGBT folks in these countries are not captured groups, as candidates from all political parties in a sense feel the pressure to campaign for their votes.

An example of this is the 2010 vote in Argentina legalizing same-sex marriage. In this case, all political parties publicly freed their members to "vote their conscious."[30] In the course of this campaign, we saw socialist candidates vote against the bill, but other elected officials from very eco-nomically conservative parties giving impassioned speeches supporting the bill.

Does this mean that parties are unimportant here? Quite the contrary. Within each of these countries where LGBT peoples have gained more equality in areas of nondiscrimination, hate crimes, and partnership rights, parties have played a clear organizational role in terms of moving policies through the legislative process. In fact, these relationships be-tween activists and parties become so strong at times that some fear that LGBT social movements might become co-opted into the larger party machine.[31] The central role of activists becoming embedded in these structures is reinforced in a number of studies.[32] Regardless of whether public opinion is strong, gains would not be realized on behalf of LGBT peoples if politicians working through parties guiding legislation.

CONCLUSION

This chapter hopefully demonstrates a couple of things about the relationship between LGBT peoples and the Left in Latin America today, as well as points to some directions for future research. First, there have been some dramatic changes in how the Left treats issues of sexuality today. For the most part, LGBT peoples had a very difficult time finding political supporters in any country in the region just ten years ago, but in the past decade several strong elite allies have emerged.

But this does not mean that all political parties are equal: Most support for LGBT groups has come from those parties that are today considered the Moderate Left. The Contestatory Left, on the other hand, has done less in terms of gay rights, but it is unclear whether this is because of the very low public opinion support for gay marriage in these countries or because of residual homophobia, and it could be a great area for future research. Finally, while states led by right-wing leaders have seen little in terms of progress for gay rights, these heads-of-state have also not been anti-gay crusaders. This is good news for LGBT groups in these countries because they are able to maintain the wins made at the local level or at least the status quo. Also, having a president from the Right does not necessarily mean no progress on gay rights, as is demonstrated in Chile.

Unlike in the United States, though, these partnerships have not emerged along partisan lines, as LGBT groups have found allies among elites in political parties on the both the Left and the Right. This does not mean, however, that political parties themselves have not played an important role in advancing issues concerning sexuality. On the contrary, some of the most important advancements have been made when LGBT groups use their connections within the parties, and the party infrastructures themselves, to move issues through the institutions of the state.

Overall, what recommendations can we give to lesbian and gay activists in Latin America based on this research? Clearly, public opinion is very important and movements should devote their resources to gaining the public's support. There is a very clear connection between public support for same-sex marriage and the level of partnership recognition. However, this does not seem to be enough because some of the most supportive countries on this list have run into hurdles. As public opinion increases, activists then should focus their efforts on securing allies with the political parties to advance legislation. Consequently, we can say that changing public opinion on homosexuality, and not the pink tide, better explains the lavender tide that is sweeping Latin America.

NOTES

1. Omar G. Encarnación, "Latin America's Gay Rights Revolution," *Journal of Democracy*, 22, no. 2 (2011), 104–18.

2. Jason Pierceson, Adriana Piatti-Crocker, and Shawn Schulenberg, *Same-Sex Marriage in the Americas: Policy Innovation for Same-Sex Relationships* (Lanham, MD: Lexington Books, 2010).

3. Cynthia Arnson, ed., *The "New Left" and Democratic Governance in Latin America* (Washington, DC: Woodrow Wilson Center, 2007); Maxwell A. Cameron, "Latin America's Left Turns: Beyond Good and Bad," *Third World Quarterly*, 30, no. 2 (2009), 331–48; Maxwell A. Cameron and Eric Hershberg, eds., *Latin America's Left Turns: Politics, Policies, and Trajectories of Change* (Boulder, CO: Lynne Rienner Publishers, 2010); Jorge G. Castañeda, "Latin America's Left Turn," *Foreign Affairs*, 85, no. 3 (2006), 28–43; Matthew R. Cleary, "Explaining the Left's Resurgence," *Journal of Democracy*, 17, no. 4 (2006), 35–49; Elisabeth Jay Friedman, "Introduction: How Pink Is the 'Pink Tide'?," *NACLA Report on the Americas*, 40, no. 2 (2007), 16; Latinobarómetro, *Informe Latinobarómetro 2006* (Santiago: Corporación Latinobarómetro, 2006); Steven Levitsky and Kenneth M. Roberts, eds., *The Resurgence of the Latin American Left* (Baltimore: Johns Hopkins University Press, 2011); Mitchell A. Seligson, "The Rise of Populism and the Left: Challenge to Democratic Consolidation?," in *Challenges to Democracy in Latin America and the Caribbean: Evidence from the Americasbarometer 2006–2007* (Nashville, TN: Latin American Public Opinion Project, 2008); Kurt Weyland, Raúl L. Madrid, and Wendy Hunter, eds., *Leftist Governments in Latin America: Successes and Shortcomings* (New York: Cambridge University Press, 2010); Marc Zimmerman and Luis Ochoa Bilbao, eds., *Giros Culturales En La Marea Rosa De América Latina* (Houston: LACASA Books, 2012).

4. Friedman, "Introduction: How Pink Is the 'Pink Tide'?"; Deborah J. Yashar, "The Left and Citizenship Rights," in *The Resurgence of the Latin American Left*, eds. Steven Levitsky and Kenneth M. Roberts (Baltimore: Johns Hopkins University Press, 2011).

5. I have intentionally left all Caribbean nations (with the exception of Cuba) out of this study because of a variety of significant historical differences they have with Central and South American countries: the lack of a traditional Marxist left/right split; different political cultures and racial compositions; and, finally, many of their legal traditions are rooted in Anglo-Saxon instead of Napoleonic Law.

6. James N. Green and Florence E. Babb, "Introduction," *Latin American Perspectives* 29, no. 2 (2002), 3–23.

7. Green and Babb, "Introduction," 11.

8. Green and Babb, "Introduction," 13.

9. Green and Babb, "Introduction," 12–13.

10. And this only happened as the result of significant international pressure.

11. Encarnación, "Latin America's Gay Rights Revolution."

12. Whether these right parties should actually be in power is contested in some of these cases. Honduras would have a leftist President, but the military forced him out of office in 2009 at the behest of the Congress and the Supreme Court. Likewise, leftist President Fernando Lugo was ousted in 2012 under questionable circumstances by the Congress.

13. Latinobarómetro, *Informe Latinobarómetro 2006*, 86.

14. Castañeda, "Latin America's Left Turn," 35.

15. Castañeda, "Latin America's Left Turn," 38.

16. John D. French, "Many Paths, One Left? Chávez and Lula," in *Latin America's Left Turns: Politics, Policies, and Trajectories of Change*, eds. Maxwell A. Cameron and Eric Hershberg (Boulder, CO: Lynne Rienner Publishers, 2010).

17. Cameron, "Latin America's Left Turns: Beyond Good and Bad."

18. Weyland, Madrid, and Hunter, eds., *Leftist Governments in Latin America: Successes and Shortcomings*.

19. Kurt Weyland, "The Performance of Leftist Governments in Latin America: Conceptual and Theoretical Issues," in *Leftist Governments in Latin America: Successes and Shortcomings*, eds. Kurt Weyland, Raúl L. Madrid, and Wendy Hunter (New York: Cambridge University Press, 2010), 3.

20. Weyland, "The Performance of Leftist Governments in Latin America: Conceptual and Theoretical Issues."

21. Some may question my choice to classify each administration by the historical origin of its party instead of looking at its actual policy outputs on economic issues. For example, I have coded the Menem administration in Argentina in the 1990s as a leftist party because his party (the Peronist party) has a historical foundation in representing organized labor. Some may argue that his government should instead be classified as a right party because he ushered in Neoliberalism and governed very far to the right on economic issues. However, because I am concerned with whether or not parties have changed over time, this provides a stronger test. Moreover, I run into tautology issues if I use policy outputs as both my independent and dependent variables.

22. Germán Lodola and Margarita Corral, "Support for Same-Sex Marriage in Latin America." I use this as a general proxy for public support for LGBT people. Although it might be better to include public opinion data on wider range of issues concerning sexuality (for example, whether homosexuality is morally wrong, whether lesbians and gays should be protected from workplace discrimination, and so on), this is one of the few cross-national studies that asks the same question to people in all countries, allowing for methodological consistency.

23. Shawn Schulenberg, "The Construction and Enactment of Same-Sex Marriage in Argentina," *Journal of Human Rights*, 11, no. 1 (2012), 106–25.

24. Shawn Schulenberg, "Policy Stability without Policy: The Battle for Same-Sex Partnership Recognition in Brazil," in *Same-Sex Marriage in the Americas: Policy Innovation for Same-Sex Relationships*, eds. Jason Pierceson, Adriana Piatti-Crocker, and Shawn Schulenberg (Lanham, MD: Lexington Books, 2010).

25. It may be too early to lump Humala in the Contestatory Left camp as his administration only took office in July 2011. This classification is solely based on his rhetoric from the past, and may be quickly refuted by his early moderate cabinet picks.

26. For a larger discussion of the process of legalizing abortion in Chile, see Mala Htun, *Sex and the State: Abortion, Divorce, and the Family under Latin American Dictatorships and Democracies* (New York: Cambridge University Press, 2003).

27. At the time of this writing, the PRI was just elected back into power, so it is difficult to see how it will deliver on LGBT issues after being out of power for 12 years. Similarly, the Right also just came into power in Paraguay recently, but it is difficult to say how it will govern.

28. Geoffrey Layman, *The Great Divide: Religious and Cultural Conflict in American Party Politics*, Power, Conflict, and Democracy (New York: Columbia University Press, 2001).

29. Charles Anthony Smith, "The Electoral Capture of Gay and Lesbian Americans: Evidence and Implications from the 2004 Election," *Studies in Law, Politics, and Society*, 40, no. 2 (2007), 103–21.

30. Schulenberg, "The Construction and Enactment of Same-Sex Marriage in Argentina."

31. Alejandra Sardá, "Resisting Kirchner's Recipe (Sometimes): 'Lgbttti' Organizing in Argentina," *NACLA Report on the Americas*, 40, no. 2 (2007), 30–32.

32. Rafael De la Dehesa, *Queering the Public Sphere in Mexico and Brazil: Sexual Rights Movements in Emerging Democracies* (Durham, NC: Duke University Press, 2010), 62; Schulenberg, "Policy Stability without Policy: The Battle for Same-Sex Partnership Recognition in Brazil"; Schulenberg, "The Construction and Enactment of Same-Sex Marriage in Argentina."

THREE

Support for Same-Sex Marriage in Latin America

Germán Lodola and Margarita Corral

Gay marriage has recently been a subject of intense discussion in many countries in the Americas. Disputes over the issue are marked by sharply conflicting opinions among citizens, social organizations, religious groups, the highly influential Catholic Church, and policymakers. In Latin America, these debates have engendered outcomes that vary sharply from country to country. Same-sex marriage has been constitutionally banned in Honduras (2005), El Salvador (2009), and the Dominican Republic (2009). In Bolivia, the new constitution (2009) limits legally recognized marriage to opposite-sex unions. In Costa Rica, the Supreme Court ruled against same-sex couples seeking the right to be legally married (2006), while a national referendum on the subject remains a possibility. Yet same-sex civil unions, which give homosexual couples some of the rights enjoyed by heterosexual couples (including social security inheritance and joint ownership of property, but excluding adoption rights), have been legalized in Uruguay (2008), Ecuador (2008), Colombia (2009), Brazil (since 2004), and in a few Mexican states.[1] Within this diverse regional context, and despite numerous protests organized by the Catholic Church, rightist organizations, and conservative legislators, Argentina became the first Latin American country to legalize same-sex marriage nationwide, granting gays and lesbians more rights than civil unions, including the right to adopt children.[2]

This chapter looks at citizens' opinions with respect to same-sex marriage. First, we examine levels of support for same-sex couples having the right to marry. Then, we assess both individual- and national-level determinants of variation in that level of support. To evaluate these issues, we query the 2010 round of the American Public Opinion Project (LAPOP) survey.[3] In this survey, 42,238 respondents from twenty-five nations in North, Central, and South America and the Caribbean[4] were asked this question: "How strongly do you approve or disapprove of same-sex couples having the right to marry?" Responses were given based on a 1–10 scale, where 1 meant "strongly disapprove" and 10 meant "strongly approve." These responses were then recalibrated on a 0–100 basis to conform to the LAPOP standard, which facilitates comparability across questions and survey waves.[5]

Figure 3.1 displays each country's average score with its confidence interval. The average level of support for same-sex marriage in the Americas is only 26.8 points on a 0–100 scale. However, there is striking variation across countries. At the one extreme, citizens of Canada, Argentina, and Uruguay express relatively high levels of support and fall on the high end of the 0–100 continuum, with mean scores of 63.9, 57.7, 50.5, and 47.7 points, respectively. At the other extreme, El Salvador, Guyana, and Jamaica (where sexual acts between men are punishable with jail) show the lowest levels of support: 10.3, 7.2, and 3.5 units, respectively. The remaining countries lie in between these extremes, with those nations in which same-sex civil union has been legalized (Brazil, Mexico, and Colombia) ranking in relatively high positions. Notably, despite the fact that the newly approved constitution grants full rights to homosexual civil unions, Ecuador is positioned well below the regional average with 18.4 points on the 0–100 scale.

What factors explain variation in support for same-sex marriage? To assess this question, we first focus on the potential impact of individual-level factors by means of a linear regression model.[6] Following the publication of seminal research on political tolerance that examines the impact of religious values toward homosexuals,[7, 8] we include two variables that are considered to be key: importance of religion and religious group participation. The former measures how important religion is in the respondent's life.[9] The latter measures the respondent's self-reported level of attendance at meetings of any religious organization.[10] Several scholars have found that disapproval of homosexual rights is highest among individuals with strong religious identities and who attend religious services frequently.[11, 12, 13, 14, 15, 16, 17] Therefore, we expect these variables to have a negative impact on support for same-sex marriage. Beliefs about homosexuality and support for gay rights have been found to vary substantially by religion. Therefore, we also included two dummy variables, Evangelical and atheist, in order to capture the effect of religious affiliations. While atheists are expected to express tolerance toward minorities' rights, membership in evangelical denominations has been found to be linked to intolerance of homosexuals in the United States.[18] While this finding could be partly attributed to differences in demographic or politi-

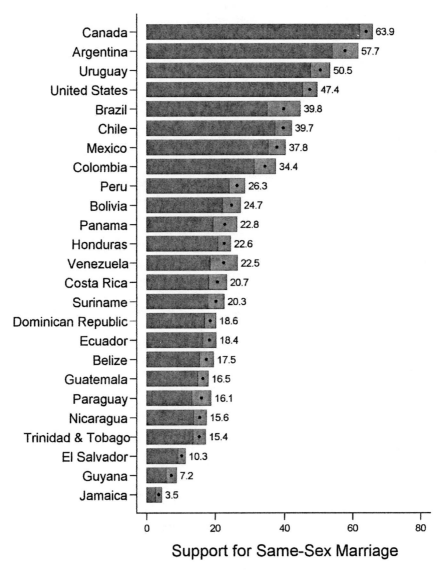

Support for Same-Sex Marriage

95% Confidence Interval (Design-Effects Based)

Figure 3.1.   Average Support for Same-Sex Marriage in the Americas, 2010. AmericasBarometer by LAPOP.

cal variables, or to general religiosity, Wilcox and Jelen[19] demonstrated that intolerance among Evangelicals persists even after controlling for these considerations.

Also included in the regression is a variable that captures the respondent's political ideology. This variable is based on a 1–10 scale, where 1 means left or liberal and 10 means right or conservative. For obvious reasons, we expect more conservative respondents to be less prone to support same-sex marriage than liberal ones.

Finally, the regression model includes a number of variables measuring basic socioeconomic and demographic characteristics that are thought to play a role in shaping public opinion towards homosexuality. We thus include education, age, gender, wealth, and city/town size.[20] We expect more educated individuals to have more liberal sexual attitudes and therefore express higher levels of support for same-sex marriage than less educated persons.[21, 22, 23, 24] Similarly, we expect older people to be less tolerant toward gays/lesbians than younger people, more because of the eras in which the former were socialized than to the aging process itself.[25, 26] As found in prior research, we also expect men to be more inclined to disapprove of homosexuality than women,[27, 28, 29] and people with higher incomes to be more tolerant than people with lower incomes.[30] Following research by Stephan and McMullin,[31] we expect urbanism (in our model, individuals living in larger cities) to be positively associated with tolerance toward homosexuals and, thus, support for same-sex marriage.

The results of this regression analysis are shown in Figure 3.2. Each variable included in the model is listed on the vertical (y) axis. The impact of each of those variables on support for same-sex marriage is shown graphically by a dot, which if falling to the right of the vertical "0" line implies a positive contribution and if to the left of the "0" line indicates a negative impact. Only when the confidence intervals (the horizontal lines) do not overlap the vertical "0" line is the variable statistically significant (at .05 or better). The relative strength of each variable is indicated by standardized coefficients ("beta weights").

We find strong empirical evidence supporting our expectations. First, even when controlling for socioeconomic and demographic factors and the impact of country of residence (the "country fixed effects"), both the importance of religion and attendance at religious meetings variables have a statistically significant negative impact on support for same-sex marriage. Specifically, the more important religion is to respondents' lives and the more frequently they attend religious meetings, the lower the support they express for same-sex couples having the right to marry. Second, we find that Evangelicals, compared to individuals who profess other religions, are significantly less likely to support same-sex marriage, while those who say that they are Atheists or agnostic about religion are more likely to support gay marriage. Third, holding all other variables constant, respondents' ideological self-placement works as we expected. The statistically significant negative impact of the political ideology vari-

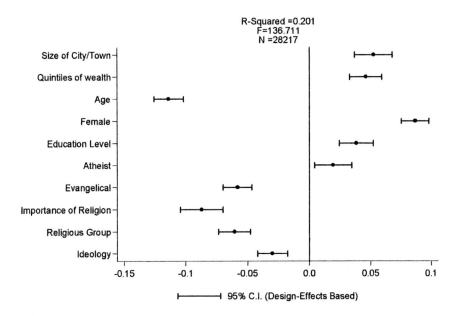

Figure 3.2. Support for Same-Sex Marriage in Latin America and the Caribbean, 2010. AmericasBarometer by LAPOP.

able indicates that the more conservative respondents are, the lower the level of support for same-sex marriage they express.

We also find that all the socioeconomic and demographic variables included in the model are statistically significant in the theorized directions. First, size of the geographic area of residence is positively linked to our dependent variable, indicating that residents of large cities express higher levels of support than those living in rural areas and small cities. Second, citizens with more years of completed education express higher support than individuals with less formal education. Third, both wealthier and younger persons express more tolerance toward homosexual marriages than poorer and older people. Fourth, the positive effect of the gender (female) dummy variable indicates that women express higher levels of support than men.

PREDICTING SUPPORT FOR SAME-SEX MARRIAGE: THE EFFECT OF CONTEXTUAL VARIABLES

In addition to the individual-level characteristics analyzed above, other factors at the country level of analysis may help explain variation in the degree to which citizens in the Americas support same-sex marriage. Extensive research on political tolerance in democratic regimes has underscored the important effects of economic development and education on acceptance of diversity. To empirically test these propositions, we estimated separate multilevel regression models.[32] The models include the respondents' individual characteristics alongside measures of each country's level of economic development or education, depending on the model. These variables are measured by GDP per capita and a composite index of adult literacy and gross enrollment, respectively.[33]

The statistical results of the multilevel models are graphically shown in Figures 3.3 and 3.4. As they show, the impact of individual characteristics remains almost unchanged when compared to our previous results, while the contextual variables have the expected positive relationships to support for same-sex marriage. More concretely, citizens who live in richer and more educated countries express significantly higher levels of support compared to those who live in poorer and less educated nations.

The specific effects of economic development and education at the national level on support for same-sex marriage are displayed in Figures 3.5 and 3.6, respectively. These figures show the fitted lines from the two multilevel regression models using national GDP per capita and the education index. Holding constant all the individual-level variables at their mean value, the models predict similar results compared to the ranking depicted in Figure 3.1. As a noteworthy exception, Trinidad and Tobago dramatically improves its position in Figure 3.5 compared to Figure 3.1.

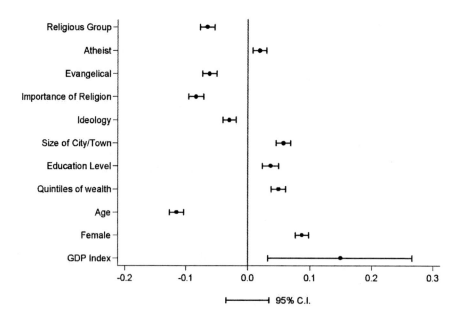

Figure 3.3.   A Multilevel Analysis of the Determinants of Support for Same-Sex Marriage in Latin America and the Caribbean, 2010: The Impact of GDP. AmericasBarometer by LAPOP.

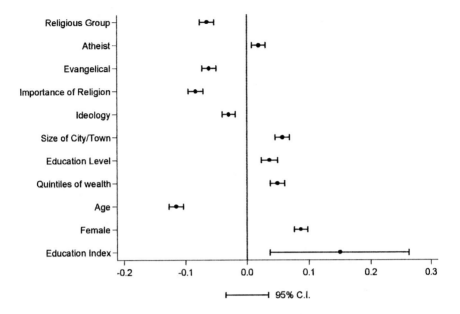

Figure 3.4. A Multilevel Analysis of the Determinants of Support for Same-Sex Marriage in Latin America and the Caribbean, 2010: The Impact of Education. AmericasBarometer by LAPOP.

This suggests that the country is strongly influenced by other variables not included in our model.

Nonetheless, the results show that higher levels of economic development and education predict substantially higher levels of support for same-sex marriage. Substantively, if a citizen from Nicaragua with a given set of socioeconomic characteristics were to move to Argentina, *ceteris paribus*, and none of her personal characteristics were to change, this person would demonstrate a level of support for same-sex marriage that would be about 20 points higher on average than if this individual were to remain in Nicaragua.

CONCLUSION

We began this short report by pointing out that citizens in the Latin American and Caribbean region, on average, express relatively low levels of support for same-sex marriage. However, we have underscored that there is also significant cross-national variation. At the individual level of analysis, our statistical analysis indicates that strong religious values and more conservative ideologies have a significant negative impact on individual support for homosexuals having the right to marry. In addition, we found that levels of support are higher among wealthier people, indi-

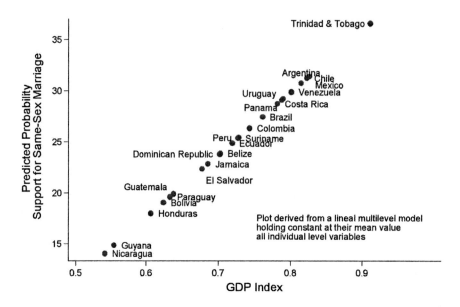

Figure 3.5.   The Impact of Economic Development on Support for Same-Sex Marriage in Latin America and the Caribbean, 2010. AmericasBarometer by LAP-OP and UNDP (Human Development Report 2009).

viduals living in larger cities, and women. In our analyses of national-level factors, we found strong empirical evidence supporting the classic claim that both economic development and education increase tolerance for homosexual rights.

These results are consistent with those for studies of tolerance over a broad range of minority rights issues, which collectively highlight the significance of education at both the individual and national level. To promote tolerance of minority rights, policymakers, and politicians should consider the importance of expanding access to education among their citizens.

Although some have argued that tolerance of diversity might have no real consequences for democracy,[34] others have found strong evidence of its positive effects on the construction of democratic policies.[35] An important implication of this report is that the vision offered by liberal democratic theorists of a society that accepts diversity and protects minority rights is more likely to develop to the extent that policymakers pay close attention to improving citizens' well being and education. Higher economic development and education tend to be linked with greater tolerance because they stimulate individual value priorities that are conducive to greater openness to diversity.

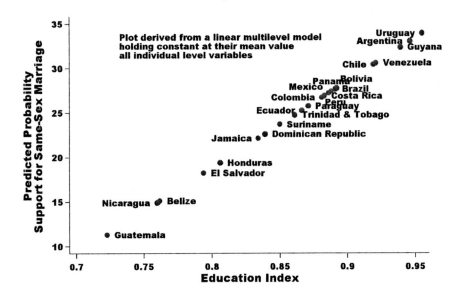

Figure 3.6. The Impact of Education on Support for Same-Sex Marriage in Latin America and the Caribbean, 2010. AmericasBarometer by LAPOP and UNDP (Human Development Report 2009).

APPENDIX

Table 3.1. Determinants of Support for Same-Sex Marriage

	Coefficient	t
Ideology.............................	-0.030*	(-4.86)
Religious Group....................	-0.061*	(-9.28)
Importance of Religion.........	-0.087*	(-9.90)
Evangelical.........................	-0.058*	(-9.91)
Atheist	0.020*	(2.50)
Education Level...................	0.038*	(5.46)
Female...............................	0.087*	(15.02)
Age....................................	-0.114*	(-18.85)
Quintiles of wealth...............	0.046*	(6.80)
Size of City/Town................	0.052*	(6.61)
Mexico...............................	-0.088*	(-7.92)
Guatemala	-0.166*	(-16.27)
El Salvador	-0.213*	(-22.19)
Honduras	-0.148*	(-13.75)
Nicaragua	-0.189*	(-16.24)

Costa Rica	-0.161*	(-13.31)
Panama	-0.146*	(-10.49)
Colombia	-0.106*	(-9.38)
Ecuador	-0.253*	(-18.01)
Bolivia	-0.217*	(-13.18)
Peru	-0.148*	(-13.52)
Paraguay	-0.192*	(-16.57)
Chile	-0.104*	(-8.21)
Uruguay	-0.044*	(-4.08)
Brazil	-0.104*	(-5.50)
Venezuela	-0.172*	(-12.87)
Dominican Republic	-0.164*	(-15.67)
Jamaica	-0.238*	(-24.71)
Guyana.............................	-0.220*	(-20.31)
Trinidad & Tobago............	-0.196*	(-19.15)
Belize..............................	-0.175*	(-14.36)
Suriname..........................	-0.172*	(-12.53)
Constant..........................	0.025*	(2.69)
R-Squared.........................	0.201	
Number of Obs...................	28,217	

* $p<0.05$
Country of Reference: Argentina

Authors' elaboration based on AmericasBarometer 2010.

NOTES

1. In Colombia, a same-sex couples bill was defeated by the Senate in 2007 but was later legalized by a Constitutional Court decision. In Mexico, same-sex civil unions are only legal in the state of Coahuila, whereas in Mexico City the state assembly recently recognized same-sex marriage with adoption rights.

2. Same-sex marriage is also legal in the Netherlands (2001), Belgium (2003), Spain (2005), Canada (2005), South Africa (2006), Norway (2009), Sweden (2009), Iceland (2010), and Portugal (2010). Israel (2006), France (2008), and Japan (2009) legally recognize same-sex marriages performed in other countries. In the United States, the federal government is banned from recognizing marriages of same-sex couples by the Defense of Marriage Act, although courts have recently ruled parts of the law as unconstitutional. Same-sex marriage is permitted in the states of Connecticut, Iowa, Massachusetts, New Hampshire, Vermont, and the District of Columbia.

3. Much of the funding for the 2010 AmericasBarometer round was provided by the United States Agency for International Development (USAID). Other important sources of support were the Inter-American Development Bank (IADB), the United Nations Development Program (UNDP), and Vanderbilt University.

4. The final version of the 2010 wave will include 26 countries; at the time of this report, the survey is being implemented to a sample of 6,000 individuals in Haiti.

5. Around 1,500 respondents were interviewed face-to-face in each country, except in Bolivia and Ecuador, where the samples were approximately 3,000. The Canada and the United States are Web-based surveys. Nonresponse to this question was 3.23 percent for the sample as a whole.

6. All statistical analyses in this paper were conducted using STATA v10 and results were adjusted for the complex sample designs employed. Given that levels of support for same-sex marriage vary across countries, dummy variables for each country were included. In all models, Argentina is considered as the base or reference country. Results for the whole model are presented in the Appendix, Table 1.

7. Gibson, James L. and Kent L. Tedin, "Etiology of Intolerance of Homosexual Politics," *Social Science Quarterly* 69 (1988): 587–604.

8. Golebiowska, Ewa, "Individual Value Priorities, Education, and Political Tolerance," *Political Behavior* 17, no. 1 (1995): 23–48.

9. This variable is based on the following question: Q5B. "Please, could you tell me how important is religion in your life? Very important; rather important; not very important; not at all important."

10. This variable is based on the following question: CP6. "Do you attend Meetings of any religious organization? Do you attend them once a week, once or twice a month, once or twice a year or never?"

11. Ellison, Christopher G. and March A. Musick, "Southern Intolerance: A Fundamentalist Effect?" *Social Forces* 72, no. 2 (1993): 379–98.

12. Herek, Gregory M., "Heterosexuals' Attitudes toward Lesbians and Gay Men: Correlates and Gender Differences," *Journal of Sex Research* 25, no. 4 (1988): 457–77.

13. Herek, Gregory M. and John P. Capitanio, "Black Heterosexuals' Attitudes toward Lesbians and Gay Men in the United States," *Journal of Sex Research* 32, no. 2 (1995): 95–105.

14. Herek, Gregory M. and John P. Capitanio, "Some of My Best Friends: Intergroup Contact, Concealable Stigma, and Heterosexuals' Attitudes toward Gay Men and Lesbians," *Personality and Social Psychology Bulletin* 22, no. 4 (1996): 412–24.

15. Olsen, Laura R., Wendy Cadge and James T. Harrison, "Religion and Public Opinion about Same-Sex Marriage," *Social Science Quarterly* 87, no. 2 (2006): 340–60.

16. Seltzer, Richard, "AIDS, Homosexuality, Public Opinion, and Changing Correlates over Time," *Journal of Homosexuality* 26, no. 1(1993): 85–97.

17. Wilcox, Clyde, and Robin Wolpert, "Gay Rights in the Public Sphere: Public Opinion on Gay and Lesbian Equality," in *The Politics of Gay Rights*, edited by Craig A. Rimmerman, Kenneth D. Wald, and Clyde Wilcox (Chicago: University of Chicago Press, 2000).

18. Jelen, Ted, "Sources of political intolerance: The case of the American South," in *Contemporary Southern Political Attitudes and Behavior*, edited by Robert P. Steed, Laurence W. Moreland, and Todd. A. Baker (New York: Praeger, 1982).

19. Wilcox, Clyde and Ted Jelen, "Evangelicals and Political Tolerance,"*American Politics Research* 18, no. 1 (1990): 25–46.

20. Citizens in Canada and the United States hold sharply higher levels on many socioeconomic characteristics; for this and because we select to focus this report on Latin America and the Caribbean, we excluded these cases from the analysis.

21. Ellison, Christopher G. and March A. Musick, 1993.

22. Gibson, James L. and Kent L. Tedin, 1988.

23. Herek, Gregory M. and John P. Capitanio., 1996.

24. Treas, Judith, "How Cohorts, Education, and Ideology Shaped a New Sexual Revolution on American Attitudes toward Non-marital Sex, 1972–1998," *Sociological Perspectives* 45, no. 3 (2002): 267–83.

25. Davis, James Allan, "Changeable Weather in a Cooling Climate atop the Liberal Plateau: Conversion and Replacement in Forty-Two General Social Survey Items, 1972–1989," *Public Opinion Quarterly* 56, no. 3 (1992): 261–306.

26. Herek, Gregory M. and Eric K. Glunt, "Interpersonal Contact and Heterosexuals' Attitudes toward Gay Men: Results from a National Survey," *Journal of Sex Research* 30, no. 3 (1993): 239–44.

27. Herek, Gregory M., "Gender Gaps in Public Opinion about Lesbians and Gay Men," *Public Opinion Quarterly* 66, no. 1 (2002): 40–66.

28. Kite, Mary E., "Sex Differences in Attitudes toward Homosexuals: A Meta-Analytic Review," *Journal of Homosexuality* 10, no. 1/2 (1984): 69–82.

29. Kite, Mary E. and Bernard E. Whitley, Jr., "Sex Differences in Attitudes toward Homosexual Persons, Behaviors, and Civil Rights: A Meta-analysis," *Personality and Social Psychology Bulletin* 22, no. 4 (1996): 336–53.

30. Hodges Persell, Caroline, Adam Green, and Liena Gurevich, "Civil Society, Economic Distress, and Social Tolerance," *Sociological Forum* 16, no. 2 (2001): 203–30.

31. Stephan, Edward G. and Douglas McMullan, "Tolerance of Sexual Nonconformity: City Size as a Situational and Early Learning Determinant," *American Sociological Review* 47, no. 6 (1982): 411–15.

32. This analysis was carried out using multilevel regression techniques (Raudenbush and Bryk 2002; Raudenbush, *et al.* 2004) as implemented by LAPOP on STATA 10. The model simultaneously takes into account both individual- and country-level (in other words, contextual) factors, and produces correct regression estimates that are impossible with standard OLS regression. We estimated separate models because national economic development and education are correlated at a moderately high level in our sample (r = .6, $p > .05$).

33. To measure national wealth we rely on the UNDP's GDP index. This index, which can take values between 0 and 1, is based on GDP per capita in purchasing power parity terms in U.S. dollars. To measure national education, we drew upon the UNDP's Education index which is measured by the adult literacy rate (with two-thirds weighting) and the combined primary, secondary, and tertiary gross enrollment ratio (with one-third weighting). For more details on how these indexes are constructed, see UNDP's 2009 Human Development Report.

34. Mueller, John, "Trends in Political Tolerance," *Public Opinion Quarterly* 52, no. 1 (1988):1–25.

35. Gibson, James L., "The Political Consequences of Intolerance: Cultural Conformity and Political Freedom," *American Political Science Review* 86, no. 2 (1992): 338–56.

FOUR

Variations in the Judicialization of Same-Sex Marriage Politics in Latin America

Jason Pierceson

The judicialization of politics occurs when courts begin to make decisions on policy traditionally made by the legislative and executive branches of government. Judicialization also may involve an increase in the invocation of rights rhetoric in the political arena in an attempt to challenge majoritarian politics.[1] In the Western Hemisphere, the increased judicialization of politics has occurred from Argentina to Canada and in many countries in between, in both common law and civil law contexts. However, few studies have explored judicialization within the context of LBGT rights and equality. In this area, particularly that of same-sex relationship equality, the record of judicialization is not clear and uniform. Most studies of judicialization have focused on cases where judicialization is obvious in a policy area, but it is also important to explore policy areas without such a clear outcome and where judicialization has not taken place in many national contexts.[2]

Strong evidence of judicialization exists in some Latin American jurisdictions, such as Brazil, Colombia, and with a more mixed picture in Argentina and Mexico. However, despite increasingly active judiciaries in Latin America, change (or resistance to change) is still largely a product of non-judicial factors. Policy advances in most nations, such as Mexico, Argentina, and Uruguay, have been led by legislatures, parties, interest groups, and executives. In most countries in Latin America, courts are weak or nonexistent actors in this policy area. The issue of relationship equality largely remains one of non-judicial politics, where political parties, interest groups, presidents, and legislators matter more than judges. And this type of politics is more easily constrained by traditionalist opposition to LGBT-supportive policies. While there may be movement away from judicial deference and restraint in civil law regimes, this may be constrained by the policy area. In other words, the reluctance of courts to move aggressively may be linked to the cultural status of homosexuality in many jurisdictions. The judicialization of politics is not uniform among national jurisdictions or within national jurisdictions.

THE JUDICIALIZATION OF POLITICS IN CIVIL LAW VERSUS COMMON LAW SYSTEMS

The divide between civil law and common law systems is a significant variable affecting the processes of judicialization. In common law systems, judges have tremendous power to shape the law. Judge-made law rivals, and often trumps, law from legislatures. Lawyers and judges in these systems, especially in Canada and the United States, are trained and socialized as legal innovators, and this often affects public policy. As Patrick Atiyah and Robert Sommers describe this dynamic, "Law is not seen as a body of authoritative doctrine, so much as an 'instrument of political, economic and social policy.'"[3] Conversely, in civil law systems, law is often seen as "authoritative doctrine," with lawyers and judges deferring to legislative enactments. A good example is Argentina, where, according to Laura Saldivia, "judges still consider themselves technocrats, who must solve problems in concrete and individual cases following . . . the codes of law or the constitution."[4] This obviously inhibits the judicialization of politics in most jurisdictions in Latin America.

However, as will be explored later in the chapter, in the cases of Argentina, Brazil, and Colombia, this dichotomy may be breaking down with increasing judicial assertiveness. One of the reasons for this is the globalization of legal doctrine. Increasingly, common law, rights-based jurisprudence is finding its way into the legal treatises and legal opinions in civil law systems.[5] Thus, the notion that rights exist outside of statutes or code law is beginning to be enforced by judges in Latin America, particularly in cases of rights derived from constitutions. Javier Couso notes two important reasons for this shift: the training and socialization of many Latin American academics in U.S. law schools and the rejection of deference and formalism that was the hallmark of judges during the era of military dictatorships.[6] As he summarizes, "the great transformation experienced by Latin America's constitutional scholarship can be described as the path from a 'formalist and anti-judicial review' position, to a 'quasi-natural law and pro-judicial review' new orthodoxy."[7] As yet, however, this is not a total transformation, and the case of sexuality presents a challenge to emerging judicialization and transformation of civil law systems, as this paper argues. The cases that follow show a mixed record of judicialization of relationship equality policy in South America. As institutional and cultural constraints, norms that limit judicialization are still powerful in most jurisdictions.

This generally reflects that state of affairs worldwide concerning the creation of relationship equality policies. In mostly civil law Europe (where a strong form of relationship recognition exists in roughly twenty countries—and counting), litigation has been at the margins of the creation of same-sex marriage or civil/registered partnerships. This is also true of common law jurisdictions, like the United Kingdom, Australia, and New Zealand, where the norm of parliamentary sovereignty is strong. However, in South Africa and Canada, new constitutions with strong equality protections and recently activist judiciaries strongly contributed to the rapid legalization of same-sex marriage in those countries. Judicialization is also a hallmark of the politics of same-sex marriage in the United States, but change had neither been as rapid or as uniform, largely owing to the jurisdiction of states, not the federal government, over family policy and the relative power of the religious right.

SEXUALITY, CULTURE AND PUBLIC OPINION IN THE AMERICAS

Ahmed Khanani and Jean Robinson argue that the question of equality for sexual minorities "troubles" liberal democracies: "Specifically, we contend that the formation of lesbians and gay men—as individuals, then individually and also in collectives—as politically relevant minorities threatens several dimensions of liberal democratic theorists and institutions' imaginaries, including the relationship between state and church, the range of issues that constitute the political, and the role of reason in a democracy."[8] Indeed, while established and emerging liberal democracies in the Americas have been successful, to varying degrees, at incorporating some political minorities and at establishing an emerging range of individual and group rights, equality and rights for sexual minorities have proven more difficult to uniformly achieve.

Corrales and Pecheny view progress on LGBT rights as part of the recent trend toward democratization in the region, but they note that progress has been sporadic and has lagged behind gains by other marginalized groups. They also provide a useful set of variables for putting into context this lack of consistent progress. Some of these variables may be similar to those in other regions while some are unique to Latin America. The opposition of organized religion is perhaps the factor most common to other regions, particularly the role of the Catholic Church (and increasingly Evangelical Protestant churches) in opposing rights for sexual minorities. While they note that religious communities are increasingly diverse on questions of sexuality, churches "often serve as veto players, objecting to non-heteronormative behaviors, if not in a person's life, at least in the policy realm."[9] In the political realm, while leftist parties would seem to be a vehicle for change, tension has existed between LGBT movements and these parties, often stemming from homophobia within the parties and opposition to non-class-based politics. Culturally, Corrales and Pecheny explain that family structure in Latin America inhibits movement-building, as LGBT youth stay at home longer and have fewer opportunities for coming out, a key to creating political awareness. There is also more cultural compatibility with same-sex acts in the context of traditional marriage, especially for men. Finally, "the struggle for LGBT rights is often a postmaterialist concern: it is likelier to rise to the top of the agenda when material concerns become less urgent."[10]

Tremendous variation in public opinion on the question of same-sex marriage exists in the Americas, as noted by Lodola and Corral in this volume. Despite an overall low level of support in the Americas (26.8 points out of 100), "there is striking variation across countries. At one extreme, citizens of Canada, Argentina, and Uruguay [and the U.S.] express relatively high levels of support . . . with mean scores of 63.9, 57.7, 50.5, and 47.7 respectively. At the other extreme, El Salvador, Guyana and Jamaica (where sexual acts between men are punishable with jail) show the lowest levels of support: 10.3, 7.2, and 3.5 units respectively."[11] In addition, Lodola and Corral found that higher levels of education and economic development explain greater support for same-sex marriage.

Finally, it is important to note the influence of the legalization of same-sex marriage in Spain in 2005 on the conversation in Latin America. Activists were inspired by this development and used Spain's actions as leverage, especially in Mexico and Argentina.[12] While judicialization may not explain outcomes in each country, the globalization of rights for sexual minorities is having an effect. Indeed, Argentina's approval of same-sex marriage has propelled a new level of discussion in other South American countries. As noted by Piatti-Crocker in this volume, internal barriers to the acceptance of equality for sexual minorities are being challenged by external political and legal norms, but it is too soon to tell what will be the full effects of this phenomenon.

THE APEX OF JUDICIALIZATION: COLOMBIA

Outside of Argentina and Uruguay, Colombia offers the most advanced national recognition of and set of policies for same-sex couples in Latin America. This policy change resulted almost entirely from mandates of the Colombian Constitutional Court.[13] The decision stemmed from a challenge to exclusion by LGBT activists in the country in 2008, an explicit decision to judicialize the issue. Indeed, attempts at policy change in the political realm stalled, largely as a result of opposition from the Catholic Church. This legislative action began the same year of a limited, but favorable, ruling (health and social security benefits) for same-sex couples from the Court in 2007 and after a ruling granting inheritance rights. After the decision, the government of President Alvaro Uribe proposed a bill with benefits for same-sex couples, and bills passed both houses of the Colombian Congress.[14] However, the bill was defeated during attempts to reconcile each chamber's bills and after strong objections and lobbying by the Catholic Church.

The 2009 decision of the Constitutional Court mirrored a decision of the Supreme Court of Canada in *M. v. H.* (1999), in that it mandated the same benefits and rights open to common law heterosexual couples be made available to same-sex couples cohabitating for two years. These recent decisions are notable, given that in 2001 the Constitutional Court ruled narrowly (five to four) that same-sex couples were not entitled to social security benefits.[15] The decision in 2009 was nearly unanimous, with eight of nine judges siding with same-sex rights.[16] The litigation, commenced in 2005 (including the cases mentioned above), possessed all the hallmarks of a judicialized U.S. or Canadian-style litigation strategy, with public interest law groups, *Colombia Diversa*, the Centre for Law, Justice and Society, and the Group of Public Interest Law at the University of the Andes, coordinating their efforts. The lawsuit called for benefits for same-sex and unmarried heterosexual couples.[17] Using court decisions to frame public debate was also part of this strategy. As Marcela Sanchez, executive director of *Colombia Diversa*, stated in reaction to the decision on property rights, the first success, "This is not only an advance for equality between heterosexuals and gay men and lesbians, but also a great achievement for the public interest, especially for all who are committed to creating a more fair and open society in which differences are respected."[18]

Litigation strategies are an attractive option for activists in Colombia because access to the courts on constitutional matters is quite open, through *tutela* suits. These lawsuits are authorized to challenge violations of constitutional rights and may be brought by anyone. Thus, "Colombia has, perhaps, the most open system of judicial review."[19] In addition, this litigation was aided by the fact that a large portion of litigation concerns economic rights, such as health and retirement benefits. In other words, the litigation on behalf of same-sex couples fit into already-established litigation pathways.

These pathways led to a 2011 Constitutional Court decision after activists went back to court to argue the unconstitutionality of the Civil Code's definition of marriage. Marriage was defined a being between one man and one woman for the purposes of procreation. The Court ruled that same-sex couples had a constitutional right to form a family. This was notable, given the seemingly heterosexist definition of family in Article 42 of the Constitution: "The family is the basic nucleus of society. It is

formed on the basis of natural or legal ties, by the free decision of a man
and woman to contract matrimony or by their responsible resolve to
comply with it." However, the court ruled that same-sex families were
not precluded by this language, and the previous line of cases frowning
on discrimination against same-sex couples was applied to this case.
However, in a nod to the sweeping nature of the decision, the court did
not mandate the recognition of same-sex families but gave Congress two
years to change the law to comply with the court's reasoning. If the
legislature does not act within the timeframe, couples will be able to get
married before a judge or notary public, according to the decision.[20]

Despite the victories, political battles remain to ensure compliance
with the court decisions, and homophobia in Colombian culture and in
government persists, despite the more liberal court decisions.[21] But it is
clear that the legal process pushed policy beyond what was possible in
the political arena—an obvious case of the judicialization of politics. According to Lodola and Corral, public support for same-sex marriage in
Colombia registers only 34.4 points out of 100.

Scholars have noted Colombia as one of the countries with a significantly judicialized politics.[22] Confirming the element of judicialization
described by Ran Hirschl, the court was created out of a conflict between
political parties concerning economic policies; it was designed to be an
institution supportive of neoliberal, individualistic economic policies. At
the same time, a new, individual-rights-protective constitution was created (1991), and judges (as in the case with the Charter of Rights and
Freedoms in Canada) began to judicially enforce these rights.[23] Colombia
fits Charles Epp's framework of rights revolutions stemming from the
existence of support structures that encourage legal mobilization around
rights claims. The *tutela* process in Colombia simply offers a low-cost
avenue for litigation.[24] In addition, and reflecting institutional factors,
judicialization in Colombia, like Canada and South Africa, also resulted
from a newer constitution and a reordering of the relationship between
branches of government, with more power migrating to the courts. As a
result, Colombia has become one of the most judicialized political systems in the Americas and certainly the most judicialized in Latin America. However, this level of advanced and thorough judicialization has
occurred only in one nation in Latin America.

NOTABLE JUDICIALIZATION: ARGENTINA AND BRAZIL

Argentina

In July 2010, Argentina became the first nation in South America to
legalize same-sex marriage. The action sent shockwaves around the
world; however, the policy conversation had been taking place for some

time and was accelerated when judges in Argentina began to marry same-sex couples in the year before the legislative enactment. This judicialization was not as strong as that of Canada and Colombia. Even though judges have become more active in making policy in Argentina, barriers to judicialization remain in this civil law country. In the end, the result in Argentina was arguably more political than legal, with the judiciary pushing the political process toward legalizing same-sex marriage.

The Argentine political system shows clear signs of judicialization.[25] Similar to *tutela* suits, *amparos* in Argentina can be brought against government officials for violations of statutorily or constitutionally defined rights. Judges are now arguably less constrained by traditional civil law approaches (especially the rule that decisions only apply to the direct parties and do not create a precedent) and are increasingly attempting to set broad policy grounded in rights-based jurisprudence, though this trend is far from uniform. According to Saldivia, the Supreme Court's jurisprudence has become increasingly favorable to sexual minorities, largely influenced by international norms.

Serious attempts to gain recognition for same-sex couples nationally in Argentina began in the early 2000s, spurred by the establishment of civil unions in Buenos Aires (2002) and the legalization of same-sex marriage by the Socialist government in Spain (2005). This was followed by the enactment of civil union laws in the province of Rio Negro (2007) and the city of Villa Carlos Paz (2007), largely as the result of the actions of left-wing parties.[26] Indeed, despite a rift among activists concerning civil unions versus same-sex marriage, a great deal of lobbying legislators and the president, Cristina Kirchner. In other words, before judges began marrying same-sex couples in 2009, much political mobilization had occurred and much groundwork had been laid for the same-sex marriage bill that eventually passed.

The bill narrowly passed after a highly visible debate in the Senate. This occurred after a committee in the Senate appeared to kill the bill, but lobbying and clear support from President Kirchner turned the tide in favor of the bill, despite the usual conservative opposition and strong opposition from the Catholic Church. Interestingly, it appears that the opposition of the Church was a factor in the bill's passage, as Kirchner made a speech from China comparing the actions of the Argentine Church to the "times of the Crusades." This was part of a larger movement to secularize Argentine politics as a part of the process of democratization, especially as the Church was historically linked to military dictatorships and is generally unpopular in many circles. Kirchner's position can be seen as an attempt to shore up her popularity with the left.[27] This also makes sense politically, given that Argentina possesses the second highest level of public support for same-sex marriage in the Americas, as indicated previously.

The issue of same-sex marriage in Argentina was undoubtedly given greater visibility and urgency by a series of court and administrative actions granting marriages to same-sex couples. To initiate litigation and to engage in civil disobedience, couples applied for marriage licenses. In one high-profile example, a couple was initially granted a license in Buenos Aires after a judge ruled that the ban on same-sex marriage was unconstitutional, but this was overturned by a different judge. The couple then found supportive officials in Tierra del Fuego to marry them late in 2009. This marriage was later nullified by a yet another judge. At the time of the legislative enactment, the Supreme Court was considering the couple's appeal.[28] Even though these decisions technically would apply only to the couples involved, judges ruling in favor of same-sex marriage claims certainly bolstered the political efforts to enact same-sex marriage.

Summarizing the Argentine case, judicialization did not lead to the legalization of same-sex marriage in Argentina, as it did in Canada and Colombia, at least in terms of courts replacing legislators as policymakers. Courts may have served as catalysts, but the enactment of same-sex marriage was mostly the result of more traditional political processes. Rights talk, however, was present throughout the process. For example, the governor of Tierra del Fuego called the issue of same-sex marriage "an important advance in human rights and social inclusion."[29]

Brazil

Despite the fact that Brazil was the site of the first formal legislative proposal for same-sex relationship recognition in the Americas in 1995, and despite same-sex unions being recognized in one state, Rio Grande do Sul, national policy recognizing same-sex relationships has stagnated in Brazil, and activists do not necessarily prioritize the issue. Shawn Schulenberg describes the policy terrain:

> Over the years, various actors have tried to clarify the law on the issue—in effect, set a policy—but institutional features have thus far prevented the federal government from doing so. The executive and legislative branches have so many veto players that it is nearly impossible for any policy—either for or against—to even receive a full up or down vote. As a result, Brazil is a country that has had extreme policy stability of this issue . . . even though there is no clear policy, leaving same-sex couples in a perpetual state of legal limbo.[30]

However, relevant to the issue of judicialization, Schulenberg notes that activists have turned to the courts in an attempt to take advantage of constitutional ambiguities, with limited initial success. This approach was not initially coordinated by established activist groups but by citizens feeling blocked by the political process.[31] This is obviously a type of judicialization, indicating an increased rights consciousness among citizens and a tendency to view courts as the proper forum for vindicating rights. However, Brazil's civil law system presents significant barriers to full-scale judicialization. Despite this, an opportunity exists for greater judicialization stemming from a 2004 constitutional amendment broadening the Supreme Federal Court's (*Supremo Tribunal Federal* or STF) policy-making authority by making its decisions binding on lower courts.[32]

The level of judicialization was elevated in 2011. The STF ruled unanimously that same-sex couples were entitled to the rights and benefits of "stable unions," Brazil's cohabitation legal framework for heterosexual couples. Several elements contributed to this outcome. As noted above, the STF has broad powers and can hear constitutional challenges from political parties, public officials, and some nongovernmental organizations. In other words, as in Colombia, it is fairly easy to judicialize politics by bringing challenges directly to the STF. In addition, the 1988 Citizens Constitution contains robust equality protections. While the inclusion of sexual orientation as a protected category was rejected during the document's drafting, courts have added this through interpretation. For the STF, equality principles trumped the constitution's heterosexist definition of marriage. The decision was the result of an abstract case commenced by the attorney general and the governor of Rio de Janiero. The court's approach was reflected in the words of Minister Carmen Lucia: "Those who make their choice for civil union cannot be unequal in their citizenship. No one can be considered a different and lower class of citizens, because they make their emotional and sexual choice apart from the majority."[33]

Following this decision, several judges began to grant same-sex marriages to couples in stable unions in response to the couples' requests. After other judges denied these requests, the Superior Court of Justice (STJ), the highest civil law appellate court, overruled these judges, stating that "sexual orientation should not serve as a pretext for excluding families from the legal protection that marriage represents."[34] Thus, after many years of political stagnation, the politics of relationship equality in Brazil has recently become significantly judicialized. As Javier Corrales notes, "the Brazilian case demonstrates that when prospects for gay rights seem tough—that is, when homophobia is widespread, when legislators are reluctant and when churches launch major homophobic campaigns—there is still hope: the court system."[35]

NO (OR RECENT) JUDICIALIZATION, BUT POLICY CHANGE: MEXICO AND URUGUAY

Significant policy change concerning same-sex relationships has occurred in Latin America with little or only very recent involvement from courts.

In Uruguay, change has occurred without a history of judicialization. Mexico has experienced judicialization, but not on the issue of relationship equality for same-sex couples until quite recently. A policy process to recognize same-sex couples that began legislatively in Mexico City was expanded by the Supreme Court of Mexico to the rest of the country.

Uruguay

In 2007, Uruguay enacted a civil union law that included same-sex couples, making it the first jurisdiction in South America to enact such a substantial policy. The law did not include parenting rights, however, thus falling short of full marriage equality. The process was purely legislative, reflecting that Uruguayan politics is marked by low levels of judicialization and continues to adhere to the norms of civil law systems. Progress here was supported by positive public opinion, a leftist government supportive of LGBT rights, and a progressive political culture that often reflects attitudes in Western Europe.[36] Indeed, since the enactment of the civil union law, the government in Uruguay has lifted the ban on gays and lesbians in the military and enacted legislation potentially making it easier for gays and lesbians to adopt children. After the enactment of same-sex marriage in neighboring Argentina, discussions began about upgrading civil unions to marriage.[37]

The outcome in Uruguay reflects party politics. The civil union law was enacted a few years after the left-leaning Broad Front Party took control of the presidency and parliament in 2004. A popular progressive legislator who has also been involved in women's rights, Margarita Percovich, authored the bill and pushed it through the legislative process, viewing it as a first step toward full marriage equality. Further illustrating the legislative origin of this policy, LGBT grassroots in Uruguay are not well organized, certainly not to the point of substantially contributing to the enactment of such a radical change in public policy. Supportive public opinion undoubtedly played a role as well. According to Lodola and Corral, public support for same-sex marriage in Uruguay registers 50.5 points out of 100, the third-highest level of support in the Americas. Thus, a progressive party in a progressive country enacted a liberal gay and lesbian rights policy and continues to create new and more protective policies in this arena.

Mexico

Developments in Mexico echo the party-centered approach in Uruguay, though the policies enacted have been much more limited geographically, specifically Mexico City and the northern state of Coahuila. The lack of judicialization of the issue stands in contrast to a more active Supreme Court. However, the more powerful Supreme Court is, by design, mostly focused on resolving disputes among political branches and has not become active in defining and promoting individual rights.[38]

The government of Mexico City enacted a civil union law in 2006 and legalized same-sex marriage in the city in 2009. As previously indicated, this was mostly driven by leftist party politics in the city and the activism of lesbian-feminist and other queer activists, including a public demonstration in support of the civil union bill that included symbolic same-sex union ceremonies on Valentine's Day, 2001.[39] In other words, unlike Uruguay, the process involved a close collaboration between activists and elected officials. Genaro Lozano also places the enactment of civil unions in the broader context of change resulting from the historic 2000 election in Mexico that challenged one-party rule and signaled further democratization. The election also brought a leftist mayor to the city, Andrés Manuel López Obrador, who as a candidate spoke favorably of sexual minorities. As Lozano summarizes the conditions that led to the civil union law,

> the simultaneous rise to power of Vicente Fox to the Presidency, and of López Obrador to the Office of the Mayor in Mexico City, along with the weakening of the once omnipotent PRI, and the arrival of LGBT elected officials . . . to the local assembly of Mexico City, marked the first years of the Mexican transition to democracy, spurring the discussion of democratic values, and opening a window of opportunity for advancing the LGBT agenda, particularly the discussion of same-sex civil unions.[40]

Activists never considered a legal strategy, but instead hoped to use a rights-based political strategy to protect same-sex couples in the city. This dynamic continued with the amending of the civil code in the city to include same-sex couples in marriage rights and benefits, including parenting rights, in late 2009, again driven by the leftist Democratic Revolution Party (PRD).[41]

In an attempt to judicialize the issue, conservative opponents, specifically federal prosecutors from the nationally governing National Action Party (PAN) challenged the law in court.[42] However, this move backfired significantly. Not only did the Supreme Court validate the Mexico City law, the justices ruled that all Mexican states must recognize same-sex marriages performed in Mexico City as a result of a constitutional provision guaranteeing the interstate recognition of contracts.[43] According to one Justice, "Those of us who are in favor of this [the same-sex marriage law] are in favor of diversity and tolerance."[44] Thus, the court affirmed the policy derived from a left-wing party and used the country's constitution to broaden the policy to the entire nation, obviously agreeing with the substance of the policy. The response of more conservative forces in the national government and the states to this judicialization remains to be seen.

OTHER DEVELOPMENTS IN LATIN AMERICA: LIMITED OR
NEGATIVE JUDICIALIZATION

Other countries in Latin America have seen legal and political activity concerning relationship equality, both positively and negatively. A new constitution was approved by voters in Ecuador in 2008, and this document reflects the potential and pitfalls of the semi-authoritarian presidentialism that persists in many Latin American nations. The constitution was championed by the popular president Rafael Correa who campaigned against corruption and oligarchy. In terms of LGBT rights, the constitution bans same-sex marriage and adoption (at the request of the Catholic Church) but allows same-sex civil unions. In general, the constitution expanded rights, but it also expanded the powers of the executive. According to Selena Xie and Javier Corrales, the gay rights progress was the result of relatively weak LGBT groups allying with more established feminist groups. The negative components were the result of Correa's own homophobia and that of elements of his party, in addition to the influence of the Church. Recent events in Ecuador, then, reflect a constitutionalization of LGBT policy but not judicialization, combined with the typical party and religion dynamics of Latin America.[45]

Venezuela is a country where the rift between the Left and the LGBT movement is pronounced, but with advocates attempting to make the case that equality for sexuality minorities is part of the legacy of leftist revolution. According to one pro-gay member of parliament, Romelia Matute, "the revolution is about taking care of those who have been excluded."[46] The veto power of the Catholic Church has also been at play, most notably in the Church's lobbying against a provision outlawing sexual orientation discrimination in the current constitution. Despite the efforts of some on the left, prospects for the enactment of a civil union law in the country are uncertain at best. In 2008 and 2009, attempts to enact a law were sharply rejected by the government.[47]

This is particularly noteworthy, given that the Supreme Court ruled in 2008 that same-sex couples were not protected by the constitution and declared that the issue is one for legislative determination. This was the result of an appeal brought by an LGBT advocacy group, Affirmative Union, influenced by international legal norms and "an ethical, neo-Kantian interpretation of human rights as a set of universal, cross-cultural values," according to a member of Affirmative Union.[48] Here, again, we see evidence of judicialization trumped by the usual factors in Latin America. In addition, judicialization in Venezuela has not moved in the direction of assisting the powerless. Instead, courts have been drawn into disputes between Hugo Chavez and his opponents.[49]

In Chile, attempts by marriage equality activists to judicialize the politics of relationship equality have failed, but the legislative process has been engaged. Activists have also taken their cause to a supranational court, hoping to tap into international legal norms. After years of little movement in the political arena, the group Movement for Homosexual Integration and Liberation (MOVILH) initiated litigation after couples (some of whom had been married in Argentina and Canada) applied for a marriage license but were denied. However, the Constitutional Tribunal ruled in 2011, in a 9-to-1 decision, that same-sex marriage was not constitutionally required—a rather stunning rejection. Two of the judges thought that same-sex marriage was unconstitutional, three upheld the denial of licenses but asserted that same-sex marriage was not unconstitutional, while the four most liberal judges invited legislation to correct the discriminatory situation.[50] All perspectives reflected a distinct lack of desire to be judicially innovative. MOVILH subsequently took its case to the Inter-American Commission on Human Rights, arguing equality and religious discrimination violations of the American Convention on Human Rights in a May 2012 complaint.[51] The court recently overturned a decision from the Chilean Supreme Court denying child custody to a lesbian based on the fact that she was in a same-sex relationship.[52]

In 2011, President Sebastián Piñera declared his support for civil unions and submitted legislation, but the legislation is stalled. The legislature only recently enacted a sexual-orientation-inclusive antidiscrimination law in response to high profile anti-gay hate crimes in the country.[53] Religious opposition to relationship equality is high and public support is low in this country where divorce was legalized as recently as 2004. Lack of judicial leadership likely means slower progress for relationship equality in Chile.

Central America and the Caribbean continue to be regions inhospitable to LGBT rights claims, reflecting the role of religious opposition and leftist parties. Costa Rica has a more progressive reputation and has experienced a significant judicialization of its politics. However, this judicialization has not been applied consistently to sexual minority equality. Like Venezuela, the Supreme Court rejected an attempt to legally mandate the recognition of same-sex relationships in 2006. Conversely, the Supreme Court recently struck down a proposed referendum on civil unions, citing doctrine that sexual minority rights are not up for a vote, perhaps indicating a turn toward increased judicialization. The court viewed the right to form civil unions as a fundamental human right, though one to be enacted legislatively.[54]

CONCLUSION

The range of judicialization in the Americas on the issue of relationship equality clearly demonstrates that the judicialization of politics is neither present nor uniform in all nations. The necessary institutional and cultural setting must be present for judicialization, but, even then, judicialization appears to be dependent on the policy area. Indeed, most judicialization has occurred in Latin America around political and economic rights, or rights with a lot of potential beneficiaries, not the rights of traditionally marginalized minorities. In other words, judicialization often is linked with majoritarian politics.

With the exception of Colombia and Brazil, and to a lesser extent Argentina and Mexico, policy change in Latin America was driven almost exclusively by non-judicial politics, or it has stagnated as a result of cultural forces such as heteronormativity and the influence of organized religion. Thus, sexuality is an arena where policy change is constrained by a variety of factors and where courts can be a forum for change, but this change is not guaranteed. Courts are increasingly a crucial part of the policy process as civil law norms erode in some jurisdictions, but they are not the definitive policymaker in most nations in Latin America.

These findings potentially alleviate the concerns about the undemocratic nature of judicialization, a central concern in the scholarship of judicialization. However, the findings also point to the need for continued political action on the part of relationship equality activists. In the proper national context, courts may be an ally, but they seldom will be the sole policymaker. Judicialization is connected to particular national institutional contexts, and it is not uniform throughout Latin America. However, where the institutional setting is favorable, the judiciary can push policy beyond the boundaries of politics defined by electoral politics and public opinion. Similarly, litigation and rights-framing can be used as leverage by activists to assist in achieving their policy goals, especially as the line between civil law and common law norms is increasingly blurred.

NOTES

1. Charles Epp, *The Rights Revolution: Lawyers, Activists, and Supreme Courts in Comparative Perspective* (Chicago: University of Chicago Press, 1998); Ran Hirschl, *Towards Juristocracy: The Origins and Consequences of the New Constitutionalism* (Cambridge, MA: Harvard University Press, 2004); Ran Hirschl, "Judicialization of Politics," in *The Oxford Handbook of Law and Politics*, Keith E. Whittington, R. Daniel Kelemen, and Gregory A. Caldeira, eds. (New York: Oxford University Press, 2008), 119–141; C. Neal Tate and Torbjorn Vallinder, eds., *The Global Expansion of Judicial Power* (New York: New York University Press, 1995).

2. Javier A. Couso, Alexandra Huneeus, and Rachel Sieder, "Cultures of Legality: Judicialization of Political Activism in Contemporary Latin America," in *Cultures of Legality: Judicialization and Political Activism in Latin America*, Javier A. Couso, Alexandra Huneeus, and Rachel Sieder, eds. (New York: Cambridge University Press, 2010), 3–21: 18.

3. Patrick Atiyah and Robert Sommers, *Form and Substance in Anglo-American Law* (New York: Oxford University Press, 1987), 377.

4. Laura Saldivia, "The Argentine Supreme Court and the Construction of a Constitutional Protection for Sexual Minorities," in *Same-Sex Marriage in the Americas: Poli-*

cy Innovation for Same-Sex Relationships,* Jason Pierceson, Adriana Piatti-Crocker, and Shawn Schulenberg, eds. (Lanham, MD: Lexington Books, 2010),73–92: 73.

5. Javier A. Couso, "The Transformation of Constitutional Discourse and the Judicialization of Politics in Latin America," in *Cultures of Legality*; Saldivia.

6. Couso, 148–49.

7. Couso, 157.

8. Ahmed Khanani and Jean Robinson, "Democracy, Discursive Frames, and Same-Sex Unions: A Cross-National Analysis," in *Same-Sex Marriage in the Americas: Policy Innovation for Same-Sex Relationships,* 15–36: 16.

9. Javier Corrales and Mario Pecheny, "The Comparative Politics of Sexuality in Latin America," in *The Politics of Sexuality in Latin America: A Reader on Lesbian, Gay, Bisexual, and Transgender Rights,* Javier Corrales and Mario Pecheny, eds. (Pittsburgh: University of Pittsburgh Press, 2010), 1–30: 22.

10. Corrales and Pecheny, 18.

11. Germán Lodola and Margarita Corral, "Support for Same-Sex Marriage in Latin America," this volume.

12. Genaro Lozano, "Same-Sex Relationship Equality in Mexico," in *Same-Sex Marriage in the Americas: Policy Innovation for Same-Sex Relationships,* 129–159; Adriana Piatti-Crocker, "Constructing Policy Innovation in Argentina: From Gender Quotas to Same-Sex Marriage," in *Same-Sex Marriage in the Americas: Policy Innovation for Same-Sex Relationships,* 37–72.

13. Tony Grew, "Colombian Court Confirms Equal Rights for Same-Sex Couples," *Pink News,* January 29, 2009, http://www.pinknews.co.uk/news/articles/2005-10938.html.

14. "Colombian Court Recognises [*sic*] Same-Sex Rights." *Pink News,* February 8, 2007, http://www.pinknews.co.uk/news/articles/2005-3663.html/; "Colombia Set to Introduce National Gay Rights," *Pink News,* June 16, 2007, http://www.pinknews.co.uk/news/articles/2005-4659.html; "Colombian Court Rules in Favour [*sic*] of Equal Rights for Gay Couples," *Pink News,* October 6. http://www.pinknews.co.uk/news/articles/2005-5666.html; Decision C-075/2007.

15. Manuel Jose Cepeda Espinosa, "The Judicialization of Politics in Colombia: The Old and the New," in *The Judicialization of Politics in Latin America,* Rachel Sieder, Line Schjolden, and Alan Agnell, eds. (New York: Palgrave Macmillan, 2005), 67–103:83.

16. Helda Martinez, "Colombia: Equal Rights for Same-Sex Partners," *Inter Press Service News,* March 2, 2009, http://ipsnews.net/news.asp?idnews=45944; Decision C-029/2009.

17. Grew, "Colombian Court Confirms Equal Rights for Same-Sex Couples."

18. "Colombian Court Recognises [*sic*] Same-Sex Rights." *Pink News.*

19. Cepeda Espinosa, "The Judicialization of Politics in Colombia," 74.

20. Decision C-577/11. Decision summary found at http://www.matrimonioigualitario.org/p/en-el-congreso.html.

21. Helda Martinez, "Colombia: Equal Rights for Same-Sex Partners." *Inter Press Service News,* March 2, 2009, http://ipsnews.net/news.asp?idnews=45944; Gregory Theintz, "Colombia: Liberal in Theory, Homophobic in Practice," *Colombia Reports,* April 30, 2010, http://colombiareports.com/opinion/89-from-the-editor/9273-colombia-liberal-in-theory-homophobic-in-practice.html.

22. Cepeda Espinosa, "The Judicialization of Politics in Colombia;" Rodrigo Nunez, "Redistributive Justice in a Neoliberal Context: The Colombian Constitutional Court and the Promotion of Social Rights." Paper presented at the Annual Meeting of the American Political Science Association, August 30–September 2, 2007.

23. Nunez.

24. Karina Anasolabehere, "More Power, More Rights? The Supreme Court and Society in Mexico," in *Cultures of Legality,* 78–111.

25. Saldivia; Catalina Smulovitz, "Judicialization in Argentina: Legal Culture, or Opportunities and Support Structures?" in *Cultures of Legality,* 234–53.

26. Piatti-Crocker, 53.

27. Alexei Barrionuevo, "Argentina Senate to Vote on Gay Marriage." *New York Times*, July 13, 2010, http://www.nytimes.com/2010/07/14/world/americas/14argentina.html?_r=1; Dan Fasterberg, "A Brief History of International Gay Marriage," *Time.com*, July 22, 2010, http://www.time.com/time/world/article/0,8599,2005678,00.html.

28. Vanessa Hand Orellana, "Buenos Aires Grants First Marriage License to Gays," *Associated Press*, November 16, 2009; Almudena Calatrava," Gay Marriage in Argentina is 1st in Latin America," *Associated Press*, December 29, 2009; "Argentine Judge Voids Latin America's First Gay Marriage," *AFP*, April 15, 2010, http://www.google.com/hostednews/afp/article/ALeqM5gHZQigoSe3zAo3TzK790ykQDFXQA.

29. Calatrava.

30. Shawn Schulenberg, "Policy Stability without Policy: The Battle for Same-Sex Partnership Recognition in Brazil," in *Same-Sex Marriage in the Americas*, 93–127: 94.

31. Schulenberg, 112.

32. Schulenberg, 118–19.

33. English summary of the STF decision in ADI 4277 (*Attorney General v. National Congress*) and ADPF 132 (*Governor of the State of Rio de Janeiro v. Courts of Justice of the States*), May 5, 2011, http://www2.stf.jus.br/portalStfInternacional/cms/destaquesClipping.php?sigla=portalStfDestaque_en_us&idConteudo=179046; Schulenberg, 100–103, 112–115. The equality provisions include Article 5, "All are equal before the law, without distinction." In addition, Article 3, Paragraph 4 states that the republic must "promote the well-being of all, without prejudice as to origin, race, sex, color, and any other forms of discrimination;" Javier Corrales, "Brazil's Recognition of Same-Sex Unions," *Americas Quarterly*, May 11, 2011, http://www.americasquarterly.org/node/2528.

34. "Brazil High Court Allows Gay Marriage," News24.com, October 26, 2011, http://www.news24.com/World/News/Brazil-high-court-allows-gay-marriage-20111026; "Decision: Fourth class admits marriage between same-sex," STJ website, October 25, 2011, http://www.stj.jus.br/portal_stj/publicacao/engine.wsp?tmp.area=398&tmp.texto=103687.

35. Corrales, "Brazil's Recognition of Same-Sex Unions."

36. Adriana Piatti-Crocker and Jason Pierceson. "Introduction," in *Same-Sex Marriage in the Americas: Policy Innovation for Same-Sex Relationships*, 1–13:4–5.

37. "Questions Raised over Uruguay's 'Gay Adoption' Law." *Pink News*, September 16, 2009, http://www.pinknews.co.uk/news/articles/2005-14108.html; "Uruguay and Paraguay could be next to debate gay marriage." *Pink News*, July 20, 2010, http://www.pinknews.co.uk/2010/07/20/uruguay-and-paraguay-could-be-next-to-debate-gay-marriage.

38. Karina Anasolabehere, "More Power, More Rights? The Supreme Court and Society in Mexico," in *Cultures of Legality*, 78–111.

39. Genaro Lozano, "Same-Sex Relationship Equality in Mexico," in *Same-Sex Marriage in the Americas*, 129–59: 140.

40. Lozano, 136.

41. Jennifer Gonzalez, "Mexico City Spproves Gay Marriage," *AFP*, December 21, 2009, http://www.google.com/hostednews/afp/article/ALeqM5h4_uOzElZivyqR7ZpWRTnJdAJ5dg.

42. Ioan Grillo, "Mexico City's Revolutionary First: Gay Marriage." Time.com, December 24, 2009, http://www.time.com/time/world/article/0,8599,1949953,00.html.

43. David Agren, "Mexican States Ordered to Honor Gay Marriages," *New York Times*, August 10, 2010, http://www.nytimes.com/2010/08/11/world/americas/11mexico.html.

44. Rex Wockner, "Mexico City Gay Marriage Law Upheld," *Bay Area Reporter*, August 12, 2010, http://www.ebar.com/news/article.php?sec=news&article=4988.

45. Piatti-Crocker and Pierceson; Selena Xie and Javier Corrales, "LGBT Rights in Ecuador's 2008 Constitution: Victories and Setbacks." In *The Politics of Sexuality in Latin America*, 224–229.

46. Rex Wockner, "Conflicting Reports on Venezuelan Civil-Union Bill." *Seattle Gay News*, April 3, 2009, http://www.sgn.org/sgnnews37_14/page9.cfm.

47. Jose Ramon Merentes, "Gay Rights in Venezuela under Hugo Chavez, 1999–2009," in *The Politics of Sexuality in Latin America*, 220–223.

48. Merentes, 223.

49. Rogelio Perez Perdomo, "Judicialization and Regime Transformation: The Venezuelan Supreme Court," in *The Judicialization of Politics in Latin America*, 131–159.

50. Bridgette P. LaVictoire, "Chile's Constitutional Tribunal Set To Reject Same-Sex Marriage Case," lezgetreal.com, October 31, 2011, http://lezgetreal.com/2011/10/chiles-constitutional-tribunal-set-to-reject-same-sex-marriage-case. The blog post is based on and contains an excerpt from a news story in the *Santiago Times* from October 30.

51. Hunter T. Carter, "Same-Sex Marriage in Chile," *Americas Quarterly*, June 7, 2012, http://www.americasquarterly.org/same-sex-marriage-in-chile.

52. Stephen Gray, "Chile: Lesbian Judge Whose Sexuality 'Put Daughters at Risk' Wins Legal Battle," *Pink News*, March 23, 2012, http://www.pinknews.co.uk/2012/03/23/chile-lesbian-judge-whose-sexuality-put-daughters-at-risk-wins-legal-battle.

53. Eduardo Ayala, "A Case for Gay Rights in Chile," *Americas Quarterly*, April 26, 2012, http://www.americasquarterly.org/node/3598.

54. Piatti-Crocker and Pierceson; Michael McDonald, "High Court Rules Against Referendum on Same-Sex Civil Unions," *Tico Times*, August 10, 2010, http://www.ticotimes.net/dailyarchive/2010_08/081020101.cfm.

Part II

Countries

FIVE

Same-Sex Partnership Rights in Central America: The Case of Panama

Shawn Schulenberg

Same-sex partnership recognition has become a salient issue for lesbian and gay movements in many parts of the world as activists have achieved some notable successes over the past decade in parts of the United States, Europe, Latin America, and Africa. However, scholars have not studied all of these regions equally: Most of the research until now has just focused on the United States and Europe. While recently a small handful of pieces are beginning to extend this coverage to other parts of the world, including Latin America,[1] even these works have focused on the "success stories" in the richer, more developed countries of Latin America where strong laws have been codified (such as Argentina, Brazil, Mexico, and Uruguay), while still paying scant attention to the poorer nations, many of which have yet to see much progress.

This chapter is a preliminary attempt to fill this void by looking at the progress (or lack thereof) of LGBT issues in Central America. Specifically, I hope to explain why we have seen such little development in the advancement of partnership rights to same-sex couples in Central America compared to other parts of the Americas. To do this, I deploy a combination of the approaches on social movements and public policy within the context of a single Central American country: Panama.

Ultimately, I find that the central issue here is the nascent and weak nature of the LGBT social movement organizations within Panama; with their lack of experience and very few resources at their disposal, they remain ill equipped to challenge the powerful heterosexism and homophobia in society required to change public opinion and gain access to

73

elite allies within the government. Most promise for future success relies on increasing the organizational capacity of the social movement organizations and building stronger ties between them and international allies. Both strategies may eventually allow LGBT movements to win many new rights, including the legal recognition of same-sex relationships.

LITERATURE REVIEW

Lesbians and gays as a group represent what can be considered a social movement, so this literature seems like a reasonable place to start. Sidney Tarrow defines social movements as "collective challenges, based on common purposes and social solidarities, in sustained interaction with elites, opponents, and authorities."[2] How are social movements different from parties, interest groups, and protests? Mario Diani sets out three distinguishing features: 1) They rely on a mass base of individuals, groups, and organizations linked by social interaction; 2) they organize around a mix of political and cultural goals; and 3) they rely on a shared collective identity.[3] Baer and Bositis come up with a similar formulation but add to it that social movements typically represent the "have-nots" in society as opposed to those with greater clout.[4]

In more recent years, the majority of the social movement literature has coalesced around three theoretical approaches to explain the emergence of collective action: 1) resource mobilization, 2) political opportunities, and 3) framing processes. Used together, these traditions have added to our understanding of why individuals sometimes decide to challenge the state in mass, while at other times they stay at home.[5] These paradigms are useful for understanding a great deal about how social movements work and even point to some important clues about what makes for social movement success in public policymaking.

The first perspective, known as resource mobilization (RM), can be defined as "those collective vehicles, informal as well as formal, through which people mobilize and engage in collective action."[6] Initially articulated by McCarthy and Zald,[7] this approach examines the internal dynamics and resources of movements. While variants of the approach have focused on the less formal dynamics of social movements, such as the informal networks that bind various actors, the majority of work in this tradition focuses on formal organizations themselves.[8] The primary hypothesis of resource mobilization is that social movements should be more successful in influencing public policy when they have strong organizations fighting for their interests. Variables such as capable leadership, strong organizational capacity, and wealth are especially important to this perspective.[9] In the case of LGBT movements, we should expect to see more success when they are well organized and have a lot of resources.

However, LGBT social movement organizations do not exist within a vacuum; this is where the second perspective—political opportunity structures (POS)—comes in handy. Political opportunity structure is defined as "the broader set of political constraints and opportunities unique to the national context in which they are embedded."[10] As opposed to just concentrating on the organizations themselves, it focuses on the characteristics of the broader structural environment within which social movements operate to explain when they achieve success.[11] Without an adequate understanding of what movements are up against, it is difficult to predict when they can advance their public policies. Two of the most important variables within the political opportunity structure that may influence a social movement's success at passing a public policy are public opinion[12] and the presence of elite allies.[13]

One school of thought argues that public opinion is the most crucial variable to look at to understand when social movements influence public policy. Paul Burstein, for example, uses what he calls the "theory of democratic representation" to argue that social movements usually do not, and should not, influence policy decisions in democratic societies when their positions are at odds with majority.[14] Since politicians are primarily concerned with reelection, it would be politically dangerous for them to defy the majority in favor of minority interests.[15] A number of studies confirm that the opinion-policy link is important.[16]

While the social movement literature is useful for looking at the success/failure of social movements as broadly understood, we need to also consider what studies on public policy can teach us as LGBT movements shift from the society at large to the political arena. Roger Cobb, Jennie-Keith Ross, and Marc Howard Ross were some of the first to write specifically about how groups in society can get their policy items onto the governmental agenda.[17] Analytically, they make a distinction between the public agenda and the formal governmental agenda. The first refers to those topics that are on the consciousness of the public, whereas the latter refers to items that the government seriously has on its agenda to pass.[18] They present what they call the "outside initiative model" of agenda building to explain how a nongovernmental group can get an issue onto the formal agenda.

The first two steps refer to identifying that there is a problem and proposing a solution. In the case of civil unions, this would refer to realizing that there are inequalities between heterosexual and homosexual relationships, and then petitioning the government for equal legal recognition of the bonds. The third step refers to seeking to expand the issue beyond just the actors who are specifically interested in the topic to the wider public. If a movement is successful at this, it will raise the salience of the issue to the public, and politicians will add it to the formal governmental agenda. The actions of politicians then are just a mere reflection of public opinion and public will, according to this point of view.

Another perspective, known as the "elite access model," focuses on the connections between interest group elites and political elites. According to it, a social movement's success often hinges on its ability to secure the help from third-party "insiders" to pass legislation.[19] With similarities to the political opportunity structure perspective of the social movement literature, this view supports the idea that interest groups have more sway when they have strong connections with policymakers.[20]

Politicians, not the public, are ultimately the ones who decide what goes on the policy agenda, and they will introduce anything that will garner them more votes.[21] Even if an issue is not a pressing concern for the public at large, a social movement may be able to get it on the agenda if it can convince enough politicians that it will enhance their prospects for reelection. Burstein's model assumes that the policy agenda is merely a reflection of the public's preferences (in other words, those issues with both high public support and high issue salience). However, this is not the only route items can take to get there.

In many ways, this line of reasoning reverses the causal mechanisms of Burstein's model between the politicians and the public: Instead of politicians being passive recipients of whatever the population demands, politicians add items to the governmental agenda and then try to convince the population that they are important. In other words, politicians have much more agency: Even if the public is not too concerned about an issue, politicians can try to "make it an issue" to activate certain groups if they believe it will secure them more votes. This argument is consistent with Praveena Gunaratnam's finding that politicians play a much larger role than either opinion or whether an issue makes its way onto the governmental agenda and is ultimately passed.[22]

Both of these models seem compelling. On one hand, the outside initiative model makes sense as politicians rarely defy public opinion when setting policy: Usually there is a strong convergence between the two. On the other hand, one can think of examples where politicians do take actions that the public is against in order to satisfy other desires (for example, personal gain, or activating an interest group that will better help its electoral success). For the purposes of this essay, I will assume that both models represent feasible pathways for LGBT movements to pass laws recognizing same-sex relationships.

To understand the battle for same-sex unions in Panama, we need to assess how these variables play out in the case of Panama. Specifically, from the political opportunity perspective model, we can borrow the variables of public opinion and elite allies: what kind of battle are LGBT groups up against? If neither of these looks good, we can also borrow from the resource mobilization perspective the variable of organizational capacity: Do LGBT social movement organizations have the capacity to change public attitudes and curry favor with elites?

Unfortunately, looking at all three of these variables in the case of Panama suggests that same-sex unions will not likely be recognized anytime soon: Public opinion remains very negative, elites from none of the major political parties are supportive of LGBT issues, and the main lesbian and gay organization is not yet capable of strong mobilization.

PANAMA

To begin, it is important to look at the status quo: What does the law say about same-sex unions and what processes or procedures would need to be followed to change it? This will determine how social movements might be able to get the state to recognize their relationships, and which actors would have the power to do it. If discrimination is codified in the Constitution, for example, change will be much more difficult than if the heterosexist language is only written in the statutory law. Unfortunately for the Panamanian LGBT movement, both the Constitution and the Civil Code (Family Law) establish that marriage and its associated rights are exclusively reserved for opposite-sex couples.

THE LAW (STATUS QUO)

The current constitution of Panama was drafted in 1972, but it saw revisions in 1978, 1983, 1993, 1994, and 2004.[23] Earlier versions did not mention anything about the biological sex of those entering into the relationship until the latest revision in 2004, where the words "opposite sex" were added as one of the requirements of a common law marriage (I will discuss the politics of this later). As a result, Article 58 of the constitution currently reads, "The de facto union between persons *of opposite sex* legally capable of marrying, maintained for five consecutive years in conditions of exclusiveness and stability, shall have all the effects of civil marriage."[24] The language here is unambiguous: Not only is common law marriage exclusive to opposite-sex couples but so are even the benefits that accompany it.

Even though the constitution does have clear language on marriage, there are two articles that may be relevant because they might apply to LGBT rights generally—a non-discrimination clause and an equal protection clause. Article 19 lays out what many consider the non-discrimination clause: "There will be no privileges or discrimination based on race, birth, disability, social class, sex, religion or political views."[25] Although this section does not mention sexual orientation by name, some argue that sexual orientation can also be covered by the reference to sex (for example, because if one of the partners was born the opposite sex, then they could get married). Moreover, Article 20 lays out the equality clause: "Panamanians and foreigners are equal before the law."[26] The logic here goes that treating opposite-sex and straight couples differently violates this provision. However, while these articles do provide some interesting reasons why same-sex couples should be recognized equally before the law, it would seem that those constitutional provisions that directly reference marriage would take precedence when speaking about marriage.

The Panamanian Civil Code also explicitly prohibits giving rights and recognition to same-sex couples. Law Number 3 from 1994 establishes the foundation of Family Law in effect today. Articles 25, 34, and 54 clearly articulate that same-sex marriage is not allowed. According to Article 25, "Marriage is the union voluntarily entered between a man and a woman."[27] The sex of the participants is clearly stated. However, if there still remains even a shred of doubt about the drafters' intentions, Article 34 removes it: "They cannot marry each other: persons of the same sex."[28] Here it is explicitly listed as a disqualification for marriage. Article 54, more or less, repeats this exclusionary language.

In summary, both the constitution and the civil code are unambiguous and clear on this issue: same-sex marriage, along with any of the rights and benefits that traditionally accompany it, is prohibited. Because the ban resides in both the statutory law and the constitution, it is a difficult (but not impossible hurdle) to overcome. Luckily, there are some features of the Constitution of Panama that make it fairly easy to amend—much easier than in the United States.

Article 308 of the Constitution details the two possible avenues to amend the document itself. According to the first path, an amendment must be approved twice (with the same exact wording each time) by the legislature in two consecutive sessions (with general elections in between each vote). No other person or body must approve the change: Not the president, the provinces, nor the people in a nationwide referendum. Moreover, Panama has a unicameral legislature—the National Assembly—meaning it only must pass through one single body each time. Terms for deputies are five years, mirroring that of the president. This is much less cumbersome than in the United States, which has many more veto players in the process.

The second way to change the Constitution is similar to the first in that it must still pass two votes by consecutive sessions of the National Assembly. However, if on the second vote the Assembly modifies or amends the proposal, it can bypass need to go up for yet another (third) vote in the National Assembly if it passes by nationwide referendum. This second avenue introduces a new player in the system: the general public opinion. While adding a new veto player, it is still not overly cumbersome.

Now that we know the legal framework and how to change the law, the next place to look to understand the battle for same-sex unions in Panama is within the two variables political opportunity structure. Notably, the two things needed to change the constitution mirror those as models discussed in the literature view: 1) supportive public opinion, and 2) LGBT-friendly political elites. A supportive public is not enough for change, but it can go a long way for winning a national referendum or getting legislators to sign on board. Taken together, these are two possible routes for change.

PUBLIC OPINION AND THE OUTSIDE INITIATIVE MODEL

This fight might be easy with a supportive public; however, this just isn't the case in Panama (or Central America generally). Looking at public opinion data, the overwhelming majority of the Panamanian population is still opposed to same-sex marriage.[29] According to a poll conducted by the Latin American Public Opinion Project at Vanderbilt University, just 22.8 percent of the Panamanian population is in favor of same-sex marriage, which is far less than other countries in the Americas such as Canada (63.9 percent) and Argentina (57.7); however, these numbers for Panama are better than some other countries in Central America, like Costa Rica (20.7) and Nicaragua (15.6).

Table 5.1. Support for Same-Sex Marriage in Central America

Country	Support for SSM (%)
Panama	22.8
Honduras	22.6
Costa Rica	20.7
Belize	17.5
Guatemala	16.5
Nicaragua	15.6
El Salvador	10.3

Out of the twenty-five countries in the Western Hemisphere in this poll, Panama ranks eleven in terms of the percentage of the population that supports same-sex marriage (see Table 5.1). While this is the highest rating for any country in Central America, these numbers are still very small as the overwhelming majority of the population remains opposed to same-sex marriage. This is important because no country with an approval rating lower than Panama, (except Ecuador), has seen any progress on same-sex marriage/civil unions to date.

Just looking at these numbers alone, it doesn't appear that the "outside initiative model" of policymaking is of much use to LGBT movements until public opinion improves. Until then, change is unlikely from the status quo in this context unless lesbians and gays can convince elite leaders to change laws about partnership recognition regardless of public sentiment. Perhaps the "elite access model" might be more useful to lesbians and gays.

ELITE ALLIES AND THE ELITE ACCESS MODEL

As Carlos Guevara Mann points out, political parties in Panama are generally unresponsive to public opinion as members of the National Assembly are often motivated by considerations of personal gain and immunity from prosecution, in addition to the traditional motive of reelection.[30] In the context of negative public opinion, this could be good for LGBT rights because politicians would not necessarily need to listen to a homophobic public.

Unfortunately, the LGBT movement in Panama has had a difficult time securing elite allies in the political system as well. One of the reasons for this is that political parties in Panama are not organized around a traditional left-right dynamic. In countries such as the United States, the Republican Party is openly hostile to lesbians and gays, giving them a home in the Democratic Party. However, this alone does not ensure victories for lesbians and gays because they may become "captured," in the sense that Democrats do not need to be perfectly responsive to them as an interest group.[31] Moreover, in the U.S. case, dividing along partisan lines can actually be dangerous for LGBT peoples because one party may actively campaign to repress LGBT rights, as we saw during the 2004 presidential election. However, the Democratic Party often does propose laws that would directly benefit lesbians and gays, such as non-decimation laws and hate crime legislation, and 2012 finally added a plank supporting same-sex marriage.

It is this type of ally that the LGBT movement is missing in Panama. The country has a presidential governance system with separate elections for the president and the National Assembly. Today the country maintains a healthy multiparty system, with no party winning a majority in the National Assembly leading to coalitions. In recent elections, three parties tend to get the most votes: *Cambio Democrático* (CD), *Partido Revolucionario Democrático* (PRD), and *Partido Panameñista* (PAN). However, none presents a platform that would form a natural home for lesbians and gays. The PRD is generally considered a center-left party, but its support is almost nonexistent. This is in contrast to cases like Mexico, Brazil, and Argentina where leftist political parties have strongly advocated for same-sex marriage/civil unions in recent years. The other two parties, the CD and PAN, are both center-right parties, but neither has ever taken a stand in support of LGBT issues. On a positive note, however, no parties are rabidly antigay either; they mostly just ignore lesbian and gay rights.

In conclusion, the lack of elite allies is just as troublesome as public opinion because no major political parties advocate their cause. Because LGBT movements need to change the status quo, but they are up against negative public opinion with no domestic elite allies, they lose every time to a political culture rooted in heterosexist values from *machista* culture and the Catholic Church. For this to change, social movements must actively work to change public opinion and win over the hearts of elites. The power of the social movements then is very important.

RESOURCE MOBILIZATION AND THE POWER FOR LGBT GROUPS?

If lesbians and gays are to turn things around, they need strong social movement organizations to both counter public opinion on these issues and also convince elites to take their side. This is where the resource mobilization perspective can be useful; even if the political opportunity structure is not supportive today, strong LGBT movements can both change public opinion and win allies to their side if they know how to build the right alliances. Unfortunately, a number of factors indicate that LGBT activism in Panama is still relatively weak and incapable of passing a law recognizing same-sex couples: 1) The movement is still relatively young, 2) the organization lacks many resources including paid support staff, and 3) its priorities are split among a number of initiatives.

Unlike other parts of Latin America where LGBT movements formed many decades ago, formal activism around LGBT issues has come very late to Panama. While the first lesbian and gay movements formed in Argentina in 1967 and Brazil in 1978, Panama's first gay rights organization, *Asociación Hombres y Mujeres Nuevos de Panamá* (AHMNP, or New Men and Women Association of Panama), did not form until April 1998. According to their constitution, their missions are:

> 1) to conduct activities aimed at raising awareness among those sectors of the population facing discrimination due to their sexual orientation; 2) to contribute to the defense of those populations' rights, and to the assumption by them of their responsibilities, in such a way that they can develop their full professional, cultural, and socioeconomic potentials; 3) to identify educational, legal, labor-related, and social problems suffered by populations discriminated against on the basis of their sexual orientation, and suggest solutions. [32]

Soon after their formation, they petitioned the government to become an officially recognized organization for legal purposes (*personas jurídicas*, or legal personhood). This would grant the organization certain legal benefits allowing it to operate (for example, rent office space, fundraise, and so on). However, their original petition was denied in 2000 on the grounds that it violated Article 39 of the Panamanian constitution. According to this provision, "Companies, associations, and foundations are permitted to form that are not *contrary to the moral and legal order*, which may obtain recognition as legal persons."[33] It was not until a year later, in 2001, that they achieved success, which some attribute to lobbying from the Organization of American States.[34]

Today AHMNP remains the only legally recognized organization representing LGBT peoples, as Article 39 is still used to regularly to deny recognition to other groups. This position is pervasive throughout all of the government of Panama. For example, very recently the government denied a woman a license to register her business because the world "gay" was part of its name. In 2011, Berta Tuñon Centella submitted the forms to register her business, "Classy Gay Realty and Design," to the Ministry of Commerce and Industry. In December of that year, her petition was denied on the grounds that "in the registration request, the description of the name shows the word gay, noun or adjective, is a way to designate the male homosexual subjects, i.e., men who are inclined towards the relationship between erotic-affective individuals of the same sex." Further, they argued that this was a problem because the law prohibits the recognition of business names "that consist of words or legends containing misleading or deceptive signs likely to cause confusion, or are contrary to morality, public order or good custom." Clearly, the government is still very uncomfortable with homosexuality as it not only prohibits LGBT movements from registering as political movements, but the word gay cannot even exist in a business name.

Although AHMNP is still very young, it has taken upon itself a number of initiatives to advance LGBT rights. First, it began to organize gay pride marches in Panama City starting in 2005 to create visibility for the movement. The first march attracted around 100 activists, and these numbers have grown in recent years to nearly 300 and 500 in 2011 and 2012. While still impressive in its growth, these numbers pale in comparison to protests in other cities like Buenos Aires, Argentina, which now attracts more than 70,000 marchers, or São Paulo, Brazil, which has more than 3.5 million participants making it the largest gay pride celebration in the world. Although the population in Panama is much smaller than either of these two countries (4 million compared to 40 million and 200 million, respectively), there is a marked difference in the lack of excitement that the movement is able to generate.

Another impediment to the legal recognition of same-sex relationships is that AHMNP has prioritized other public policies. According to Ricardo Beteta, president of AHMNP, the two most pressing issues for the group are 1) passing a national non-discrimination law to include sexual orientation, and 2) allowing lesbians and gays to openly serve in the federal police.[35] This was done out of a combination of necessity and pragmatism. According to Beteta, winning a law prohibiting discrimination is more feasible in the short term than same-sex marriage or civil unions. Moreover, it is also a more pressing issue because discrimination based on sexual orientation and gender identity affects all LGBT people in Panamanian society.[36]

First, the key priority for the AHMNP is passing a law outlawing discrimination based on sexual orientation and gender identity. A draft of this law has been floating around for many years (*Anteproyecto* 50), but in 2010 this bill received the support of the president of the Commission of Government, Justice, and Constitutional Affairs, H.D. Hernán Delgado. However, this bill, while it has gained some supporters, has yet to pass out of committee, and its future is uncertain.[37]

Second, AHMNP is also very focused on discrimination within the National Police.[38] Executive Decree 204 from September 3, 1997, added several items to Article 133 of the "Internal Rules of the National Police." According to this article, lesbianism and homosexuality "are considered grave offenses of conduct." Consequently, because this is an executive decree, AHMNP is also focused on lobbying the president to change the law on this subject.

So far, neither of these initiatives has been able to pass; however, this is not to say that the LGBT movement in Panama is completely powerless. Panama was the last Spanish-speaking country in Latin America to have a sodomy law on the books, but this changed on July 29, 2008, when President Martín Torrijos signed Executive Decree 332, which effectively decriminalized acts of sodomy.[39] This action effectively repealed Article 12 of Executive Decree 149 from May 20, 1949, which penalized acts of sodomy with three to twelve months in prison and a fine.

The wording of Decree 332 is also significant for a number of additional reasons possibly relevant for other LGBT issues. First, it cited the non-discrimination clause (Article 19) of the Panamanian constitution, marking the first time that the executive branch applied this to lesbians and gays. Second, it also noted that Panama is a signatory to numerous human rights treaties of which the earlier law was in conflict. Finally, it also noted that the Ministry of Health has a policy in its STD/HIV/AIDS programs to respect sexual preferences of every kind without discrimination. All of these references represent the possibility for future success if AHMNP can more effectively organize in the future. Until then, same-sex couples will continue to be discriminated against.

AHMNP did once previously petition the government to recognize de facto same-sex unions in the forms of stable unions, but this petition backfired and the government actually made the policy *more* discriminatory (as was discussed earlier in this chapter). In 2004, AHMNP lobbied the Congress to pass its draft law *Igualdad Jurídicapara Parejas Estables*, which would have given same-sex couples all of the rights of marriage without the name but in many ways allowing it to be considered a de facto union. However, this strategy backfired as the government actually went out of its way to change the language from being gender neutral to specifically discriminating against same-sex couples. As discussed earlier in this chapter, Article 58 of the constitution today reads, "The de facto union between persons *of opposite sex* legally capable of marrying, maintained for five consecutive years in conditions of exclusiveness and stability, shall have all the effects of civil marriage."[40] This addition of the language *of opposite sex* was added because AHMNP was asking for more rights in 2004.[41] So the organization in the meantime has chosen to focus on other issues that it believes have a stronger chance of passing. Until the movement takes up this issue, the law is not likely to change soon.

CONCLUSION

Negative public opinion and a lack of elite allies within the government are the main impediments to the advancement of LGBT rights and same-sex partnership recognition in Panama. Both the society at large and elites in government are, at best, indifferent or, at worst, virulently homophobic. However, other countries in Latin American have faced a similar background not more than a decade ago. The key dilemma at this time for LGBT persons in Panama is the nascent and weak nature of the movement organizations themselves; although activists are tireless and dedicated to their cause, they lack the resources and connections to affect either of these variables. Not much will change until the movement in Panama is able to increase its organizational capacity.

This is not to say that they are without hope; on the contrary, the LGBT movement has seen some progress. AHMNP, in just a few short years and with very few resources, has been able to get one agenda item in a congressional committee even in the face of negative public opinion and very few elite allies. Moreover, public opinion in the region has slowly become more positive as regional attitudes and ideas of partnership recognition are permeating not just from places like Western Europe, but also from regional leaders in Latin America (see the chapter on political parties in this volume).

Finally, in the absence of elite allies and supportive public opinion within Panama, AHMNP has often tried to use its connections with regional and international organizations to put pressure on the Panamanian government, in the form first identified by Keck and Sikkink as the boomerang pattern.[42] In various campaigns, the organization has used its contacts within the Organization of American States, the United States Department of State, the International Gay and Lesbian Human Rights Commission, and several other organizations to apply pressure on the federal government.[43] It may be able to use this international pressure to put pressure on the government for change. Until public opinion catches up, this may be one of its best tactics.

NOTES

1. For example, see Jason Pierceson, Adriana Piatti-Crocker, and Shawn Schulenberg, *Same-Sex Marriage in the Americas: Policy Innovation for Same-Sex Relationships* (Lanham, MD: Lexington Books, 2010).

2. Sidney Tarrow, *Power in Movement: Social Movements and Contentious Politics*, 2nd ed., Cambridge Studies in Comparative Politics (New York: Cambridge University Press, 1998), 4.

3. Mario Diani, "The Concept of Social Movement," *The Sociological Review*, 40 (1992), 1–25.

4. Denise L. Baer and David A. Bositis, *Politics and Linkage in a Democratic Society* (Englewood Cliffs, NJ: Prentice Hall, 1993), 166.

5. Doug McAdam, John D. McCarthy, and Mayer N. Zald, eds., *Comparative Perspectives on Social Movements: Political Opportunities, Mobilizing Structures, and Cultural Framings*, Cambridge Studies in Comparative Politics (New York: Cambridge University Press, 1996).

6. Doug McAdam, John D. McCarthy, and Mayer N. Zald, "Introduction: Opportunities, Mobilizing Structures, and Framing Processes—toward a Synthetic, Comparative Perspective on Social Movements," in *Comparative Perspectives on Social Movements: Political Opportunities, Mobilizing Structures, and Cultural Framings*, eds. Doug McAdam, John D. McCarthy, and Mayer N. Zald (New York: Cambridge University Press, 1996), 5., italics in original.

7. John D. McCarthy and Mayer N. Zald, *The Trend of Social Movements in America: Professionalization and Resource Mobilization* (Morristown, NJ: General Learning Press, 1973); John D. McCarthy and Mayer N. Zald, "Resource Mobilization and Social Movements: A Partial Theory," *American Journal of Sociology*, 82, no. 6 (1977), 12–41.

8. McAdam, McCarthy, and Zald, "Introduction: Opportunities, Mobilizing Structures, and Framing Processes—toward a Synthetic, Comparative Perspective on Social Movements," 3–4.

9. Craig A. Rimmerman, *From Identity to Politics: The Lesbian and Gay Movements in the United States*, Queer Politics, Queer Theories (Philadelphia: Temple University Press, 2002), 8.

10. McAdam, McCarthy, and Zald, "Introduction: Opportunities, Mobilizing Structures, and Framing Processes—toward a Synthetic, Comparative Perspective on Social Movements," 3.

11. Doug McAdam, *Political Process and the Development of Black Insurgency, 1930–1970* (Chicago: University of Chicago Press, 1982); Sidney Tarrow, *Struggling to Reform: Social Movements and Policy Change During Cycles of Protest* (Ithaca, NY: Cornell University, Western Societies Program, Occasional Paper No. 15, 1983); Charles Tilly, *From Mobilization to Revolution* (Reading, MA: Addison-Wesley Pub. Co., 1978).

12. Paul Burstein, "Social Movements and Public Policy," in *How Social Movements Matter*, eds. Marco Giugni, Doug McAdam, and Charles Tilly (Minneapolis: University of Minnesota Press, 1999).

13. Doug McAdam, "Conceptual Origins, Current Problems, Future Directions," in *Comparative Perspectives on Social Movements: Political Opportunities, Mobilizing Structures, and Cultural Framings*, eds. Doug McAdam, John D. McCarthy, and Mayer N. Zald (New York: Cambridge University Press, 1996), 27.

14. Burstein, "Social Movements, Protest, and Contention."

15. Keith Krehbiel, *Information and Legislative Organization*, Michigan Studies in Political Analysis (Ann Arbor: University of Michigan Press, 1991).

16. Paul Burstein and April Linton, "The Impact of Political Parties, Interest Groups, and Social Movement Organizations on Public Policy: Some Recent Evidence and Theoretical Concerns," *Social Forces*, 81, no. 2 (2002), 380–408; Burstein, "Social Movements, Protest, and Contention; Paul Burstein, "Bringing the Public Back In: Should Sociologists Consider the Impact of Public Opinion on Public Policy?" *Social Forces*, 77, no. 1 (1998), 27–62; Paul Burstein, *Discrimination, Jobs, and Politics: The Strug-

gle for Equal Employment Opportunity in the United States since the New Deal (Chicago: University of Chicago Press, 1985); Anne N. Costain and Steven Majstorovic, "Congress, Social Movements and Public Opinion: Multiple Origins of Women's Rights Legislation," *Political Research Quarterly,* 47, no. 1 (1994), 111–35; Paul Burstein, "The Impact of Public Opinion on Policy: A Review and an Agenda," *Political Research Quarterly,* 56, no. 1 (2003), 29–40; Robert S. Erikson, "The Relationship between Public Opinion and State Policy: A New Look Based on Some Forgotten Data," *American Journal of Political Science,* 20, no. 1 (1976), 25–36; Marco Giugni and Florence Passy, "Social Movements and Policy Change: Direct, Mediated, or Joint Effect?," in *American Sociological Association's Section on Collective Behavior and Social Movements: Working Paper Series* (1998); Benjamin I. Page and Robert Y. Shapiro, "Effects of Public Opinion on Policy," *American Political Science Review,* 77, no. 1 (1983), 175–90; Benjamin I. Page, "Democratic Responsiveness? Untangling the Links between Public Opinion and Policy," *PS: Political Science and Politics,* 27, no. 1 (1994), 25–29.

17. Roger W. Cobb, Jennie-Keith Ross, and Marc Howard Ross, "Agenda Building as a Comparative Political Process," *American Political Science Review,* 70, no. 1 (1976), 126–38.

18. Cobb, Ross, and Ross, "Agenda Building as a Comparative Political Process," 130.

19. Tarrow, *Power in Movement: Social Movements and Contentious Politics.*

20. McAdam, McCarthy, and Zald, "Introduction: Opportunities, Mobilizing Structures, and Framing Processes—toward a Synthetic, Comparative Perspective on Social Movements."

21. John W. Kingdon, *Agendas, Alternatives, and Public Policies* (Boston, MA: Little, Brown, 1984), 70.

22. Praveena Gunaratnam, "Drug Policy in Australia: The Supervised Injecting Facilities Debate," in *Policy and Governance,* ed. Asia Pacific School of Economics and Government (Australian National University, 2005).

23. The full text of the current constitution (2004) can be found at http://www.binal.ac.pa/buscar/const197204.htm.

24. Translation and emphasis mine.

25. Translation mine.

26. Translation mine.

27. Translation mine.

28. Translation mine.

29. Germán Lodola and Margarita Corral, "Support for Same-Sex Marriage in Latin America," *AmericasBarometer Insights Series 44.* (2010), http://www.vanderbilt.edu/lapop/insights/I0844.enrevised.pdf.

30. Carlos Guevara Mann, *Political Careers, Corruption, and Impunity: Panama's Assembly, 1984–2009* (Notre Dame, IN: University of Notre Dame Press, 2011).

31. Charles Anthony Smith, "The Electoral Capture of Gay and Lesbian Americans: Evidence and Implications from the 2004 Election," *Studies in Law, Politics, and Society,* 40, no. 2 (2007), 103–21.

32. International Gay and Lesbian Human Rights Commission, "Panama: Victory! First Gay and Lesbian Organization Is Formally Registered," (2001), http://www.iglhrc.org/cgi-bin/iowa/article/takeaction/globalactionalerts/714.html.

33. Translation mine, italics added for emphasis.

34. International Gay and Lesbian Human Rights Commission, "Panama: Victory! First Gay and Lesbian Organization Is Formally Registered."

35. Ricardo Beteta, Personal Correspondence. July 3 (2011).

36. Beteta.

37. Eric Jackson, "Historic First Hearing for Gay Rights in Panama Law to Bar Discrimination against Gays Unlikely to Pass This Year," *The Panama News.* September 23 (2010), http://www.thepanamanews.com/pn/v_16/issue_10/news_05.html.

38. One of the consequences of the United States' invasion of Panama in 1989 is that the country no longer has a military; therefore, the question of whether the armed forces allow lesbians and gays to serve openly is moot.

39. The full text for Executive Decree 332 can be found at http://www.asamblea.gob.pa/APPS/LEGISPAN/PDF_GACETAS/2000/2008/26095_2008.PDF.

40. Translation and emphasis mine.

41. In the previous version of the Constitution of Panama, this language was numbered as Article 54, not Article 58.

42. Margaret E. Keck and Kathryn Sikkink, *Activists Beyond Borders: Advocacy Networks in International Politics* (Ithaca, NY: Cornell University Press, 1998).

43. Beteta.

SIX

The Creation of Civil Partnerships in Uruguay

Diego Sempol

In 2007, Uruguay passed a civil partnership (*Unión Concubinaria*) law that regulated, among other things, same-sex couples, and it became the first country in Latin America to sanction this type of legislation nationwide. Previous regional examples had been more limited. A civil union law had been adopted in Argentina in the autonomous city of Buenos Aires and in the Province of Rio Negro, while Mexico had passed a same-sex marriage law but only for its federal capital. The bill was sanctioned as the result of a double process: the electoral victory of the *Frente Amplio*[1] (FA) in the first round, which granted it a majority in both chambers of parliament; and the consolidation of profound transformations within the lesbian, gay, transgender, bisexual, and queer (LGBTQ) movement in Uruguay, with significant capacity to mobilize in public spaces. The final wording of the law and its legislative process demanded negotiations among the various sectors that make up the FA, which led to limited legislative achievements and a continuous dialogue with LGBTQ social organizations for their support of a bill that did not fully respond to their demands.

Since the return of democracy in 1985, Uruguay had not discussed homosexuality and its status in society in such an extensive and prolonged way in the public realm until 2007. The proliferation of news articles and television reports enabled the mass media to discuss the profound changes in family structure that Uruguayan society had been experiencing since the 1970s, the growth of various "family arrange-

89

ments," and the existence of a democratic deficit due to the gap between these changes and the legislation in force.

This chapter intends to track the debate produced throughout this period in order to answer the following questions: How was the agenda construed? What notions of the family circulated in the debate? What rhetoric was used by the various players involved on how the state should engage with the "homosexual family" and how it should acknowledge it? Can civil partnership be considered a regulation that reinforces heteronormativity? What type of integration entailed sanctioning a law that seeks to regulate couples considered socially "different" (an "other") regarding married heterosexual couples?

SOCIAL CHANGES

The civil partnership bill sought to provide legal solutions for major changes that had been quietly taking place in the Uruguayan family structure in the last decades. Within the Latin American context, Uruguay's population had an early participation in the first demographic transition. Already in the early twentieth century, the 1908 census revealed strong social changes in this sphere: a drop in birth and death rates and an aging population. Uruguayan historiography and demography tried to explain this early change emphasizing the process of social disciplining in the social, economic, and political modernization experienced in the last three decades of the nineteenth century, as well as the impact of European immigration in a cattle ranching society, which enabled the growth of urban areas after the state's attempts at agricultural colonization failed.

The "breadwinner system" was extended in this period, with its typical example of a married father and mother and their biological offspring. The system reproduced the division of heteropatriarchal skills. While the father had the role of sole provider, occupying the public space and maintaining the whole family structure, the mother carried out the domestic chores in the private space and took charge of social reproduction through the caring for and education of the children.

This model, according to Filgueira, went into crisis in 1960s Uruguay because of the impact of profound demographic, economic, and sociocultural changes.[2] By then, clear signs had emerged at the end of that first transition while a new phase was in place, characterized by a rise in life expectancy, changes in the age structure, and relative population aging, aspects that affected the family structure. The uniformity that had apparently existed in the first half of the twentieth century was replaced by a diverse number of alternatives: the number of single-person households grew, as well as the number of nuclear families without any children ("empty nest") and female-headed households, while there was a similar rate of extended and stepfamilies. Thus, already in 1996, the typical nuclear family, formed by a couple and their children, represented only 37 percent of all Uruguayan households. These changes were related to the progress made by women in the work force, a phenomenon that, starting in the 1970s, also included married women. Thus, the single breadwinner model was gradually replaced by another, with multiple breadwinners, even among the lower income sectors, where women were key in sustaining the family as they headed the household. The multiple breadwinner model enabled new negotiations within the family, along with the social and cultural changes regarding the role of sexuality in the lives of individuals, the so-called divorce revolution and the progress made for gender equality by the local feminist and women's movements. The marrying and reproduction age rose among middle class sectors, and starting in 1971 there was a generalized fall in the number of marriages (especially in Montevideo), a process that has intensified since 1988. In parallel, de facto relationships grew among lower income sectors, a phenomenon that gradually spread to the younger middle class generations.

These profound social transformations were not acknowledged by the legal system, although Uruguay had been in the past a pioneer in Latin America in the recognition of family rights. The secular drive had made civil marriage obligatory in 1885, eliminating its religious counterpart which had been adopted by the 1869 Civil Code. In 1907, the reformist drive passed law 33245, which enabled divorce by mutual consent and by grounds for divorce (abandonment of the home, prison sentence of ten years or more for one of the spouses, and so on), while in 1913 another bill was sanctioned enabling divorce by the woman's sole will. This tendency to innovate did not cease, not even during the military dictatorship (1973–1984) since the Council of State (the ruling junta) introduced a new change in 1978, despite opposition from the Catholic Church, allowing men to divorce of their own accord, thus updating the legal doctrine.[3] Once these changes were consolidated, divorce was no longer considered punishment: it was now a "remedy," where finding a guilty party became irrelevant, and offered legal solutions to a relationship that was actually dissolved.

Socially, the cohabitation of de facto couples during the last decades of the twentieth century was de-stigmatized, and this also reached the custody of children out of wedlock. But de facto relationships, called *concubinato* in Uruguay, suffered a significant legal vacuum. Once they ended, by separation or death, partners were defenseless regarding inheritance, property, social security, and paternal obligations and rights. The solution to these issues depended on a judge's discretion and his/her ethical and ideological convictions, a weakness that increased when the case brought to court was that of a same-sex couple. In the best of cases, sensitive court officials muffled the injustices produced by this legal vacuum and resorted to legal terms such as "de facto society" or "unjust enrichment," terms that were originally meant to solve other problems.

THE LEFT AND THE LGBTQ MOVEMENT

The *Frente Amplio's* electoral victory in 2005 consolidated the political work that the party's youth had carried out since 2001 on sexual diversity and gender, because many of its members were elected to Parliament for the first time, such as deputies Pablo Álvarez, Diego Cánepa, Edgardo Ortuño, and Javier Salsamendi. These policymakers were crucial in the adoption of the civil partnership law, while the support of Senator Margarita Percovich (*Vertiente Artiguista*, FA), to the bill was indispensable.

Since the mid-1990s, the FA has gradually shifted toward the political center and the development of *"progresismo"* (progressiveness) with reformist social change strategies, and an appreciation of democracy facilitated the development of new agendas.[4] Human rights, sexual and reproductive rights, discrimination on the grounds of sexual orientation, gender identity, and ethnic origins came to the fore. The first years of the twenty-first century witnessed rainbow flags appearing in the FA's major demonstrations, along with the creation of the multisector group *Gays y Lesbianas de Izquierda* (Left-Wing Gays and Lesbians), while something similar took place in the most iconic commemorations of Uruguayan social organizations, such as those of May 1 (workers' day) and August 14 (the student movement's celebration).

The FA's rise to power also consolidated a new framework of opportunities[5] for the LGBTQ movement's political action, which contributed significantly to its social mobilization. The political system had opened up and the LGBTQ movement's influence had grown significantly, while allies among the elites were willing to carry out an agenda focused on recognizing the rights of these groups, traditionally excluded.

The first gay organization appeared in Uruguay in 1984, while the first public demonstration against discrimination on the grounds of sexual orientation and gender identity took place in 1992. The first political contacts between organizations and legislators of all parties were held in the late 1990s. As a result, an anti-discrimination law was passed in 2003, stipulating up to two years of jail for "incitement of hatred" on the grounds of gender identity and sexual orientation, among others. The first negotiations between sexual diversity activists, such as Fernando Frontán and Diana Mines, and legislator Percovich took place during this period to propose a bill that would regulate same-sex couples.

Starting in 2004, the groups that had been working since the mid-1990s[6] were joined by a slew of new organizations,[7] including the *Colectivo Ovejas Negras* (Black Sheep Collective).[8] This group successfully sponsored a change of the interpretation frameworks within the movement,[9] abandoning the stress on identity aspects in order to advocate an intersectional conceptualization of discriminations that enabled the construction of stronger alliances among LGBTQ organizations and student, feminist, afro-descendant and workers' movements. Primarily, the sexual diversity movement started using on its discourse, terms such as "equality" and "social justice," which facilitated engagement with the Uruguayan Left (not so with the traditional parties).[10]

Also, the mobilization of the sexual diversity movement grew significantly and, with it, its ability to influence and press the various political sectors. In good measure, this change was the result of a growing social politicization of sexuality and of a radical shift in the movement's political strategy, which resorted to the category of "diversity," understanding the need to fight against a collective imagination that encouraged strong social homogenization because of social hyperintegration produced by the reformist drive. This transformation reinforced an intersectional view and an expansion of social mobilization, which enabled an exponential growth in the attendance of diversity marches (called "pride" marches in the 1990s) growing from an average of 200 attendants in 2004 to 13,000 in 2010. These changes, along with the local impact of Spain's same-sex marriage law in 2005, were part of the setting for the parliamentary and social debate that finally enabled the approval of the civil partnership bill.

This progress encountered its largest resistance from members of the Catholic Church's hierarchy, who continued to spread pathological views of sexual diversity. In 2003, Montevideo's Archbishop Nicolás Cotugno said in public that homosexuality was a "contagious disease" and "aberrant," and that gays should be "isolated" from the rest of society.[11]

WRTING THE BILL

Strong social change in Uruguayan society (changes in family structure and a growing visibility of sexual diversity) and the new legal problems they were causing led Parliament to provide solutions. Thus, several bills were introduced since the beginning of the new century that were never passed, but were taken as inputs for the final bill: Deputy Díaz Maynard introduced a bill on May 9, 2000; deputies José Falero, Pablo Mieres, Iván Posada, and Felipe Michelini introduced another bill on May 16, 2000; the FA deputies introduced a third bill on October 9, 2002, that was reintroduced by the FA Senators; and finally an alternative bill was introduced by Senator Percovich which, with some changes, was finally passed by both chambers.

This law regulated couples with five years of uninterrupted cohabitation and, in section 2, defined "civil partnership as the de facto union derived from the community of life of two people—whatever their sex,

identity, orientation or sexual option—who maintain an affective relationship of a sexual character, of an exclusive, sole, stable and permanent
nature, without being united by matrimony itself."[12] Civil partnership
recognizes reciprocal assistance and, once the bond is dissolved, a partner may request alimony, if applicable. Recognition of the bond may be
requested by one or both partners. Also, any interested party may do so
once the legal proceedings for inheritance of one or both partners begin.
Recognizing a partnership guarantees property rights, if so desired, may
include the same rights as in marriage and automatically dissolves any
previous partnership or marriage by the couple, even when there was no
formal divorce. The formalization and dissolution of the partnership is by
judicial decision at the request of any of the partners, upon death or by
declaration of absence. Also, the court decision in case of dissolution
must decide on the custody and support of their children (if any) and
determine who will remain in the family's home. In the case of death, the
surviving partner has the same inheritance rights the Civil Code recognizes to spouses in cases of marriage.

However, the law does not mention the possibility of adoption by civil
partnership couples. In the bill's original version, section 10 expressly
stated that only opposite-sex partners could adopt jointly. At the time,
Percovich argued that "society was not prepared" to accept this right for
same-sex couples, that there was an urgent need to provide these relationships with a legal solution given the problems caused by the death of
one of its members due to the HIV/AIDS pandemic, and finally that there
were reasons of legislative strategy, since in her opinion this was the only
way to reach an agreement for the bill in the FA. When asked about this
limitation during an interview in early 2005, Percovich elaborated on
these three arguments:

> We thought Uruguayan society had to debate this issue much more.
> That society was not sufficiently prepared and that it was more urgent
> to first recognize the civil partnership between homosexuals: many
> times one of its members is HIV-positive and many families refuse to
> accept this reality. . . . My position in this regard has been absolutely
> tactical: we had evaluated it in depth with the lawyers and had decided
> to ensure its approval. This bill will once again be much debated. And
> sincerely, I do not believe yet that in Uruguay we have the luck to be
> able to legally recognize adoption by homosexuals, although it is a
> reality already in place: it is a fact that single men and women in
> Uruguay can adopt and that many of them are homosexuals. I am
> willing to battle for the bill once it is discussed, and see what chances it
> has. In the Chamber of Representatives, when I introduced it in 2003,
> some would have signed it if I had left out the part about homosexual
> adoption."[13]

Some sexual diversity organizations, such as *Grupo Diversidad, Encuentro
Ecuménico para la Liberación de las Minorías Sexuales,* CIEISU, and *Hermanas*

de la Perpetua Indulgencia had advocated since the late 1990s for the need of legislative progress in the recognition of gay and lesbian couples.[14] The Percovich Bill, which had been consulted with several organizations at different times, was received with ambivalence: It was accepted as a major step in the recognition of rights, but it was considered "minimal" because it only recognized couples and did not cover other forms of cohabitation (friends, groups with distant consanguinity bonds, communities). Nor did it recognize adoption by gay and lesbian couples, and the original wording of section 10 was considered a legislative setback. Activist Diana Mines, from the group *Diversidad*, stated,

> [T]he bill reserves adoption rights for "partners of different sex," by which it ends up innovating in a negative way, since Uruguayan legislation had lacked so far discriminatory clauses. . . . [T]he numerous cohabiting couples that are already raising children will see the recognition of their rights unfairly postponed. . . . As an activist, my duty is to advocate for all the rights our society does not recognize to lesbian, gay, transvestite, transsexual, intersexual, and bisexual people. A politician's job is to find the way to pass their bills, which many times force them to compromise clauses and wordings. However, I do not believe it is convenient to modify a text outright, in order to consider others' prejudices, and even less to fragilize [*sic*] the future debate by admitting that "society is not prepared" to accept certain changes. . . . Also, what data sustain this statement? Public opinion—which is a tide in constant movement—has evolved rapidly in Uruguay."[15]

Percovich's bill was introduced on March 16, 2005, to the Senate's Constitution and Legislation Commission, signed by 16 *Frente Amplio* legislators,[16] with several changes (such as the exclusion of any mention of adoption) and was passed by that chamber on September 12, 2006. The Chamber of Deputies introduced new changes and passed it on November 28, 2007. It was finally passed by an extraordinary Senate meeting on December 18 that year. The bill was passed with the vote of FA legislators, who had a majority in both chambers, and received support from National Party (PN) deputies (Beatriz Argimón, Sandra Etcheverry, Álvaro Lorenzo, and Pablo Iturralde) when section 2 recognizing homosexual couples was voted, and from the Colorado Party in the Senate (Julio M. Sanguinetti). The main public resistance and critiques came mostly from the National Party and the Catholic Church.

DEFINITION OF THE "PROBLEM"

When arguing for the bill, its advocates constantly referred to academic research that confirmed the existence of profound social changes in the family, as well as the undeniable progress of de facto unions in Uruguayan society. Summaries and texts circulated among legislators' offices, and researchers were abundantly quoted in order to argue in favor of the law. Academic information was presented as "reality," as unquestionable, resorting to the legitimacy that statistic indicators have acquired in Uruguayan society, thus successfully establishing the reasons and the need to debate the bill and advance legislatively in that direction.

These changes (which had left the nuclear family, married with children, in the minority, as some argued) demanded a legislation update that anticipated legal solutions for conflicts of interests among the members of a de facto couple. This, in turn, would allow for the recognition of individual rights and guarantee the property and equality of those involved. The principles of non-discrimination and equality were the second pillars that sustained the bill and the way found to include same-sex couples in section 2. The legislative change sought to take "a step" toward the recognition of same-sex couples, regulating some of its basic rights and enabling them to form a partnership of assets. This recognition reinforced the similarity that exists between same-sex and opposite-sex couples (they build reciprocal affections and responsibilities, they generate property). In practice, it incorporated the obliteration of sex and the variety of its sexual practices, limited the "citizens' freedom of choice," and included the demand of a compulsory and proven monogamy of at least five years. Finally, the bill was presented as a "conservative" measure, anticipating potential resistance, given that its purpose was not to assimilate civil partnership with marriage or seek the forced formalization of couples that had chosen to cohabit, and it also required a large number of conditions, including five years of cohabitation.

Also, by focusing the argument on the need to update and modernize legislation in order to adapt it to change and respond to the needs of the majority, its detractors were placed in a difficult situation under the dichotomy "inevitable change"/"irrelevant reaction," which forced them to argue against the recognition of rights while advocating for a model of family organization that was now in the minority, whose social legitimacy had been strongly eroded, questioned, and denaturalized in practice through the divorce revolution.

The ruling party, taking a pragmatic stance, argued that this recognition did not seek to equate cohabitation with marriage but responded to a new reality about which there was no need to moralize. This strategy sought to lower the debate's profile on this issue (what is family?) and was based on a dual tradition when arguing for the recognition of all citizens' rights without seeking to impose a moral or specific model to the rest: the humanistic "Batllism" tradition, which recognized the need to defend those most vulnerable, and the left-wing tradition, with its basic principles of equality and dignity.[17]

The introduction of a bill including same-sex and opposite-sex couples indistinctly, based on a pragmatism that refused to moralize (although with a strong ethical view about the place morality holds in the state), forced opposition sectors to argue by moralizing and explaining the existence of ontological differences in status between homosexuals and heterosexuals, thus exposing their religious or moral views, of very little influence in Uruguayan society. The civil partnership bill was not construed as a matter of philosophy or beliefs, but as an issue of citizenship and rights, of social inclusion and legal solution for the social heterogeneity of the existing types of family. This was the framework for the debate that managed to obtain a consensus among FA legislators to approve the bill, and also enabled legislators from traditional parties to vote in favor.

NORMATIVE FAMILY VERSUS REALITY

National Party legislators were the main opponents in both chambers to the bill and, particularly, to the inclusion of same-sex couples. Argumentation during the debate deployed a "strategic secularism,"[18] which, resorting to legal and philosophical rhetoric, sought to defend traditional religious positions supported by many legislators, but who avoided expressly referring to the official doctrine of the Catholic Church. The debate took three different paths that often intermingled in the speeches but, for reasons of clarity, will be presented here separately: The "average" morality is not prepared for this legislative change; same-sex couples cannot reproduce, and therefore are not a family, and a regulation of their bonds should not be included in family law; and it is unconstitutional to include same-sex couples in this law.

Senator Eber Da Rosa (*Alianza Nacional*, PN) recognized the bill's pragmatism but nonetheless added that its compatibility with social principles, values, or notions about family life should be assessed. In order to confront the reality/needs argument that favored reforming the legal framework and to avoid expressly discriminatory considerations, Da Rosa proposed debating the family as a value (and not as a reality), referring to, and building upon, a sort of average public opinion that considered the inclusion of homosexuals excessive, violent, and conflictive, a factor that would force the deferral of their inclusion in the law:

> [W]e believe there are basic concepts in our society—including that of the family—that, although not the only or definite ones in the life of humanity, have a certain degree of acceptance in the average culture of society, at a certain time. Thus, many times, the definition we have to give or the decision we must take on this issue, has to be referred to the existing or current concept in the average culture of society. . . . Section 2 states the possibility of homosexual unions, which we understand affects the concept that in the average culture of our community defines the family today. Perhaps, in an x number of years, there may be

another more encompassing definition that avoids any doubt on this issue; the doubts that now haunt us are, precisely, due to this.[19]

This discourse aimed to elliptically silence and justify excluding LGBTQ people by blaming those that sought to expand the recognition of rights of excess and a lack of "peacefulness" because they did not accept the average values of Uruguayan society.

The argument that a society "is not mature" enough for a change of this sort was added to the need of clearly defining what type of bonds can be conceptualized as "family" based on current legislation. This reasoning sought to limit the discussion to juridical aspects and exclude demographic and sociological aspects that point to the existence of profound social changes in Uruguayan society. In short, it confronted the "weight of reality" versus the weight of Uruguay's current legal system, reframing the discussion in order to lead it to the realm of the definition of the family, thus avoiding a discussion focused on individual rights and the need to set guarantees for individuals who decide to live together. In this sense, Senator Francisco Gallinal (*Correntada Wilsonista*, PN) developed, in his numerous speeches, a line of reasoning that sought to determine the characteristics of the "normative family" and how it was conceptualized inseparably with a couple's reproductive potential. This, of course, implied an insurmountable barrier for the inclusion of non-heterosexual couples.

> [S]ection 40 [of the Constitution] establishes the family as the basis of our society and gives the state the responsibility to safeguard its moral and material stability, with an addendum that is practically part of all definitions of the concept of family—at least, of those appearing in the Constitution of the Republic—that is, the potential, which is not necessarily fulfilled, that a family has to generate descendants. That is where I believe lies the limit of the notion of the family. . . . Not by chance section 40 of the Constitution stipulates—and I repeat part of what was already said: "The family is the basis of our society. The State shall safeguard its moral and material stability so that children may be properly reared within that society." Also, in one part, section 41 states: "The care and education of children, so that they may attain their fullest physical, intellectual, and social capacity, is the duty and the right of parents." It means that that potential—which, I repeat, does not necessarily have to be fulfilled because we all know that many times there are impediments of a various nature—is today a part of that definition.[20]

This legal interpretation led to claims that the bill was unconstitutional, thus avoiding other sorts of evaluations, which would have implied a higher political cost. Senator Gustavo Lapaz (*Herrerismo*, PN) pointed out:

The protection of the stable cohabitant relationship is understood as a way to protect the heterosexual family, which is the basis of society, according to section 40 of the Constitution. Its evident procreative finality deserves a special protection and consideration, which certainly does not happen with homosexual relationships. To equate them is a serious mistake and an assault on the Constitution, which protects the family as the basis of society and not homosexual relationships which, for sure, will never be the basis of society; insomuch as the original sense of the word, "matrimony" derives from the word "mother", and in order to be so the maternal experience has to be necessarily lived through. It is serious craftiness to include in the law situations that are substantially diverse and to pretend to assimilate them in rights, when they do not fulfill the same functions nor have, for sure, the same relevance.[21]

Thus, the bill's opponents emphasized traditional and heteronormative arguments about marriage. For example, an editorial in *El Observador*, which is linked to the Catholic Opus Dei, sought to limit the family label only to the nuclear family, and added that those in favor of the civil partnership bill were mistaking these arrangements with the family:

One issue is the notion of the family. The other covers the legal rights of those who make up non-married couples, between two people of different or same sex. These unions are a reality that cannot be overlooked because their addition to our society and that of many other countries has grown. . . . But it is a profound and dangerous mistake to mix their rights with the role of the family. They are two different and irreconcilable things. . . . The law under parliamentary discussion . . . disperses the word family in a cloudy mist. Its advocates state that there is no longer one single model of the family, there are several. But that is not so. It is important to call things by their name. . . . Whoever supports that position attempts to deform and crack a structure which is a central and irreplaceable pillar of an orderly society.[22]

Catholic Church authorities and representatives of its dependent institutions followed the same argument, trying to reinforce that restrictive conceptualization of the family, leaving aside the elliptic formulations that are typical of Uruguayan political culture (laden with nonconfrontational gestures), to explicitly condemn not only the potential regulation of homosexual couples, but also that of unmarried heterosexuals. This was accompanied by assessments that sought to magnify the impact of the suggested reforms, and also emphasized pathological views of homosexuality.

The chairman of the Uruguayan Episcopal Conference, Bishop Pablo Galimberti, believed the ratification of the bill "would be approving deviate behavior and turning it into a model for society. In no way can it be accepted that homosexual cohabitation can be equated with marriage."[23] Galimberti considered homosexual unions or heterosexual domestic partnerships as "devaluations of the original bond."[24] The discourse of the local church hierarchy reproduced that of the Congregation for the Doctrine of the Faith, which stated that homosexuality was "objectively disordered."[25] The bill was seen as a threat to the current sexual order and its hierarchic systems, and every means was sought to reinforce the forms of heteronormative regulation, which reserved legal legitimacy and recognition only for the models of the hetero-patriarchal reproductive family. The bill was also conceptualized as a threat to the centrality of the traditional nuclear family and an erosion of its symbolic weight and hierarchy in society.

Opponents also sought to confront the bill's implicit constructivism, appealing to essentialist views of the family which put "nature" as basis for its interpretation. Ana Maria Abel, from the Uruguayan Family Institute, believed that "the new models cannot be equated with the family because they imply an exclusion of commitment, of exclusiveness and, in many cases, also of descendants while nature demands descendants for the continuation of the species."[26] These players supported the idea of "fair discrimination," which differentiates justice from equality, where the alleged differential traits and goals of homosexual and heterosexual couples ought to be preserved in the law. Thus, the opposition sought to lead the debate to a new field, leaving aside the argumentative strategy focused on the recognition of individual rights, to start discussing which types of bonds are a family and which are not, in order to define who can be benefited by the new legislation and the proper form in which the state should regulate this new and unquestionable social heterogeneity. Opponents were willing, as stated by several legislators, to accept recognition of rights for homosexual couples as long as it did not imply providing a status of legality to those bonds as another alternative of the family. The equation made by the bill, which included homosexual and heterosexual couples indistinctly, was deemed unacceptable since it silenced the "different natures" of two types of bonds.

On one extreme was the stance of the Catholic Church and its social and institutional allies seeking to preserve all the rights and legitimacy for married heterosexual relationships. On the other, a majority of the National Party's legislators, who were closer to a non-intervening liberalism that sought to publicly ignore the existence of same-sex couples because they lack the "same relevance" as heterosexual ones and to recognize the latter given their overwhelming presence in society. This allowed the players to take their positions in the debate stating their rejection to the inclusion of homosexuality while, at the same time, denying that they were discriminating. As Senator Lapaz said, "I should clarify that for the homosexual person we have the utmost respect. Even the Catholic Church . . . points out that homosexuals shall be received with respect, compassion and delicacy, avoiding any sign of unfair discrimination against them. But that does not justify in any way their assimilation with rights for natural families."[27] However, the Catholic Church forged a strong link on these issues with the National Party, and the social diversity movement seized this support strategically in parliament from FA legislators. This path allowed the FA to reinforce its differences with the traditional parties in its own "secular" or "post-materialist" agenda, an area that is highly sensitive for its constituents.

How did the political and social sectors in favor of the bill react to this shift in the debate? The first reaction was to avoid such a debate and to return to the original discussion: to recognize individual rights and remedy a legal vacuum caused by changes in social reality. Further reaction was to avoid discussing the conceptualization of family and instead refer to "family arrangements" to prevent a confrontation with the more traditional views that had assigned this category exclusively to heterosexual and reproductive nuclear families. The strategy developed a pragmatic rationale that sought a swift legislative approval of the bill, avoiding cultural confrontation on the different family models and their legitimate stance in society.

This strategy was also used by other FA legislators. However, in their speeches, conceptual shifts occurred that turned the discussion into a cultural debate, pointing out that family arrangements (including the typical family) are all different versions, but generating the same rights, of what could be called a family. For example, the Deputy presenting the bill in the lower chamber, Diego Cánepa (*Nuevo Espacio*, FA), stated,

> We believe that social reality demands acknowledging that, apart from matrimony, the traditional element for the configuration of the home, there are other, informal, family arrangements but with equal affective, economic, sexual, emotional bonds that are not marriages, but they are families. Consequently, we think it is necessary that the law covers situations that are the result of social change and that it allows for the application of the constitutional axiom, recognizing other models of family arrangements, like that of civil partnership. The restrictive interpretation of the constitutional postulate with marriage as the only way of forming a family leads to ignoring real families in our society that are in utter neglect.[28]

The LGBTQ organizations, which were in constant communication with FA's legislators, also applied in different degrees the strategy originally outlined by the ruling party. Some emphasized the legal vacuum and the need to address it, while others challenged the traditional view and fought the cultural debate about the existence of different family types.

The ruling party's pragmatic strategy was also resisted by the *Colectivo Ovejas Negras*, which agreed that it was important to pass the bill, but also to provoke a social debate that would launch the fight against discrimination in Uruguay. "Although discrimination situations here do not include savage aggressions, there are those that continue to consider homosexuality a pathology,"[29] said Mauricio Coitiño, a member of the group. This was the underlying reason for some legislators to oppose the bill, he added. It was indispensable to launch a cultural debate on family models and to advocate for the legitimacy of other "arrangements." According to Coitiño, "a family is a group of two or more people joined by affectionate bonds with a common project. It is a conception that exceeds the reproductive role and covers groups of people who like to live together. There is a commitment of reciprocal assistance with loyalties deriving from the bonds, which dissolve when the relation collapses."[30]

In this view, family and reproduction are not mutually exclusive, and people that at a certain time share a common project and solidarity bonds could be included, without the need for affective-erotic relationships or exclusiveness of any kind. A taxative definition was avoided and individuals were recognized the capacity to self-identify what kind of bond they considered a family. Thus, this loose notion of the family attempted to integrate all the different arrangements and solidarity nets that many gays and lesbians build on a daily basis, as an alternative to overcome the loss of family relationships with legal legitimacy owing to the exclusion they experienced because of homophobia in their families.

The original way the "problem" was construed was very productive in parliament since it enabled, apart from the criticism of sexual diversity groups and opponents to the reform, legislators from the traditional political parties to justify their support to the bill without entering into the cultural debate about the meanings condensed by the notion of family. For example, Deputy Beatriz Argimón (*Alianza Nacional*, PN) said she would vote for the bill: "I'm convinced it does not affect the legitimate family at all. Basically it serves to sort the existing bonds in society."[31]

Arguments about the bill's unconstitutionality were repeatedly refuted, even by Colorado Party members. During his intervention in the Senate, former President Julio María Sanguinetti (Colorado Party) defended the significance of such a bill and stated that constitutional law had always handled a wide notion of the family, since it had recognized early on the rights of the children born out of wedlock. In a similar sense, Senator José Korseniak (Socialist Party, FA) mentioned article 75 of the 1952 Constitution as a precedent, which granted Uruguayan citizenship to foreigners in a three-year period under the condition they had "formed a family" in the country and were unmarried.

All of these perspectives, beyond their different nuances and emphasis, shared a common point of view: Democracy should not defend only one morality and the state cannot be limited to not condemning (non-intervening liberalism), but must intervene to recognize and guarantee effectively the same rights to all individuals, addressing their particular situations. Cánepa developed this idea as follows, during his defense of the bill in the Chamber of Deputies: "There is a very different step between tolerating, which is a minimum deed in democratic cohabitation, and protecting a right so it can be effectively exercised and enjoyed and that it is not only a statement, so it can be transformed into a permanent exercise."[32]

THE LAST STAGES OF THE DEBATE

The mass media constructed the debate around the recognition of same-sex couples and different types of families, mostly because legal discourse is not media-friendly. While the media as public space filters and amplifies the discourses and interpretation frameworks of other public spaces, it is interesting to note how openly opposing media to the FA government (*El País*) and in some cases close to the Catholic Church (*El Observador*) turned this issue into one of their strong subjects (appearing on several covers and editorials) and repeatedly denounced the end of the typical family. Meanwhile, the coverage of independent left-wing publications (*Brecha, La Diaria*) was more balanced and also included the voices of LGBTQ groups and their criticisms, while stressing the similarity of arguments by the National Party and the Catholic Church.

In addition, because the bill had the support of the ruling party, which had enough votes to pass it through the Chamber of Deputies, during the debate in the legislature, National Party legislators devised a new strategy: They criticized the bill from an apparent a more "progressive" perspective than the ruling party's. For example, Álvaro Lorenzo (*Alianza Nacional*, PN) criticized the demand of five years of cohabitation to access the benefits as excessive. Others, such as Julio Basanta (*Alianza Nacional*, PN) stated that individual freedoms and other rights would be affected only if one of the partners was allowed to create a civil partnership without the consent of the other. This would amount to an invasion of privacy of people who sought relationships unregulated by the state, said Basanta. Finally, Luis Lacalle Pou (*Herrerismo*, PN) mentioned that the bill was actually a kind of undercover and "degraded homosexual marriage," which needed another discussion and a different kind of legislative mechanism.

This change in strategy among PN members in the lower chamber can also be interpreted as an attempt to undermine the ruling party's discourse, for which the approval of the bill was an historical benchmark, and updated the political imagination of a Batllist matrix.[33] In very different ways, allusions to this political tradition were constantly present in the speeches of the ruling party legislators. For example, Deputy Edgardo Ortuño (*Vertiente Artiguista*, FA) said during the debate that passed the bill, "When we began our task here in this Legislature we said we aspired for the Uruguayan parliament to recover its place among the vanguard of social legislation that it once had exactly a century ago, which distinguished it from the rest of Latin America."[34]

The dispute over the Colorado Party's Batllism tradition, which some FA sectors such as *Vertiente Artiguista* were timidly undertaking since the late 1990s, was reflected in this bill. A series of bills under that tradition enabled the spread and reinforcement of the left-wing government's re-founding nature through its rhetoric. Ortuño considered the civil partnership bill a pearl in a long necklace of legal victories that recognized the rights of the most vulnerable social sectors:

> We are changing. This is not an isolated bill, it is part of a group: the law that guaranteed union rights to workers, the law that guaranteed rights for domestic employees, the law that set safeguards for construction workers, such as the unemployment fund, the law that for the first time established equal opportunities for men and women, recognizing gender rights, law Nº 18.059, which for the first time in this country referred to racial equity and recognized the contribution and the rights of Afro-descendants, overcoming the inequalities that have affected us, as well as the laws that have addressed the situation of Uruguayans abroad or those that have guaranteed the rights of former political prisoners. And now the rights of those who freely decide to live in civil unions, whatever sexual orientation they may have, are guaranteed.[35]

Secularization and an early recognition of divorce rights, the rabid anti-clericalism of a part of Batllism and the sanction of important social legislation during the first decades of the twentieth century are a founding part of the local political culture which, although broken in the late 1960s, was brought up to date significantly during those debates. The stated strategy not to challenge the traditional family but to seek the recognition of a plurality of existing situations reinforced the social imagination focused in a secular and plural state which recognized vanguard rights to its citizens, and which had coincided with one of the foundational moments of the welfare state and Uruguay's social and economic development.

However, a significant difference is salient in the attempt to imitate this tradition: Social changes, instead of being construed and encouraged by the state, as it happened during Batllism, are only recognized once they have taken root in social reality. While Batllism acted with foresight, trying to anticipate and avoid social injustice even before social demand from a specific sector emerged, the recognition of civil partnership was only taken into consideration after sexual diversity organizations demanded it. The attempt during the debate by several FA legislators to bring Batllism's political imagination up to date can be interpreted not only as a dispute with the Colorado Party, owing to its political tradition and symbolic capital, but also as a challenge to that exclusion, and as claiming a place in a political genealogy that was and is socially considered as foundational landmark of the modern Uruguayan state.

CONCLUSION

Demands for rights can be made from different discursive places. The irony of claiming equality from a place of difference is a recurring problem of contemporary politics which introduces a discussion on the risks of normalization entailed by political action. In what measure has civil partnership, instead of attacking "normality," reinforced the heteronormative model? There is no simple answer. The law only recognizes couples and not other types of arrangements, and requires an exclusive bond (monogamy) and five years of uninterrupted cohabitation, aspects that reinforce the erotic-affective-monogamous bonds as a vector for the allocation of rights. Also, the possibility of formalization at any time gives guarantees to a bond and, thus, builds a new social sexual hierarchy in terms of legitimacy and rights, excluding other arrangements.

This equation caused resistance. The argumentation of the Catholic Church did not accept differences quietly, nor did it conceive them as a matter of indifference. Almost intolerantly, it claimed the need neither to promote nor legalize traits of social life that could compromise "public morality" or the "social order." Its alarm was linked to the "danger" of spreading moral relativism that would expand constitutionally protected equality to the realms of sexuality and the family, undermining heterosexism that advocates a "natural order" view and the centrality of the sacrament of matrimony. Thus, the secular state was ignored and, in practice, legal norms were being equated with religious morality and provisions.

In general, the National and Colorado parties' legislators, who opposed the bill embodied a conservative discourse emphasizing the differences (reproductive, normative) between same-sex and opposite-sex couples in order to justify the need for separate and different rules to address the particularity of each situation. This implicitly established different hierarchies between both types of bonds and a certain "resigned acceptance"[36] of the different, as long as the other accepts their place and does not seek an equality which may compromise the system's social basis or that which is socially accepted.

On the contrary, the bill's advocates developed a discourse that identified them going beyond the idea of tolerance and recognized equality within the difference and, in order to generate equity, guaranteed rights for that particularity. The rights of individuals were recognized above any moral appraisal and this position was presented as plural and pragmatic (family reality has changed), since it expanded the recognition of rights overcoming the traditional separation between the public and the private in the assumption that, far from weakening the democratic system, it guaranteed and strengthened it.

However, in practice, this discourse has shown its limitations since the sanctioned law recognizes differences in two levels: There are oppo-

site-sex couples who do not want to marry, and there are same-sex couples. The new law addresses these differences so that they do not turn
into an excuse to deny individual rights. All those (opposite and same-
sex couples) who fulfill the conditions are now considered "family arrangements" with practically the same rights as those the Civil Code
guarantees for the traditional married family. This equation in terms of
rights between subordinate and hegemonic forms, apart from being a
path to social integration seeking to generate equity in the difference,
pluralized (with clear limits) the ways the state recognizes families.

But this progress coexists with a legal system where opposite-sex couples can get married at any time, while civil partnership is the only alternative that same-sex couples have to formalize their bond. Equality is not
achieved without modifying the legal structure, which bars same-sex
couples from marrying and adopting children. This hierarchy, which determines different rights according to sexual orientation, is reinforced
even more at a nominal and symbolic level by calling this new institution
a partnership. Although for heterosexuals it works as recognition of an
alternative vital decision, in the case of same-sex couples it is not an
option and thus, reinforces their place of social exclusion and subordination. In addition, the partnership needs a legal recognition, which aggra-
vates the problem since couples have to expose their intimate and affective lives to third parties and prove their five years of uninterrupted
cohabitation in a monogamous relationship. The legal process is quite
costly, since each of the couple's members must hire an attorney and
obtaining a judicial decision takes months.

The whole process is close to what Baumann and Gingrich[37] define as
"grammar of encompassment": The inclusion is thought of as something
abstract, as if the others were part of what is conceptualized as "us," but
the differences of what socially works as an "other" in the presence of
married heterosexual couples are undermined (only monogamous couples with five years of living together are recognized). Also, many "others" are excluded: nonmonogamous hetero/homosexual couples, other
types of arrangements, and homosexual couples wishing to adopt.

In short, the law was a step toward recognition and equality, but at
the same time, old hierarchies were left in place, preserving the right of
adoption for heterosexual married couples. This limitation of rights was
irritating for LGBTQ groups and was remedied two years later with the
reform of the adoption system, which recognized in all civil partnerships
the right to adopt as couples.[38] The decision to fragment the recognition
of these rights into two stages is explained by the strategy thought up by
senator Percovich to obtain the necessary consensus from her own political party and make their approval feasible. Her strategy first sought to
recognize civil partnerships and then to incorporate them into the new
adoption system with full rights, making it more difficult politically for

opponents to emerge within the FA, since this type of bond had been already legally recognized.

But the difficulties in the negotiations in spite of the FA majority in both chambers revealed the limited commitment the left-wing coalition had with this agenda, as well as the persistence of a political perspective that continues to think of inequality in a unidimensional way (social class) while the intersections with ethnic groups and sexual orientation are scarcely problematized and recognized. This difficulty persists, as is evident in the current postponement by Parliament to address an "Equal Marriage" bill as a priority. The bill seeks to reform the Civil Code in order to allow same-sex couples to marry, and was presented to the Constitution, Code and Legislation Commission of the Chamber of Deputies in 2011 by the *Colectivo Ovejas Negras*, together with deputy Sebastian Sabini (*Movimiento de Participación Popular*, FA).

These difficulties within the FA, together with significant levels of social violence against the LGBTQ community, must be taken into account when evaluating the law. Without denying that its approval was a form of integration from subordination, it is also impossible to rule out, as some groups do,[39] the significant progress meant by its approval. As Fraser[40] points out, there is no recognition without redistribution since, when one type of bond becomes legal, a redistribution of rights has taken place, implying the access to a system of social benefits and the right of naming oneself without shame. Finally, the approval of Civil Partnership implied also a first criticism and deconstruction of the social views that conceptualize the family as prediscursive and alien to power relations in Uruguayan society, which expanded the political field and made feasible the rest of legal conquests achieved during the period.

NOTES

1. The *Frente Amplio* (Broad Front) is a coalition of left-wing and center-left parties founded in 1971 whose electoral growth has been constant since the return of democracy in 1985. This political force, with Dr. Tabaré Vázquez as its candidate, won the elections for the first time in the history of Uruguay in 2004, with 50.7 percent of the vote.

2. Carlos Filgueira, *Sobre revoluciones ocultas: la familia en Uruguay* (Montevideo: CEPAL, 1998).

3. Law 14.766 was passed on April 18, 1978, and modified several aspects: Adultery was now considered equal for both sexes, the property penalty that used to affect the woman (she would lose the right to marital property) was eliminated, and voluntary separation without interruptions for more than three years was now a cause for divorce.

4. Jaime Yaffé, *Al Centro y adentro. La renovación de la izquierda y el triunfo del Frente Amplio en Uruguay* (Montevideo: Linardi y Risso, 2005).

5. Doug McAdam, "Orígenes terminológicos, problemas actuales, futuras líneas de investigación" in Doug McAdam, et al., eds. *Movimientos sociales: perspectivas comparadas* (Spain: Istmo, 1999).

6. *Grupo Diversidad, Encuentro Ecuménico para la Liberación de las Minorías Sexuales, ATRU, Hermanas de la Perpetua Indulgencia, La Brújula Queer, Amnistía Internacional Uruguay/Grupo GLTB, Biblioteca y Banco de Datos GLTTB, CIEISU, Voces del Arcoiris, Asociación de Lesbianas del Uruguay.*

7. New organizations emerged in this period: *Llamale H, Área Académica Queer Montevideo, 19 y Liliana, AMISEU, La red, Centro de Estudios de Género y Diversidad Sexual, Entre Nosotras, Osos Uruguay, Kilómetro 0 and Club Leather Sección Uruguay.*

8. The Collective was formed in 2004 and is made up of a permanent core of thirty people, while about twenty-five more collaborate in specific activities and tasks. Gays, lesbians, trans women, trans men, bisexuals, heterosexuals, and queer persons take part in the group, who work under the assembly format, where everybody can speak and vote. There are several working commissions: Institutional and International Relations, Community (workshops in social and educational facilities), Health, Communications, Interior, Legal, Education, Parliament, and Finances. None of the activists is paid for his or her work. All of the activities are funded through monthly contributions made by some 250 subscribers and occasional funds obtained nationally or abroad. The organization lacks offices of its own and meets weekly in labor union facilities in Montevideo.

9. Diego Sempol, "Sexo-género y sexualidades políticas. Los nuevos desafíos democratizadores" in *La aventura uruguaya. ¿Naides más que naides?* Volume 2, Rodrigo Arocena and Gerardo Caetano, eds. (Montevideo: Sudamericana, 2011).

10. The Colorado and National parties are known as the "traditional parties," founded in the nineteenth century.

11. *Brecha*, August 28, 2003, 14.

12. Meetings Journal of the Chamber of Representatives (DSCR) N 3468 60ª *Sesión (Extraordinaria) XLVI Legislatura*, November 28, 2007, 149.

13. *Brecha*, April 8, 2005, 29.

14. Organizations such as *La Brújula Queer* opposed all state regulation of same-sex couples, believing it was a form of political and social assimilation.

15. Brecha, April 8, 2005, 29.

16. The signatory legislators included all of the FA's major sectors and those with parliamentary representation: Susana Dalmás, Mónica Xavier, Lucía Topolansky, Margarita Percovich, Víctor Vaillant, Eduardo Lorier, Alberto Cid, Enrique Rubio, Jorge Saravia, Leonardo Nicolini, Alberto Breccia, José Korzeniak, Alberto Couriel, Eduardo Ríos, Enrique Pintado, Rafael Michelini.

17. J. Barránand B. Nahum, *Batlle, los estancieros y el imperio británico, Un diálogo difícil (1903–1910)*, volume 2 (Montevideo, 1981).

18. Juan Marcos Vaggione, "Sexuality, Religion and Politics in Latin America." Paper presented at the Regional Dialogues. Rio de Janeiro, August, 2009.

19. Meetings Journal of Chamber of Senators. *2do Período Ordinario de la XLVI Legislatura. 38ª sesión ordinaria.* N 113, Volume 435, September 12, 2006, 319.

20. Ibid., 321.

21. Ibid., 324.

22. *El Observador*, May 12, 2007, 22.

23. *Búsqueda*, May 3, 2007, 32.

24. *El Observador*, May 5, 2007, 3.

25. Document "Considerations regarding proposals to give legal recognition to unions between homosexual persons," approved by the Congregation for the Doctrine of the Faith, June 3, 2003.

26. *El Observador*, May 5, 2007, 3.

27. Meetings Journal of the Chamber of Senators. 2nd Ordinary Period of the XLVI Legislature, 324.

28. Meetings Journal of the Chamber of Deputies, Meeting N 3468 60 (Extraordinary) XLVI Legislature November 28, 2007, 105.

29. El Observador May 5, 2007, 3.

30. Ibid.

31. *Búsqueda*, May 3, 2007, 32.

32. Meetings Journal of Chamber of Deputies, Meeting N 3468 60, 106.

33. Henry Finch, *Historia económica del Uruguay contemporáneo* (Montevideo: EBO, 1980).

34. Meetings Journal of Chamber of Deputies, Meeting N 3468 60, 133.

35. Ibid., 135.

36. Michael Walzer, *Tratado de la tolerancia* (Barcelona: Paidós, 1998).

37. Gerd Baumann and Andre Gingrich, eds., *Grammars of Identity/Alterity. A Structural Approach* (New York: Berghahn Books, 2004), 10.

38. The reform of the Code of the Child and the Adolescent, approved on September 9, 2009, recognized the legal parity of all children, beyond their "family arrangements," thus enabling homosexual couples who had a legally declared civil partnership to legally adopt children.

39. For example, a leaflet from the group Anarquía, handed out during a concentration against homophobia in 2010 stated, "Do we want to ask the state for a law? The same state that oppresses, discriminates, marginalizes, pursues and points at us? A law will not change the homophobic and sexist way of thought that the system imposes on us from childhood. The laws are a set of interests only for the bourgeoisie, for a few." *Grupo Anarquía*, May 2010.

40. Nancy Fraser, *Iustitia Interrupta. Reflexiones críticas desde la posición "postsocialista"* (Colombia: Siglo del Hombre Editores, 1997).

SEVEN

Same-Sex Couples in Colombia: Three Models for their Legal and Political Recognition

Daniel Bonilla[1]

Since the enactment of the 1991 Constitution, the Colombian Constitutional Court has ruled on the legal status and rights of same-sex couples on seven occasions.[2] In this set of rulings, the court takes the issue of sexual minority rights seriously and provides a complex set of arguments to evaluate what legal and political status should be granted to members of the LGBT community in a liberal democracy like Colombia. With the same-sex couples jurisprudence, the Constitutional Court has taken major steps to eliminate discrimination against the LGBT community in Colombia. These rulings recognized the legal existence of same-sex couples for the first time in the history of the country and gave them an important set of legal and constitutional rights and obligations. These rights and obligations cover topics as varied as human dignity, equality, health, pensions, and the nationality of members of the same-sex couples.

This set of rulings, however, represents a major shift in the case law of the Court regarding the rights of the LGBT community. Prior to the issuance of the C-075/2007 ruling, the Court had recognized the rights of homosexuals as individuals, but had systematically refused to recognize the legal existence of same-sex couples, and therefore refused to recognize that they were collectively entitled to rights. Also, these seven rulings reveal a significant, though not definitive, shift in Colombian society's interpretation of the LGBT community. The fact that these rulings were unanimous or supported by significant majorities in a court comprised of several judges committed to conservative political positions

111

reflects the changes that have been happening in Colombia regarding the social value of sexual minorities. This shift is confirmed by the fact that the rulings were supported—or at least not questioned—by large segments of the population. Taken together, these rulings can help us to understand, evaluate, and potentially solve the problems created by the lack of legal recognition of same-sex couples.

The reasoning behind this set of rulings corresponds with three different models used to understand, evaluate, and give legal recognition to same-sex couples: the model of dignity, the model of equality, and the model of autonomy. In addition to the traditional arguments of autonomy and equality, this group of rulings calls upon the argument of dignity, less commonly used to address these problems. If the first two models are complementary, this chapter claims that, along with the model of autonomy, they are mutually exclusive. Likewise, this chapter reviews how the Colombian Constitutional Court's same-sex couples jurisprudence recognizing the legal existence of same-sex couples is based on models that are theoretically and practically in tension with each other.

Finally, this chapter will analyze how the model of dignity offers significant advantages compared with alternative models because (i) it identifies the problem at stake in the clearest, simplest, most precise and comprehensive way possible; (ii) it explains the obstacles to solving the political and legal problems involved in the lack of legal recognition for same-sex couples in a precise manner; (iii) it provides solid criteria for determining the usefulness of the mechanisms that seek to invalidate these obstacles; and (iv) it characterizes clearly the competing models and the perspective of political morality that underpin our political and legal system, namely liberalism.

This chapter is divided into three parts. The first part presents the basic structure of the Colombian Constitutional Court's decisions to legally recognize same-sex couples and grant them a significant number of rights. The second part, both analytical and critical, argues that this set of rulings constitutes an important step towards the elimination of the discrimination that exists against the LGBT community in Colombia. The third part presents the central features of the models of autonomy and equality, as well as their primary weaknesses. In this section, I also present the elements of the model of dignity and the arguments affirming that this normative perspective provides a clearer and more complete explanation and basis for the position promoting the legal recognition of same-sex couples.

THE LEGAL RECOGNITION OF SAME-SEX COUPLES IN COLOMBIA

The line of case law articulated by the Colombian Constitutional Court on same-sex couples can be divided into three stages: recognition, consolidation, and expansion. In the first stage, represented by the C-075 ruling of 2007, the Constitutional Court acknowledged the legal existence of same-sex couples for the first time in Colombian history. The Court decided that Law 54 of 1990, which regulates all matters relating to the de facto marital union, applies to both heterosexual and same-sex couples. It signaled that Article 1 of Law 54, which defined the marital union as that institution consisting of a man and a woman cohabiting for at least two years, was constitutional only if it was also applicable to homosexual couples. This conditional interpretation of Article 1 implied that the rest of the mandates of Law 54, which regulate the patrimonial aspects in the marital union, were applicable to all couples in the country, both heterosexual and homosexual.

The Court stated unequivocally that its decision was limited to Law 54 of 1990. This argument is particularly important because Article 1 of this law was the only place in the Colombian legal system where the marital union was defined in a clear and precise way. As such, it is an unavoidable reference point for interpreting the large number of provisions that specify the rights and responsibilities of individuals in de facto marital unions—norms governing matters as diverse as citizenship, auto insurance, and child support. If the Court had so desired, it could have created a global transformation of the Colombian legal system with this single sentence, so that all norms governing the marital union and its consequences would have applied equally to heterosexual and same-sex couples.[3] While the ruling did not have this effect, it opened the path for new lawsuits challenging the constitutionality of the legal norms that refer to the de facto marital union but which are applied to heterosexual couples alone.

The second stage of this line of case law, constituted by the C-811/2007, C-336/2008, C-798/2008, T-856/2007, and T-1241/2008 rulings, confirmed that same-sex couples may constitute de facto marital unions, and also extended the rights and responsibilities of same-sex couples.[4] C-811/2007 acknowledged that the norms governing heterosexual couples in the health care system also apply to same-sex couples.[5] C-336/2008 signaled that members of same-sex couples are entitled to receive survivors' pensions, as are those in heterosexual couples.[6] C-798/2008 indicated that members of same-sex couples and heterosexual ones are entitled to receive alimony from their partner once they have terminated their life in common.[7] The last two *tutela* rulings confirm the right of citizens that are part of same-sex couples to be affiliated in the contributory social security system and to receive a survivor's pension, respectively.[8] Together, these rulings solidified the rule established in previously decided cases of abstract control via two cases of concrete control of constitutionality.[9]

The third stage of this line of case law, which dramatically expands the number of rights and responsibilities available to members of same-sex couples, has a single but very important component, the ruling in the

C-029/2009 case.[10] This ruling arises from a lawsuit that challenged the constitutionality of 26 legal norms that differentiate unfairly between same-sex and heterosexual couples.[11] The norms that the Constitutional Court declared conditionally constitutional in this ruling can be grouped into the following five categories: criminal, civil and commercial, social security, political, and those relating to the armed conflict. The Court signaled that this set of legal norms aimed at heterosexual couples is constitutional only if it also applies to same-sex couples.[12]

The line of case law articulated by the Constitutional Court in these seven rulings is consistent insofar as all these rulings are based on the premise that members of same-sex couples are subjects of law and therefore entitled to an important set of individual rights and obligations. Similarly, the seven rulings are based on the same three legal pillars set forth in the C-075/2007 ruling: dignity, free development of personality (or autonomy), and equality. As the Court declared, "[i]n this scenario, for the Court, the absence of protection in the patrimonial area for the homosexual couple is harmful to the dignity of the human person, is contrary to the right to free development of personality and functions as a form of discrimination prohibited by the Constitution."[13]

The Constitutional Court defines these three legal categories by appealing to standard interpretations of the theoretical body of liberalism. Each of these, in turn, becomes the axis of one of the three models that justify the legal recognition of same-sex couples that I will discuss in the third section of this chapter (free development of personality/autonomy model; equality/model of equality; and dignity/model of dignity).

The Court has stated that dignity is both an attribute that all humans have and a principle underlying the Social State of Law (*Estado Social de Derecho*).[14] The Court argues that dignity is a quality that all persons have by the mere fact of belonging to the human species, a consequence of the ability of all individuals to choose their life plans by making use of reason. That is, dignity is an attribute that arises as a consequence of the autonomy and rationality elements of human nature. It is the characteristic that guarantees the basic equality of all human beings. The Court argues that we are all equal because we have dignity.

The Court claims that this attribute is in itself a constitutional principle, forming the premise from which our fundamental rights are deduced. These rights are the instruments that permit the defense of human dignity from the undue interventions of the state and individuals. Fundamental rights are the tools that allow human nature to flourish. Consequently, for the Court, the principle of dignity has a negative and a positive dimension.[15] On one hand, the state has the duty to refrain from any action that violates the autonomy of human beings;[16] on the other hand, it has the duty to ensure the minimum material conditions that allow for autonomy to be exercised.[17] For the Court, autonomy cannot be implemented if individuals cannot meet their basic living needs, such as those related to health or the number of calories needed to survive.

The Court has suggested that the free development of personality is a right that protects the autonomy of individuals broadly. Fundamentally, the Court understands this as the right to "be left alone," that is, the right to have the state and other individuals refrain from interfering in the space in which individuals articulate, transform and try to realize their life plans. Thus, the free development of personality summarizes, promotes, and protects the principle of human dignity.[18] The Constitutional Court, however, following liberalism's standard interpretation of individual autonomy, sees the free development of personality as a relative right. The legal order and the rights of others constitute legitimate limits to the autonomy of individuals.

Lastly, appealing again to the standard interpretation of the liberal canon, the Court understands equality as the right to have analogous cases treated in an analogous way and to have different cases treated in a different way. For the Court, then, this right implies that subjects cannot be discriminated against by the state and that any differential treatment on the part of the administration must be adequately justified—particularly when those treated differently are groups of individuals that have been historically discriminated against in the political community. This line of argument is followed closely by the other six rulings that constitute the line of case law on same-sex couples (C-811/2007,[19] T- 856/2007,[20] C-336/2008,[21] T-1241/2008,[22] C-798/2008,[23] and C-029/2009[24]).

However, in the seven main cases involving same-sex couples, the Court established a close connection between, on the one hand, the norms challenged and the actions of the administration questioned, and, on the other hand, the violation of the rights to equality and the free development of personality as well as the principle of human dignity. The Court indicates that same-sex couples and heterosexual couples are equal in all matters defined and regulated by the form of the de facto marital union. For the Court, there are no legally relevant differences for distinguishing same-sex couples and heterosexual ones on these matters. Both are forms of association that allow individuals to share their sexual and emotional lives and their patrimony. Therefore, any interpretation of these norms that excludes their application to same-sex couples is unconstitutional as an unjustifiable difference between two forms of association to which citizens are entitled in order to realize their life plans.

In turn, the norms examined by the Constitutional Court unduly restrict the autonomy of individuals.[25] The lack of legal recognition for same-sex couples discourages and makes the pursuit of a common life plan less viable for individuals with nontraditional sexual orientations. Finally, this set of norms violates human dignity, that is, the ability of humans to choose and try to materialize their life plans through reason. The Constitutional Court established that the lack of legal recognition for same-sex couples denies them full membership in the human race. This set of norms and state actions does not allow individuals to "live as they wish," to "live without humiliation," and to have access to the basic material conditions for survival.[26]

THE IMPORTANCE OF THE RULINGS

The set of seven rulings in which the Colombian Constitutional Court recognized the legal existence of same-sex couples and granted them a wide set of rights is relevant for four reasons: because the Court remedied what was in effect a two-tiered citizenry; because the Court radically changed the direction of its case law; because these rulings reflected a change in the values of Colombian society at large; and because the rulings contribute to the growing recognition of sexual difference.

First, with these decisions the Court attacks a problem that seriously undermines the Colombian legal-political order: the unjustified existence of two types of citizenship. At one end of the spectrum are heterosexual citizens, who are defined by the legal system as first-class citizens; on the other are citizens with alternative sexual orientations, who are treated by this same system as second-class citizens.

The Constitutional Court's rulings should be interpreted as a radical challenge to the use of sexual orientation as a criterion for determining who can be granted full citizenship. According to the Court, in a liberal democracy such as Colombia, the state must treat all citizens with equal consideration and respect. The state cannot make use of available resources, the law and law enforcement, for example, in order to promote the life plans of some of its citizens over others.

Life as a couple is one of the ways in which human beings try to realize their life plans. It is a medium through which they seek to realize their moral commitments. Allowing the legal system to ignore the existence of same-sex couples not only sends a message to society characterizing nontraditional sexual orientations negatively, a matter that should not to be addressed by the state, but also imposes very high costs on those who embody, for example, the social marginalization and economic expenses related to the management and liquidation of common patrimony. However, the highest price that members of same-sex couples must pay is related to the fact that the legal system denies them their full humanity. In the legal system, these individuals are not full members of the human race; their autonomy and rationality are fundamentally restricted so long as the result of their exercise is characterized negatively by the state.

Second, these rulings radically shifted in the case law of the Constitutional Court. Until the C-075 ruling of 2007, the Court had not recognized members of same-sex couples as subjects of law, although it had protected the rights of those with nontraditional sexual orientations in their capacity as individuals. Between 1991 and 2007, the Court indicated that institutions for military training cannot expel members solely based on the fact that they are homosexual,[27] that public and private schools cannot expel homosexual students because they believe their sexual orientation to be immoral,[28] and that homosexuality does not represent a lack of honor for the military or the duties of public school teachers.[29] Nevertheless, during this same period, the Court indicated that the state is constitutionally empowered to prohibit same-sex couples from adopting children,[30] that it is constitutional in Colombia to prevent a homosexual individual from joining the social security system with his or her partner,[31] and that the Constitution accepts that the law governing de facto marital unions be applicable only to heterosexual couples.

With the issuance of the C-075 ruling of 2007, the Court recognized that the legislature's discretion to regulate social practices is not unlimited in matters related to sexual orientation. The Court now accepts that the central argument that had been used to declare the constitutionality of the norms governing heterosexual couples, but which omitted all references to same-sex couples, has no foundation when structural constitutional principles (such as dignity) and the fundamental rights of citizens (such as equality and the free development of personality) are at stake. The legislature cannot refrain from regulating issues related to same-sex couples when it creates norms for regulating heterosexual couples, given that, in principle, there is no difference between both forms of association, at least in economic matters. Thus, the freedom of the legislature has negative and positive aspects. The legislature should not, in principle, regulate issues related to the sexual orientation of citizens. However, having the authority, the legislature must do so in a manner consistent with the protection of the rights and basic principles of the Social State of Law, and cannot neglect to include cases analogous to those it seeks to regulate.

However, it is important to remember that the changes articulated by the Constitutional Court are formal; that is, they are mere transformations in the legal order. The progress in recognizing the equal dignity of human beings is a legal development that simply moves the Colombian political community closer to the ideals of modern liberalism. With regard to sexual orientation, we are just now approaching the eighteenth century. Societal discrimination and violence against the LGBT community remain evident in Colombia.[32]

Nevertheless, this legal recognition has symbolic and material value. On one hand, the political community recognized the close connections between the equal dignity of all citizens and their sexual orientation for the first time. The political-legal discourse changed with this set of rulings and the rules of play in the polity were transformed accordingly. In this way, legal-political imagination was both expanded and diminished.

The set of those holding full citizenship now includes members of the LGBT community and it is no longer possible to exclude those who do not identify as heterosexual from the polity. In addition, we must not lose sight of the power of the law to change the social imaginary. The law is now on the side of sexual diversity, associated with a positive emotional role and with the coercive apparatus it has at its service. In the long term, when used properly, this fact can contribute to changing the social practices that discriminate against sexual minorities.

On the other hand, this legal transformation gave citizens a powerful tool for opposing actions of the state and private sector that violate Colombians' rights to live in accordance with their sexual orientation. Members of same-sex couples can now make use of the tools of the legal system in order to defend their rights: in particular, the *tutela* action, civil actions to offset the damage caused to victims, and criminal proceedings (which can sanction those who refuse to comply with constitutional mandates).

Third, this set of rulings provides evidence that Colombian society has changed its perceptions of sexual minorities over the last decade. The Constitutional Court is an institution composed of nine judges, many of whom defend conservative positions on social issues—perspectives that are generally influenced by the doctrine of the Catholic Church. It is revealing, then, that this set of rulings has been adopted by consensus or by large majorities in the Constitutional Court. The landmark opinion, the one that opened this line of case law, was supported by eight judges. The only dissenting vote, delivered by Judge Araujo, arose because he thought that the ruling had not gone far enough in protecting the rights of members of same sex couples. In practice, then, there was a consensus within the Court surrounding the idea that the Constitution of 1991 requires the recognition of same-sex couples.

Similarly, the fact that a good part of the political community supported—or at least did not oppose—the rulings issued by the Constitutional Court provides evidence that the country has taken a few steps towards the recognition of sexual diversity. This was made explicit in the extensive and positive coverage that the cases received in the media, and the fact that much of the Catholic hierarchy accepted these legal changes having to do with civil issues, particularly patrimonial issues related to married life.[33] A good portion of the Catholic hierarchy argued that these issues are the responsibility of the state, not the church.[34] The narrative describing sexual minorities, then, has been changing in Colombia. From a discourse focused on sin or sickness, we are making important strides towards one focused on the recognition of sexual difference.[35]

Finally, the case law of the Constitutional Court contributes to reflection on the recognition of sexual difference in a new way when making use of the principle of human dignity. When the Court invokes this principle to justify its decisions, it offers a number of conceptual tools that allow us to understand and evaluate the problems that the lack of legal recognition for same-sex couples creates for a liberal democracy in a rich, complex, and fresh way. However, while the Court also relies on the rights to equality and the free development of personality as a basis for their rulings, this argument raises some important theoretical tensions.

THE MODELS OF AUTONOMY, EQUALITY, AND DIGNITY[36]

The legal recognition of same-sex couples can be understood and justified by appealing to three different models: autonomy, equality, and dignity. However, although equality and dignity provide complementary conceptual and practical tools, the model of autonomy is incompatible with the other two normative structures. The model of dignity and that of equality interpret the problem that is an object of study in different ways and generate substantial and procedural consequences for the political community that are irreconcilable with the model of autonomy. It is important to specify that each of these models includes as its centerpiece one of the rights to which the Constitutional Court appeals in order to justify its line of case law. Similarly, it should be noted that the three models coexist, in tension, within each of the rulings issued by the Court on the legal recognition and rights of same-sex couples. Finally, the models do not appear in full in the Colombian Constitutional Court rulings; only their structural elements do. This section of the article therefore seeks to define and develop the content of these elements, to explain their foundations and to analyze their theoretical and practical consequences.

> The model of autonomy argues that issues related to sexual and emotional life concern only the individuals involved. The state does not have jurisdiction to get involved in matters having to do with the life plans of its citizens. As the model of autonomy argues, individuals have the right to "be left alone"; they have the right that the State not invade the private space in which they articulate, modify and attempt to realize their moral commitments.[37] In the terminology of the Colombian Constitutional Court: "The right to free development of personality embodies a general protection of the capacity of the Constitution to recognize individuals for self-determination, that is, to follow their own norms and develop their own life plans, provided they do not affect the rights of others or the legal order." For the Court this right is violated "when the person is prevented, in an unreasonable way, from meeting or pursuing legitimate aspirations in their lives and freely choosing or valuing the options and circumstances that give meaning to their lives and enable their realization as human beings."[38]

This model is interwoven with the traditional liberal argument advocating for the separation between the private and the public spheres. The private sphere, liberals argue, is the realm of morality, the space where the individual builds his or her life plan. The public sphere is the realm of justice, the space where we build the basic structure of the political community; the area where political power and the scarce resources controlled by society are distributed. The border that divides these two spheres has the objective of firmly defining the limits that configure the space for the legitimate action of the state, namely, defining the contours of the space for the political. The state therefore cannot cross the border that divides these two spheres without violating two of the basic principles of liberalism: that the state should treat all members with equal consideration and respect, and that each individual has the right to build and realize his or her own moral plan without the involvement of the state.

However, this model has major weaknesses. First, it is a radically individualistic perspective that understands human beings as monads without relevant connections to the community. The model of autonomy assumes a strong subject that builds (and should build) its identity in a solitary fashion. The satisfaction of this need, in the model of autonomy, is guaranteed legally and politically through the right to be free, that is, the right of individuals to be left alone. Thus, the model of autonomy looks upon human relations with suspicion, as they constitute obstacles to the free construction of the subject.

The model loses sight that autonomy is not exercised in the abstract but in contexts that limit and simultaneously constitute the individual. The webs of significance in which subjects are inevitably immersed prescribe the options available for the individual life, as well as their moral value. Autonomy is therefore exercised within the boundaries previously established by this network of interpretations of reality. The subject does not have an infinite amount of possibilities for being in the world to build his individual identity, only the alternatives that exist within the community to which he belongs.

Moreover, the model of autonomy obscures the community dimension of gender and, therefore, the political dimension of the lack of legal recognition for same-sex couples. Choosing among the roles available to each gender, violating them and being questioned, or fulfilling them and being recognized, for example, only makes sense within a social context. Individuals-monads, if they existed, would not have problems breaking out of the socially assigned gender roles to which they supposedly belong, as the construction of their individual identity does not depend in any way on the view that "the other" has of us. These subjects forget that the life of a couple is both a private and public issue: It concerns individuals in a direct and special manner, but they understand it largely through the interpretive lens that the community provides. The legal recognition of same-sex couples, then, aims to have the political community declare formally that being part of a same-sex couple is as valuable, generally speaking, as being part of a heterosexual couple. A lack of legal recognition submits members of same-sex couples to an official structure of subordination that condemns them to a position of moral inferiority in comparison with heterosexual individuals.

Second, the model of autonomy loses sight of the ways in which the lack of recognition for same-sex couples is in violation of the right to equality and the principle of human dignity. With respect to equality, the model of autonomy is unable to capture that part of the problem is rooted in the fact that same-sex couples are treated differently than heterosexual couples. The issue is not only that individuals should have the opportunity to share their lives with whomever they choose, a matter that the model of autonomy captures and protects, but the legal and political consequences of the unwarranted distinction between same-sex couples and heterosexual ones. The model of autonomy, then, obscures the problem of equality running through the case law of the Colombian Constitutional Court on same-sex couples. The Court has stated,

> The same considerations which establish that in relation to the system of inheritance of homosexual couples there is a lack of protection with respect to the constitutional order, which leads to the conclusion that the system of Law 54 of 1990 . . . is discriminatory to the extent that it applies only to heterosexual couples and excludes homosexual couples. Thus, notwithstanding the objective differences between the two types of couples, and the specific considerations which led the legislature of 1990 to establish this system of protection based on the need to protect women and family, it is no less certain that homosexual couples can be shown today as having similar requirements for protection and that there are no objective reasons for differential treatment. [39]

The marginalization of the right of equality in the way that the lack of legal recognition of same-sex couples is understood and evaluated creates two closely intertwined problems: one of weak equality and the other of strong equality. The problem of weak equality has to do with the fact that two analogous cases are treated differently, as there do not seem to be fundamental differences that justify differential treatment by the legal system. Both same-sex couples and heterosexual ones are forms of association intended to allow two people to share their emotional, sexual, and financial lives.

Strong equality is a problem in that it justifies the practice of legally recognizing heterosexual couples but not same-sex couples. The justification is made by making a deeper distinction between the members of either type of association. The former are recognized as full members of the human race while the latter are excluded. The model of autonomy is incapable of explaining that the core of the problem that the legal silence surrounding same-sex couples produces is related to the lack of recognition of members of such couples as full members of the human race. It ignores the fact that couple relationships serve as key elements of human development. This fact becomes more evident when the legal system's reasoning for excluding same-sex couples is of a religious nature and indicates that sexual and emotional relationships between individuals of the same sex are against nature.

The model of autonomy focuses all its attention on the decision taken by individuals to form part of a same-sex couple and not the content of the decision and the symbolic and material consequences it generates. The model only defends that the decision to form a couple must be respected by the state because it was a decision made by two capable adults. The subject matter of the decision is irrelevant. It does not therefore demand that the state act to recognize the existence of same-sex couples, rather, it argues that the state should refrain from acting with respect to any subject having to do with the sexual and emotional life of individuals. Consequently, it loses sight of the fact that the state has already unfairly made moves to recognize exclusively the legal existence of heterosexual couples.

With respect to the principle of human dignity, the model of autonomy is incapable of showing that behind the problem of weak equality that arises as a result of the lack of legal recognition of same-sex couples lies the problem of a lack of knowledge of the human characteristics that liberalism qualifies as a constituent of all members of the species: their autonomy and rationality. As will be discussed in detail in the next section, the model of equality (as well as that of autonomy) does not describe the problem accurately and completely: the issue is not that we have dignity because we are equal but that we are equal *because* we have dignity. The lack of legal recognition for same-sex couples violates equality in the strong sense because it violates human dignity, not vice versa.

The model of equality offers an interpretation different from that of the autonomy model on the theoretical and practical problems generated by the lack of legal recognition for same-sex couples. From this perspective, as evidenced above, the central problem is the violation of the right to equality in the weak sense and in the strong sense. Equality in the weak sense is violated when sexual orientation is used unjustifiably as a criterion for distributing basic rights and obligations among citizens. Equality in the strong sense is transgressed when distinguishing unreasonably between two groups of subjects, the members of same-sex couples and those in heterosexual couples, in order to deny the former their character as human beings. The case law of the Colombian Constitutional Court on same-sex couples focuses on the problem of weak equality. When referring to the right of equality, the argument of the Court has focused on exposing the unjustified nature of the legal order's distinction between same-sex couples and heterosexual couples. The problem of strong equality does not appear explicitly in the case law of the Court. Rather, it appears implicitly and as a problem directly related to the principle of human dignity.[40]

The model of equality has the virtue of explaining the political dimension of sexual orientation, the dialogic nature of the construction of individual identity, and the role that law plays in this process. The web of significance offered by the community in which the individual is immersed conditions and gives meaning to the decisions individuals make regarding their sexual and emotional life. This model also highlights the connections between the principle of equal citizenship and the principle that affirms the basic equality of all human beings, and it requires the state to do whatever is necessary to protect the right to equality to which members of same-sex couples are entitled.

However, the model of equality, similar to the model of privacy, is incapable of giving a full account of the central problem that the lack of legal recognition for same-sex couples generates. This model loses sight of the fact that equality in the weak sense depends on equality in the strong sense and that this, in turn, is a right that depends on the principle of human dignity. If, as the model of equality argues, what is really at stake is not whether the criteria for distinguishing members of same-sex couples are plausible, but whether or not they belong to humankind. Again, human beings do not have dignity because we are equal, but we are equal because we have dignity. The fact that it is thought that autonomy and rationality are central characteristics of human beings and that liberalism holds that all human beings are born with these capabilities is what enables all human beings to be characterized as fundamentally equal.

Similarly, the model of equality obscures the fact that the lack of legal recognition for same-sex couples also violates the autonomy of its members. The question is not, as articulated by the model of autonomy, whether the state must refrain from acting on matters related to the sexual and emotional life of individuals. Rather, it is whether same-sex couples must be legally recognized so that individuals can effectively exercise their autonomy. The state's omission in this matter sends a double message: alternative sexual orientations are morally questionable, and those who choose to live by them will have to make significant sacrifices (economic, social, political) that heterosexual individuals do not have to make.

The third model, in contrast, revolves around the principle of human dignity. This principle indicates, as has been stated previously, that all human beings have dignity in that we have the capacity to define, modify, and realize our life plan by making use of reason. This is to say that, as the case law of the Colombian Constitutional Court has continuously indicated regarding same-sex couples, members of the human species are equal in that we are fundamentally autonomous and rational beings. The model of dignity argues that these common capabilities are violated when the legal order does not recognize same-sex couples. The life plan of the majority of individuals includes a dimension of life as a couple that is radically denied to individuals with alternative sexual orientations when same-sex couples are not recognized. The state, with this omission, is preventing individuals from making an autonomous decision regarding the kind of life they want to live, provided that does not adversely affect the rights of third parties. It is limiting the power to freely choose one's own life plan in a radical and unjustifiable fashion. Through its inaction, the state indicates that it prefers one sexual orientation (the heterosexual), over another (the homosexual) and that individuals should therefore choose the former and not the latter.

The issue is not just that people should be able live with the partner of their choice without being punished by the state, but that the state should recognize the lives of same-sex couples as a valid alternative for the political community. This recognition has a powerful symbolic value (that of the recognition of members of the same-sex couples as human beings equal to heterosexuals); and a material value (related to reducing the costs of managing the patrimony in the life of a couple and the decrease in discrimination and violence against the LGBT community).

The model of dignity offers several advantages over the competing models. First, it is a comprehensive normative structure. As such, it includes a dimension of equality as well as one of autonomy. The model is not a product of a weak eclecticism that seeks to combine the model of equality with a reinterpretation of the model of autonomy. Structurally, equality and autonomy are rigged on the concept of human dignity. In fact, the rights of (weak) equality and the free development of personality are instruments derived from and used for the defense of dignity. In the model of dignity, equality is understood as basic (strong) equality of human beings. This equality is a function of the autonomy and rationality that all individuals enjoy. In fact, weak equality, which is part of the model of equality, and which depends on strong equality, is a creation and development of the latter. It is a right that grants the tools to evaluate when it is legitimate for members of the political community to be treated differently and what reasoning would challenge or support such distinctions.

In the model of dignity, autonomy is understood as a basic faculty that all human beings have and that can only be exercised effectively if two conditions are met: the satisfaction of basic material needs, such as eating a certain number of calories daily; and the existence of a broad legal-political framework that respects the various life plans that are possible within the community so that citizens have real power to choose those they consider the most valuable. In the terminology of the Colombian Constitutional Court, dignity includes three dimensions that are intertwined: the right to live as you wish, the right to live free of humiliation, and the right to a minimum standard of living.

Second, the vagueness of the principle of dignity and the potential for basing it on different perspectives makes it an ideal discursive space for reaching broad agreements within a diverse political community. The principle's high degree of generality might be interpreted against it. The meaning of human dignity, one could argue, depends on the interpreter and is therefore at the mercy of power relations within the political community. Nevertheless, this seems to be a typical feature of all principles, not just that of human dignity. Moreover, principles do not remain perpetually vague. Their content becomes more precise as they are interpreted, particularly by authoritative legal and political operators. This content becomes obligatory and therefore becomes a guide for the conduct of individuals. Similarly, the recognition that the precise content of the principle has a contingent character allows for variation as a result of transformations in the political community.

Likewise, given that the principle can be filled with content and justified by appealing to different types of arguments—moral and secular, religious and historic—a large number of people can accept that it is a principle worth defending and enter into deliberative processes that aim to clarify its content. The notion that a political community should be structured about the principle of dignity can be supported by those who believe that the principle of human dignity should be safeguarded because it is a consequence of human beings having been created in the image and likeness of divinity or those who believe that autonomy and rationality are essential characteristics of human beings or those who believe that it is a historically constructed principle to defend the goods that we find valuable.

Third, the model of dignity explains the issue at stake in a clear, precise and simple way and interprets and resolves it by tying it to an illuminating interpretation of the political tradition underlying the Colombian political-legal system: liberalism.

The models of dignity, equality and autonomy offer us a series of useful conceptual tools for approaching the problem of the lack of legal recognition for same-sex couples (in particular) and of discrimination on grounds of sexual orientation (in general). Nevertheless, we cannot forget that the ultimate goal is not to interpret the problem more richly, but to eliminate it in practice. The objectives are not only clarity, accuracy and legal and philosophical subtlety, but also political struggle and building a more egalitarian society in which the dignity of all people can be protected effectively.

NOTES

1. I would like to thank Ryan Fox for his excellent research assistance.
2. Corte Constitucional [C.C.] [Constitutional Court], February 7, 2007, M.P.: R. Escobar Gil, Sentencia C-075/07; C.C., October 3, 2007, M.P.: M.G. Monroy Cabra, Sentencia C-811/07; C.C., October 12, 2007, M.P.: H.A. Sierra Porto, Sentencia T-856/07; C.C., April 16, 2008, M.P.: C.I. Vargas Hernández, Sentencia C-336/08; C.C., August 8,

2008, M.P.: J. Córdoba Triviño, Sentencia C-798/08; C.C., December 11, 2008, M.P.: C.I. Vargas Hernández, Sentencia T-1241/08; C.C., January 28, 2009, M.P.: R. Escobar Gil, Sentencia C-029/09. In July of 2011, the Constitutional Court decided case C-577/11. In this case, the Court declared constitutional article 13 of the civil code that defines marriage as a contract between a man and a woman. However, in this case the Court also recognized same-sex couples as one of the types of family protected by the 1991 Constitution and urged Congress to legislate on matters related to same sex couples. The case has not been yet published so it cannot be examined in this article. Corte Constitucional, Comunicado de Prensa No. 30, July 26, 2011, available at http://www.corteconstitucional.gov.co/comunicados/No.%2030%20comunicado%2026%20de%20July%20de%202011.php. The Constitutional Court issues two types of rulings: the first are rulings of the "C" type, involving an abstract control of constitutionality and therefore where the argument focuses on whether there is consistency between a lower norm and the Constitution. This type of case is not tied to any individual citizen. The second are rulings of the "T" variety, in which Court reviews *tutela* cases already decided by lower courts, in which it is alleged that the state, or individuals in some cases, has violated the fundamental rights of one or more individuals by act or omission.

3. The lawsuit that challenged the constitutionality of Law 54 of 1990 requested that the Court recognize that Law 54 was a point of reference for the interpretation of other rules referring to the marital union, and as such it asked the Court to generate a domino effect that would have radically transformed the Colombian legal system. The lawsuit was filed by the Public Interest Law Group at University of the Andes and the nongovernmental organization Colombia Diversa.

4. Daniel Bonilla and Natalia Ramirez, *Grupo de Derecho de Interés Público de la Universidad de los Andes* (Public Interest Law Group of the University of the Andes), "Report for the 18th International Congress on Comparative Law," *American University Journal of Gender, Social Policy, & the Law* 19:1 (2010), 97–112.

5. *See* Corte Constitucional, October 3, 2007, M.P.: M.G. Monroy Cabra, Sentencia C-811/07.

6. See Corte Constitucional, April 16, 2008, M.P.: C.I. Vargas Hernández, Sentencia C-336/08. (That is, when a member of the couple receiving a pension dies, the survivor can replace him as the beneficiary of this right.)

7. See Corte Constitucional, August 8, 2008, M.P.: J. Córdoba Triviño, Sentencia C-798/08.

8. See Corte Constitucional, October 12, 2007, M.P.: H.A. Sierra Porto, Sentencia T-856/07; C.C., December 11, 2008, M.P.: C.I. Vargas Hernández, Sentencia T-1241/08.

9. In the T-1241/08 ruling, the Constitutional Court ordered the retirement fund of the armed forces to reform its procedures so that members of same-sex couples would be able make use of their right to transfer pensions. Nevertheless, the Court did not decide in favor of the claimant because he did not submit sufficient evidence as to the nature of his permanent companionship with the deceased, to whom the retirement fund of the armed forces was required to pay a pension. See Sentencia T-1241/08.

10. Corte Constitucional, January 28, 2009, M.P.: R. Escobar Gil, Sentencia C-029/09.

11. The lawsuit was filed by the nongovernmental organizations *Colombia Diversa* and *Dejusticia*, as well as the Public Interest Law Group at the University of the Andes.

12. The Court, however, refrained from deciding on the constitutionality of norms that include the concepts of family, relatives, or the household. The first set of norms involves a variety of criminal matters such as the right to avoid testifying, denouncing or filing a complaint against long-term partners in any disciplinary, criminal, or military matter; the benefit of dispensing with the penalty of imprisonment when the victim of a crime is the long-term companion; and increasing the penalty for the criminal actor where the long-term companion is the victim of the crime. The second set of civil and commercial norms involves such diverse topics as the constitution of the family's protected patrimony, the shielding of the family home to the end of protecting the property and housing of the partners, and the obligation to pay alimony

to the long-term partner once life is common has been terminated. The third group of norms, grouped under the category "social security," refers to the possibility of giving members of same-sex couples the health and pension benefits received by members of heterosexual couples belonging to the armed forces, and allowing individuals who are part of same-sex couples to obtain benefits received by members of heterosexual couples, such as housing and education subsidies. The fourth set of norms governs matters related the inabilities and incompatibilities of public officials, and restrictions to the access and exercise of civil service and government contracts, as well as the application of the requirements for acquiring citizenship by adoption. Finally, the fifth set of norms concerns important issues such as the rights of the long-term partners of those who have been passive subjects of heinous crimes to be considered victims and therefore to be entitled to the truth, justice, and reparation.

13. Corte Constitucional, February 7, 2007, M.P.: R. Escobar Gil, Sentencia C-075/07.

14. According to the Court, "This body has said that human dignity is a higher value and a founding principle of the rule of law, under which all people should be treated in accordance with their human nature." The Court has noted that "within the Colombian constitutional system, the principle of dignity constitutes the axiological center from which we derive the obligations of protection, respect and promotion of constitutional rights and ensuring the fulfillment of constitutional duties under the aegis of the just order." For the Court, "dignity is understood to be the supremacy the person demonstrates as an attribute inherent in a rational being, whose validation and recognition cannot be measured as the cause or the effect of someone or something (i.e., as an object), but as a higher purpose underlying him or herself" (citations omitted). Sentencia C-075/07.

15. "Generally, in accordance with constitutional case law, human dignity, as a founding principle of the State, is the essential precondition for the consecration and effectiveness of the system of rights and guarantees provided in the Constitution and therefore has absolute value that cannot be limited under any circumstances. Thus, although the Constitution imposes as a limit to the free development of personality the rights of others and the legal system, this limit cannot be taken to the extreme of exploiting anyone for the achievement of general interest under conditions affecting their dignity. Finally it should be noted that, in accordance with case law, the principle of human dignity functions as a constitutional mandate that determines not only a negative duty of non-interference but also a positive duty to protect and maintain decent living conditions." Ibid. (citations omitted).

16. This is what the Court has so tellingly called the right of individuals to "live as you wish" and "live without humiliation." See, for example, Corte Constitucional, October 17, 2002, M.P.: E. Montealegre Lynett, Sentencia T-881/02; Corte Constitucional, May 5, 1994, M.P.: C. Gaviria Díaz, Sentencia C-221/94; Corte Constitucional, October 17, 2002, M.P.: E. Montealegre Lynett, Sentencia T-881/02; Corte Constitucional, September 23, 2002, M.P.: A. Barrera Carbonell, Sentencia C-521/98.

17. This is what the Court has called the material dimension of the principle of dignity. This dimension is expressed in constitutional law on the creation of case law for a minimum vital (*mínimo vital*). See, for example, Corte Constitucional, May 20, 1998, M.P.: E. Cifuentes Muñoz, Sentencia SU-225/98; Corte Constitucional, December 9, 1999, M.P.: C. Gaviria Díaz, Sentencia SU-995/99; Corte Constitucional, September 11, 2003, M.P.: M.G. Monroy Cabra, Sentencia SU-783/03.

18. "[T]his Court has understood that the right to free development of personality embodies a general protection of the capacity of the Constitution to recognize individuals for self-determination, that is, to follow their own norms and develop their own life plan, provided they do not affect the rights of others or the legal order " (citation omitted). Sentencia C-075/07.

19. To this respect, in the C-811/07 ruling, the Court says, "[i]n order to carry out the study of the accused provision, the Court must consider the elements of doctrine set forth in the C-075 ruling of 2007, as they constitute the conceptual framework that determines the current scope of the rights of same-sex couples . . . . In effect, accepting

the doctrinal criteria outlined by the Court in the C-075 ruling of 2007, that mark the current view on the legal treatment of the issue, the barriers which the same-sex couple has to joining the Social Security in Health system by the contributory scheme constitutes a violation of their right to human dignity, free development of personality—in the conception of sexual self-determination—as well as a transgression of the prohibition of discrimination based on sexual orientation." Corte Constitucional, October 3, 2007, M.P.: M.G. Monroy Cabra, Sentencia C-881/07.

20. In sections 4 and 5 of the T-856/07 ruling, decisions C-075/07 and C-811/07 are cited as binding precedent for deciding the case of *tutela* under review. *See* Corte Constitucional, October 12, 2007, M.P.: H.A. Sierra Porto, Sentencia T-856/07.

21. The Court notes to this respect in the C-336/08 ruling, "[i]n the present case, the application of the expressions under review has allowed homosexual couples differential treatment from that afforded to heterosexual couples in that the latter are beneficiaries of the survivor's pension and the former are not, differential treatment that is discriminatory against homosexual couples, which, while not explicitly excluded from pension benefits for survivors, if they are in fact exempted from social security system, because a lack of clarity on the part of the legislature has led to the implementation of a situation contrary to the values of the Social State of Law, to the principles of recognition and respect for the dignity of the human person, and the norms from the Constitution which protect the free development of personality and its extension: freedom of sexual choice." Corte Constitucional, April 16, 2008, M.P.: C.I. Vargas Hernández, Sentencia C-336/08. *See also* section 5 of the ruling, which gathers the doctrine set forth in Decision C-075/07.

22. Sections 4.2 and 4.3 of the T-1241/08 ruling cite both Decision C-336/08 and Decision C-075/07 as the basis for the decision the Constitutional Court takes in this *tutela*. See Corte Constitucional, December 11, 2008, M.P.: C.I. Vargas Hernández, Sentencia T-1241/08.

23. The Court signals in the C-798/08 ruling, "the patrimonial system of de facto marital unions—within which the duty of alimony is defined—is contained in Law 54 of 1990, as amended by Law 979 of 2005. As is known, the C-075 ruling of 2007, the Court declared Law 54 of 1990 to be enforceable . . . on the understanding that the system for the protection of patrimonial rights of long-term partners forming a de facto marital union also applies to homosexual couples. . . . The systematic interpretation of the provisions mentioned and the judicial decisions cited above does not cast any doubt on the existence of the obligation of alimony between long-term partners, regardless of their sexual orientation. . . ." Corte Constitucional, August 8, 2008, M.P.: J. Córdoba Triviño, Sentencia C-798/08. See also Part 13 of the same ruling.

24. "However, it should be taken into account that, according to constitutional case law, the couple with a common life plan that has a durable vocation and involves mutual assistance and solidarity among its members, enjoys constitutional protection, independent of whether it has to do with heterosexual or homosexual couples, and in this context, the difference in treatment of couples who are in comparable situations may raise issues of equality and, similarly, the absence of legal provision for same-sex couples with respect to advantages or benefits applicable to heterosexual couples can give rise to a lack of protection in violation of the Constitution, insofar as it disregards a higher imperative according to which, under certain circumstances, the legal order must contemplate a minimum of protection for certain subjects, in the absence of which principles and superior rights such as dignity, free development of personality and solidarity may be compromised." Corte Constitucional, January 28, 2009, M.P.: R. Escobar Gil, Sentencia C-029/09.

25. In a paradigmatic manner, the Court indicates in the C-075/07 ruling, "[p]ut another way, the legislative decision not to include homosexual couples in the patrimonial regime provided for de facto marital unions functions as an unjustified restriction of the autonomy of the members of such couples and can have harmful effects, not only as it impedes the realization of their common life plan, but because it does not

offer an appropriate response to situations of conflict that may occur when cohabitation is ceased for any reason." Sentencia C-075/07.

26. The Court refers to the case of the members of low-income same-sex couples that survive their partners and have no right to transfer pensions, or those who, once separated from their partner or upon his or her death, do not have the right to jointly built inheritance so long as it is only in the name of the deceased or separated partner. *See* Sentencia C-075/07.

27. *See*Corte Constitucional, July 14, 1999, M.P.: V. Naranjo Mesa, Sentencia C-507/99.

28. See Corte Constitucional, March 24, 1998, M.P.: F. Morón Díaz, Sentencia T-101/98.

29. Protection for the fundamental rights of homosexual individuals is granted in Corte Constitucional, March 7, 1994, M.P.: E. Cifuentes Muñoz, Sentencia T-097/94; Sentencia T-101/98; Corte Constitucional, September 9, 1998, M. P. A. Martínez Caballero, Sentencia, C-481/98; Sentencia C-507/1999; Corte Constitucional, May 29, 2000, M. P.: A. Martínez Caballero, Sentencia T-618/00.

30. Corte Constitucional, August 2, 2001, M.P.: M.G. Monroy Cabra, Sentencia C-814/01.

31. Sentencia T-618/00.

32. See Human Rights of Lesbians, Gays, Bisexuals and Transgender Individuals in Colombia 2006–2007, available at http://www.colombiadiversa-blog.org/p/informes-ddhh.html.

33. However, the Catholic hierarchy strongly opposed the recognition of the right to marriage or adoption by members of same-sex couples.

34. The Catholic news agency ACI Prensa reported that "[i]n late September, the President of the Episcopal Conference of Colombia, Bishop Luis Augusto Castro stated that although the Church doesn't have anything to say "against the inheritance and the social security of homosexuals," these goals can be achieved without the need to "introduce a form of camouflaged marriage and without taking a harder swing at the structure of family." *See Senado colombiano aprueba ley de patrimonio para parejas del mismo sexo*, ("Colombian Senate passes law of same sex couples patrimony"), October 11, 2006, http://www.aciprensa.com/noticia.php?n=14432. Similarly, the Caracol chain reported the following: "The secretary general of the Colombian Episcopal Conference, Monsignor Fabian Marulanda, indicated that within the principles of respect and non-discrimination against homosexuals, "it is right to guarantee the inheritance rights of homosexual unions." The prelate indicated that the important thing for the Catholic Church is that same-sex couples do not reach the same level of marriage as heterosexual couples, and added that the clergy would not accept granting the right of adoption to 'gay' unions." See *Iglesia respeta fallo sobre derechos patrimoniales a los homosexuales* , ("Church respects decision about homosexuals' patrimonial rights"), Caracol.com, Feb. 7. 2007, http://www.caracol.com.co/nota.aspx?id=388585.

35. Sodomy was a crime in Colombia until 1980 and that the American Psychiatric Association, a basic reference for Colombian psychiatry, only removed homosexuality from its list of mental illnesses in 1973.

36. For my analysis in this section, I am indebted to a range of legal philosophers: Ronald Dworkin, Robert Burt, Patricia Williams, Robin L. West, Charles Taylor, Will Kymlicka, Jeremy Waldron, to name a few. Specifically, see Giovanni Bognetti, "The Conception of Human Dignity in European and U.S. Constitutionalism," in European and US Constitutionalism, Georg Nolte, ed. (Cambridge: Cambridge University Press, 2005); Robert Burt, "Regulando la sexualidad: libertad frente a igualdad," Seminario en Latino america de Teoría Constitucional y Politica - SELA, (2009), accessed October 31, 2012, http://www.law.yale.edu/intellectuallife/sela2009.htm; Ronald Dworkin, Éticaprivada e igualitarismo político (Barcelona: Paidós, 1993); Alan Gewirth, "Human Dignity as the Basis of Rights," in The Constitution of Rights: Human Dignity and American Values, Michael J. Meyer and William Allan Parent, eds. (Ithaca: Cornell University Press, 1992): 99–109; Will Kymlicka, Multicultural Citizenship: A Liberal

Theory of Minority Rights, (New York: Oxford University Press, 1996); Julieta Lemaitre, "Los derechos de los homosexuales y la Corte Constitucional: (casi) una narrativa de progreso," in Hacia un Nuevo Derecho Constitucional, Daniel Bonilla and Manuel Iturralde, eds. (Bogotá: Legis, 2005), 181–217; Julieta Lemaitre, "El amor en los tiempos del cólera: derechos LGBT en Colombia," SUR Revista Internacional de Derechos Humanos 6 (2009): 81–82; Neomi Rao, "On the Use and Abuse of Dignity in Constitutional Law," Columbia Journal of European Law, 14 (2008): 201–56; Reva Siegel, "Dignity and the Politics of Protection: Abortion Restrictions Under Casey/Carhart,"Yale Law Journal, 117 (2008); Charles Taylor, Ética de la autenticidad (Barcelona: Paidós, 1994); Patricia Williams, "On Being the Object of Property" in Feminist Legal Theory: Readings in Law and Gender, Katherine Bartlett and Rosanne Kennedy, eds. (Boulder: Westview Press, 1991), 165–80.

37. This is a model that has been used to justify the recognition of same-sex couples as well as other rights related to sexuality. It is, as we have seen, one of the arguments underlying the line of case law of the Colombian Constitutional Court recognizing the legal existence of same-sex couples. However, it has also been a model used in the Anglo-Saxon context to justify Supreme Court rulings as important as *Roe v. Wade*, 410 U.S. 113 (1973) (abortion), *Griswold v. Connecticut*, 381 U.S. 479 (1965) (the right of married couples to use contraceptives), and *Lawrence v. Texas*, 539 U.S. 558 (2003) (along with the argument for equality, it allowed for the rules punishing sexual relations between same-sex couples to be declared unconstitutional).

38. Corte Constitucional, February 7, 2007, M.P.: R.E. Gil, Sentencia C-075/07.

39. Corte Constitucional, February 7, 2007, M.P.: R. Escobar Gil, Sentencia C-075/07.

40. For the Court in the C-075/2007 ruling, "the involvement of dignity, finally, is inferred in a direct way as well, in the absence of legal recognition of personal lifestyle choices. This occurs in this case because the reality of homosexual couples and the individuals in them is not recognized and is invisible to the legal order, given that, in spite of the fact that said persons have acted in the exercise of an option protected by the Constitution, they are ignored by the legal system when it comes to solving the conflicts of inheritance that can arise from such a decision. " Sentencia C-075/07.

EIGHT

Legal Mobilization and the Road to Same-Sex Marriage in Argentina

Maria Gracia Andía

In the context of rising judicialization of politics, Argentina presents a case that is relevant for explaining the phenomenon of legal mobilization. This chapter explores the legal activism of the LGBT movement in Argentina leading eventually to the adoption of same-sex marriage legislation. It briefly analyzes the factors that made this group choose the courts as political strategy, the influence of the courts on the National Congress as well as on the media coverage, and whether social mobilization support structure[1] made any difference.

Argentina reformed its constitution in 1994, introducing some normative developments that included a catalogue of new rights, called positive or second-generation rights, and rights with collective impact including protection to the environment, socioeconomic rights, right to health care and, rights related to vulnerable/disadvantaged groups. The reform also invigorated a procedural tool for vindicating those rights, the case of the *"recurso de amparo."*[2] In fact, the individual and collective *amparo* has been a procedural tool that has been used by the diverse groups of civil society to bring their claims to the courts.[3]

Charles Epp demonstrates that the success of the rights revolution depended not solely on constitutional guarantees of rights, or even on judicial leadership, but most critically on the public support structure for such rights. For Epp, "support structure" means litigation-oriented lawyers organizing to pursue recognition of individual or group rights and grassroots organizations working with them. He contends that previous scholarship tended to leave it out non-legal factors in the evolution of rights. In addition to the "demand-side factors" for each country, which account for the turn to courts drawing especially on Epp's "support structure for legal mobilization" thesis, some scholars emphasize the "supply-side factors," namely the institutional characteristics of the judicial system. This chapter takes into account the particularities of the Argentine judicial system for the demand and supply side factors. For instance, Catalina Smulovitz argues that the increase of judicialization of politics in Argentina may not be related to how people evaluate the judiciary, but to the opportunity structure for making claims combined with the support structure of existing lawyers and a new structure of advocacy organizations that lead to the greater use of courts.[4]

ORGANIZATION AND MOBILIZATION OF LGBT GROUPS

LGBT groups are prominent examples of how groups in Latin America have attained some significant political achievements over the past decade. Normative and societal developments have created several political achievements in the 2000s for LGBT activist groups in Latin America. The Argentine same-sex marriage law, passed in 2010, is an example of this trend.

Argentina has a vibrant and well-organized civil society. After democratic restoration in 1983, the discourse and language of rights found fertile ground in which to grow, as did the groups of civil society pressuring for effective justice. The courts started to play a new role, a role that included venturing into the realm of politics.[5] In Argentina, there are several associations, NGOs, and groups that address the issue of LGBT rights. Nevertheless, only a few of them have a committed work relationship with the community that has influenced government agenda.[6] The 1960s and 1970s were decades well known for liberation, mobilization, and breaking away from old models and structures. During those two decades, a diverse number of grassroots organizations emerged. It was a time where the gay movement started to mobilize as well. The first example of social mobilization was the organization called Our World Group (*Grupo Nuestro Mundo*) founded in Buenos Aires in 1969, which was the first formal gay organization in Latin America. The second and main precedent was the Homosexual Liberation Front (*Frente de Liberación Homosexual*: FLH),[7] founded in 1971. In 1976 (a time of political violence and the year of the most virulent military coup), those organizations weakened and eventually disappeared. Currently, the two most active organizations are the Argentine Homosexual Community (*Comunidad Homosexual Argentina*, or CHA)[8] and the LGBT Federation.

CHA was the first gay organization that was legally recognized in Argentina and the second in Latin America. At that moment, ten independent activist gay groups across Argentina joined the CHA. Its main office is located in the City of Buenos Aires, and it performs a number of different activities. Its legal section, one of the most relevant in the association, receives around 1,500 cases per year and provides free legal advice in those cases. Nevertheless, they do not assume legal representation of all the cases due to financial constraints. However, occasionally CHA resorts to courts of law, and choose some of those cases if its lawyers believe that they might help set precedents for future changes. CHA's two most significant achievements have been obtaining legal recognition and becoming one of the key players in the passage of the Civil Union Law enacted by the Legislature of the City of Buenos Aires.

In 2001, CHA presented a law proposal for civil unions in the City of Buenos Aires, an initiative that was joined by other organizations. The law passed in December 2002 as Law 1,004. This successful accomplishment was tremendously difficult to achieve, and showed some flaws in the articulation of LGBT strategies. The association that participated in the "lobbying" process of the Civil Union Law, apart from CHA, was *La Fulana*.[9] *La Fulana* worked very hard in lobbying city legislators and spreading public awareness of the law before and after its passage. Later *La Fulana* recognized that involving other LGBT groups would have made the process easier. Joining forces was a crucial strategy if the groups intended to pass a national law.

The context was beneficial to embark on the struggle of adopting a national law. First, the social and political environment was favorable. Second, the positive effects of the law exceeded the rights recognized in it. Third, Spain had approved recently a marriage law for everyone (without sexual distinction). Precisely, the Spanish associative model of support and articulation, and the strategy that the Triángulo Foundation and the Spanish LGBT Federation used to achieve success in the Spanish Equality Law, inspired *La Fulana*. The Spanish social mobilization approach guided the Federation's organization and strategy. The Spanish LGBT movement did not use the courts, but it was an example to follow in the way they organized a cohesive grassroots movement. Indeed, Pedro Zerolo—Madrid's Councilman and member of the Spanish Socialist Party—became a close friend and strong activist during the same-sex marriage campaign. Similar historical, cultural, and traditional roots made the passage of that legislation an example to follow. For those reasons, *La Fulana* called for a meeting with different LGBT organizations in order to explore common goals and establish a strategy for the marriage law. Together, they established contact with the Spanish LGBT Federation to learn from their experiences as an association struggling for the approval of their same-sex marriage law. In Argentina, prior attempts to coordinate LGBT movement groups had not been successful. Therefore, they analyzed the similarities and differences between Argentina and Spain and tried to learn from the latter's experience.

The passage of the Union Civil Law in the City of Buenos Aires had significant effects in Buenos Aires and beyond the capital city. This law not only recognizes some rights, but also legitimizes "being homosexual." The law sends the symbolic messages of what is and is not acceptable in society. It was a public statement about a group that had been invisible to the state before. Some lesbians told their groups about the positive reactions of their families and colleagues. It is clear that "the use" of law, as a strategy, was very effective in influencing cultural changes in society. Additionally, it was an efficient way to work with the media. Newspapers set up the topic at the national level, mixing the words "civil union" and "marriage." Right-wing groups and the Catholic Church expressed that marriage is just between men and women, unlike a civil union.

Civil unions went beyond the borders of the City of Buenos Aires and triggered other debates. Same-sex marriage was not on the agenda of the LGBT community. Nonetheless, when they realized the cultural, social, and political changes that a gay marriage law would bring, they decided to put marriage on top of the agenda. Those responses provoked changes in how some organizations had been working. For instance, *La Fulana*, which had focused aggressively on cultural changes, from that moment emphasized strategies to achieve legal changes. In 2006, five organizations (*Asociación de Travestis, Transexuales y Transgéneros de Argentina, La Fulana, Nexo Asociación Civil, Fundación Buenos Aires SIDA*, and *VOX Asociación Civil*) founded the LGBT Federation to satisfy a concrete demand: to join forces to achieve their shared objectives. These five groups had strong track records of fifteen to twenty years of fighting for LGBT rights and grassroots commitments with the community. The Federation established five initial objectives: 1) same-sex marriage and adoption (the strategy was called "the same names, the same rights"), 2) gender identity for transsexual individuals, 3) antidiscrimination law, 4) sexual education law, and 5) the code of non-criminal wrongdoing.

THE STRATEGY: "THE SAME NAMES, THE SAME RIGHTS"

In the beginning, the LGBT social mobilization did not include same-sex marriage legalization among their demands. There were other objectives and struggles to endure. The most common strategies used to raise awareness on the public included publications in journals and popular newspapers, seminars, gay parades, lobbying, and so on. Later, and particularly after the constitutional reform in 1994, they gradually introduced in their strategy the use of the court, and more aggressively after the approval of the civil union law in Buenos Aires. This law boosted the idea of a legal change and its symbolic "revolution" in the whole society.

CHA was the first organization to use courts of law by bringing a strategic case before the 1994 constitutional reforms. The first and most relevant case with broad repercussions was the extraordinary appeal and complaint filed by CHA to the Supreme Court in 1991: *Comunidad Homosexual Argentina c/ Resolución Inspección General de Justicia s/ personas jurídicas y recurso de hecho*.[10] This lawsuit sought to overrule the prior decisions that ratified the denial of the legal entity to the association by the General Inspection of Justice (Executive Power).

Although the Supreme Court declared the file inadmissible, the significant legacy of the minority opinion and the later legal authorization for CHA to function made this lawsuit very relevant. This case opened the door to other legal challenges, such as the lawsuit brought to the Supreme Court by the *Asociación Lucha por la Identidad Travesti-Transexual* (ALITT) fifteen years later. ALITT was struggling for the legal and social recognition of transgenderism as a unique identity and for full rights for transgender citizens. ALITT presented an extraordinary appeal to the Supreme Court and filed a complaint against the Tribunal of Appeal decision. On June 29, 2008, the Supreme Court overruled the CHA decision and set an important and visible precedent. This court decision came while important transgender activism was taking place—the first national transgender parade.

The composition of the court was different in those cases. In the second decision, there were only two justices from the old court (Justice Carlos Fayt and Justice Enrique Petracchi[11]), whereas the conservative ideology of the court prevailed during the 1990s. Roberto Gargarella explains how the majority of the court decisions were conservative showing a strong defense of authoritarian and traditional morals.[12] The renewal of the court meant more independence from political power and brought some positive features: more diversity in thinking, religion, and gender. Currently, not all the justices are Catholic and there are also two women, one of them a known feminist and atheist.

After those significant cases, the first legislative achievement encouraged the use of legal strategies by the LGBT community. Following the recognition of the CHA as a subject of rights, in 2002, the Legislature of the City of Buenos Aires passed the civil union law. This law legally recognized a union between two individuals, not taking into account their sexual orientation. Argentina was the first country in Latin America with this type of legislation.

This law rules several rights for gay partners, such as the legal recognition of homosexual couples; the extension of social security benefits, health insurance, subsidies, and social programs; the option of taking loans jointly; the license of one member to take care of the other in the case of either illness or death; preferential visits in the case either of hospitalization or imprisonment; and the power to decide over the health issues of the other spouse. Notwithstanding, the scope of this law is very limited, because the attribution to legislate civil law (in this case, civil marriage) corresponds to the National Congress. The "big" issues that the civil union does not rule include patrimonial assets and adoption.

The law proposal was written by Graciela Medina, CHA's legal advisor. *La Fulana* also contributed in lobbying to pass the legislation. In this case, the LGBT community acknowledged CHA's efforts. CHA strategically decided where and when to present the law proposal. The Legislature of the City of Buenos Aires and the year 2002 were the right time and place to do so. Additionally, the Mayor of the City of Buenos Aires at that moment, Aníbal Ibarra, supported civil unions.

After the 2001 Argentine crisis, there was a collapse of political parties and a proliferation of small ones. The bipartisan system disappeared. The legislature was divided into several small parties and was formed by legislators with very different backgrounds. Party discipline did not exist. Moreover, the Constitution of the City of Buenos Aires was the only one in the country that established sexual orientation as a suspect classification in cases of discrimination. In this context, there was a better position to persuade legislators to pass the law; the conditions were there to push for policy advancements in this area. The debate on the floor took five hours. There were 29 votes in favor and 10 against.

Following the experience of the City of Buenos Aires, the province of Río Negro approved a Civil Union Law on December 17, 2002. Later, the City of Carlos Paz—in the Province of Cordoba—passed a law for freedom of consciousness with 12 votes in favor and 6 against (November 23, 2007). On May 5, 2009, in the City of Rio IV—Province of Cordoba—the city councilors followed the same path, voting unanimously.

The strategy of achieving local civil union laws in several cities or provinces, and later a national civil union law instead of national same-sex marriage law, was planned by the CHA. First of all, they were looking to end the hegemony of the institution of marriage, as it has been known. Second, its aspiration was an integral modification of the institution of marriage, including the name. Nevertheless, the experience of the city of Buenos Aires was successful and boosted LGBT community activism; it also showed the flaws of the social mobilization and the lack of union and coordination among the different organizations of the community. Also, this situation was an excellent training to understand the dynamics of the legislators and to analyze the arguments of the opposition and the Church.

On one hand, the unexpected positive repercussions as well as the weaknesses of the movement that came to light on that process resulted in the creation of the LGBT Federation, in 2006, with one clear objective: to press for the adoption of a same-sex marriage law. On the other hand, CHA presented a bill for a national civil union law in 2005 but lost parliamentary status. Since then, CHA joined the whole LGBT and focused on the same agenda.

There were several legal precedents to this bill. In the 1990s, the association Gays for Civil Rights tried to promote a proposal for civil marriage, with no results. In 1998, Congresswoman Laura Musa from Affirmation for an Egalitarian Republic (ARI), wrote a law proposal for civil unions; however, it lost parliamentary status. Margarita Stolbizer, from the Radical Civic Union (UCR), presented the same proposal in 2000. Laura Musa introduced new proposals in 2002 and 2004, to no avail. In 2005, the soon-to-be Federation and Congressman Eduardo Di Pollina from the Socialist Party introduced a project for a same-sex marriage law. This project was countersigned by other legislators from several political parties. Regrettably, it lost parliamentary status and the representative ended his tenure.

A battle had begun, at the end of the 1990s, to either pass a new law that would regulate the whole institution of the Argentine family or modify the existent marriage law by giving access to marriage to same-sex couples. Facing this scenario, the LGBT Federation decided to use the courts. Judicial decisions are important because they set precedents—not binding in the Argentine system—but they entertain a broad symbolic message to society about what is acceptable.[13] Furthermore, lawsuits generate media attention, educate the public, and provide leverage to grassroots organizations.

This legal accomplishment synthesizes many fights into one. It is a symbolic claim because it means to equalize this minority to the whole society in several aspects. The law helps construct some identities, persons, and families as "normal," while others are deemed "deviant." Those who are included in those "legal definitions" are denied basic rights to which others are entitled. The Federation was prepared to fight that battle. The social mobilization support structure that they had built was ready to go to courts. They built an organization able to lead, support, and follow up on the cases.

María Rachid took control of the political decisions of the group and pointed out the plan to follow. They were determined to use courts to advance the public policy agenda. Under her decisions as the president of the Federation, there was a group of lawyers who had been working on the strategies of the cases and other members working on their media repercussions, and they also had the support of the INADI.

The strategy was to first present three types of *amparos*. Every *amparo* has had particular features taking into account who were the people asking for the right to marriage. The approach involved different political and cultural groups of the society and had impact at national and local levels from groups from the center and from the periphery. In each case, the Federation analyzed the pros and cons of every couple, their visibility and empathy they reveal in society. The Federation prepared and coached them for media discussions and possible debates. They needed to know how to publicly and precisely defend same-sex marriage. It could not be a random couple that did not understand and support the movement's claims.

Lawsuits were brought to the Civil Tribunal taking into account the purpose of their demands. On February 14, 2007, Claudia Castro, coordinator of *La Fulana*, and María Rachid went to the City Council asking for an appointment with the Civil Registration Office to get married. The civil servant official denied the request, arguing that the civil law does not allow same-sex marriages. The civil law requires the consent of a woman and a man (articles 172 and 180, Civil Code). This unsuccessful attempt to marry had a political objective intended to bring high visibility to this case.

Soon after, María Rachid and Claudia Castro introduced an *amparo* recourse to the National Civil Tribunal of First Instance (*Juzgado Nacional de Primera Instancia en lo Civil*). Some lawyers and an interdisciplinary group of professionals who belonged to the Federation, led by Gustavo López, Florencia Krávetz, and Analía Más, drafted their lawsuit. Judge María Ofelia Bacigalupo ruled against the couple. The claimants appealed to the National Chamber and then went to the Supreme Court. However, after the passage of the *Egalitarian* Marriage Law, the case was declared moot by the Supreme Court, in August 2010.[14]

A second request to an appointment at the Civil Registration Office was sought by a pair of well-known actors, Ernesto Larrese and Alejandro Villalba, on June 27, 2007. The idea of a soap opera actor (Larrese) getting married brought the same-sex marriage matter to the people. Additionally, the witnesses were a renowned actor, Boy Olmi, and a famous actress, Mercedes Moran; former President of INADI, María José Lubertino; and Patricia Walsh, House of the City of Buenos Aires Representative. Another refusal led to an *amparo*. The lawsuit was presented again to María Ofelia Bacigalupo's Tribunal.

The last of the first series of those *amparos*[15] came from the provinces in 2008. As members of VOX, an association for LGBT rights located in Rosario, Martín Peretti Scioli and Oscar Marvich's request was rejected by the registration office. Hence, they also brought an *amparo* to the courts. The local justice of the City of Rosario studied the case and ruled against the claimants' demand (Judge Graciela Abraham of The Civil and Commercial Tribunal Number Six, located in the City of Rosario). The Civil and Commercial National Chamber of Appeal (Sala III) ratified the first instance decision and asked the Congress for a decision on this issue.

None of those *amparos* obtained a favorable court decision. Nevertheless, the most significant ramification of those cases was the introduction of a same-sex marriage bill to the House of Representatives by Representatives Di Polina and Silvia Augsburger from the Socialist Party in 2007. Six months later, Senator Vilma Ibarra introduced another bill with the support of the Federation in the Senate. Simultaneously, María José Lubertino presented another initiative through the Executive.

After the negative experiences with the cases cited above, the Federation decided to introduce legal challenges in other, less-conservative courts. The Court of Administrative Law Claims was selected. The Federation had been told that the judges of that jurisdiction were younger, less prejudiced, and less risk averse.[16] In Marc Galanter's words, the LGBT social mobilization had been developing the expertise of "repeat players," and had become much more sophisticated in their use of litigation.[17] Considering that the government of the City of Buenos Aires would appeal given its conservative ideology, the Federation's objective was to bring the cases to the Supreme Court. A favorable decision would have been expected according to previous precedents and background of this National Court. In the Contentious-Administrative jurisdiction, the new legal cases achieved favorable decisions. Surprisingly, after the first *amparo*,[18] the city's government decided not to appeal. This was a good indicator of the favorable political environment. Therefore, many parties to the case (Alex and José María, Jorge and Damian,[19] and Norma Castillo and Ramona Arévalo[20]) were able to get married. After those successful experiences, there were several other judicial presentations.[21] Those circumstances were widely covered by the media (newspaper, TV shows, radios, and magazines) with a supportive point of view.

Along with this positive development, the Federation spread the news, encouraging gay couples throughout the country to bring their cases to the courts, providing free legal advice to couples submitting *amparos*. Thousands of requests arrived to the organization. The Federation built a network with different lawyers across the country that wanted to volunteer their services. The demand was overwhelming. The Federation was not trying to judicialize all marriage celebrations. They intelligently used this tool to pressure and persuade the Congress.

Another significant *amparo* is the case of Alex Freyre and José María Di Bello.[22] They are activists from AIDS Buenos Aires Foundation and Argentine Red Cross and Positive Effect, respectively. Moreover, they live with HIV/AIDS. As with all the other couples, they went to the civil registration office asking for a date on April 22, 2009, and it was denied. A month later they sued the city of Buenos Aires (an *amparo*). The judge, Gabriela Seijas (Tribunal Number 15 on Contentious-Administrative) ruled in favor of the claimants. She declared the unconstitutionality of the Civil Code articles (172 and 188).

The city of Buenos Aires did not appeal. Thus, *res judicata* gave them a vested right to get married on April 1 (the international day for the struggle against AIDS). However, a week later the lawyer Francisco Roggero motioned for preliminary injunction to nullify Seijas's judgment with the legal representation of the Catholic Lawyers Corporation. The judge of the National Civil Tribunal (Number 85), María Marta Gómez Alsina, ruled in favor of Roggero's claim and suspended the marriage celebration.[23] Roggero stated that the LGBT community was looking for tenacious judges at hand in bringing the cases to the administrative jurisdiction.

The arguments of this court decision were that Judge Seijas had neither jurisdiction nor competence on subjects ruled by the Civil Code. Indeed, the former demands for getting married in the civil jurisdiction were dismissed. The National Chamber ratified the previous verdict on December 1, 2009. As a consequence, the official of the Civil Registration Office followed the prior mentioned civil judgments and decided not to allow the couple to marry.

Given these circumstances, the Federation looked for a LGBT-friendly province. The Governor of the Southernmost Province of Tierra del Fuego, Fabiana Ríos, had always expressed her approval of same-sex marriage and assented to support the Federation strategy. Thus, the Federation, along with INADI, organized everything in absolute secret to travel to the capital city of Ushuaia. Alex and José María went to Ushuaia and Governor Fabiana Ríos authorized the marriage following the Seijas's judicial decision and endorsing the law proposal of same-sex marriage. Alex and José María finally got married on December 28, 2009. That marriage was the first same-sex marriage in Latin America.

THE LGBT MOVEMENT BEYOND THE COURTS. THE TIME FOR A LEGISLATIVE AGENDA: EGALITARIAN MARRIAGE REFORM

Those cases had a significant media impact and provoked debates in the whole society. The debate was across TV shows: political programs, interview programs, talk shows, gossip shows, and recreational programs. Other media outlets, radio, Facebook, and Twitter followed suit. The stories occupied the front-page of newspapers, and the news websites had a special tab with the label "gay marriage." It was an issue not only discussed in academia and among interested people, but also at every kitchen table and coffee shop in Argentina.

The issue was finally at the top of the public's agenda. Thus, Vilma Ibarra—House Representative from the Encounter for Democracy and Equality Party and president of the General Legislation Commission, jointly with Juliana Di Tullio from the Peronist Party and president of the Family, Women, Children and Adolescence Commission of the House of Representatives, put the issue on the list of items to debate in the Plenary Commission on October 29, 2009. That decision was taken between Ibarra, Di Tullio, Augsburger, and María Rachid, taking into account the momentum generated by court decisions and waiting for the right moment to do it. The Plenary Commission was expected to discuss two projects: one introduced by Ibarra in 2008 and the other drafted by Silvia Augsburger.

The Federation encouraged every representative to attend the Commission's session. On October 29, 2009, the Plenary Commission reached quorum and debated the projects. There were several speakers. Representatives Augsburger and Ibarra explained and defended their initiatives as well as the president of the INADI. The constitutional law experts Roberto Saba and Andrés Gil Domínguez presented their arguments as well.

Then, the Federation, along with the representatives, established a list of twenty speakers in favor of and against the drafts. Spanish activists Antonio Poveda and Pedro Zerolo, constitutional law experts Roberto Gargarella and José Miguel Onaindia, journalist Osvaldo Bazán, psychiatrist Alfredo Grande, and president of CHA Cesar Cigliutti spoke in favor of the initiative. CHA expressed its support of the same-sex marriage project after the failure of the civil unions. After two intense days of debate, it was believed that it might be possible to obtain a commission ruling in order to discuss the drafts on the floor. However, the Civic Radical Union (UCR) and Front for the Victory (FPV)[24] did not give a quorum, seemingly because of the President's impending visit to the Pope scheduled for two days later.

With the June 2009 legislative elections, the composition of the Chamber was going to change, having a more conservative presence. Thus, the chances of debating the project and obtaining the necessary votes to approve the law by the House of Representatives were very low. At the beginning of the congressional sessions in March 2010, the Federation called a press conference in which it asked for support for the same-sex marriage drafts in order to extend the recognized rights to some couples through the courts to all the LGBT communities across the country. The key actors in the House of Representatives were at that conference.

After these demonstrations, Ibarra, then president of the General Legislation Commission, and Claudia Rucci, who had just become the new president of the Family, Women, Childhood, and Adolescence Commission, called for a plenary commission session on March 25, 2010. Once more, Ibarra and Augsburger presented their drafts for deliberation. For a second time, the same speakers of 2009 expressed their opinions. In addition, the new president of INADI, Claudio Morgado, and the judge of the first favorable decision, Gabriela Seijas, presented their arguments.

The sessions in the commission were an excellent picture of the situation. The room was divided in two. In one area of the room were the flags and signs of the LGBT movement with words and phrases like "equality" and "the same rights with the same names." On the other side of the room were signs with drawings of families and the words "I want a mom and dad." In that room, the two groups were tolerant, although they were clearly uncomfortable with each other. In any case, and especially remembering Argentina's virulent history, it was a civil and democratic celebration. On April 15, 2010, the Plenary Commission signed a ruling of the majority giving the green light to the draft to be discussed on the floor. There was also a ruling of the minority proposing a new concept of "family union."

The general session at the House of Representatives was scheduled for April 28, 2010. The agenda included other items before the civil marriage law modification. This complicated the strategy, as there were politically divisive issues that the Peronist Party wanted to avoid. The same-sex marriage issue, although originated in Congress by some independents and socialists representatives, got an important backing and support from the government. But due to those other issues that were supposed to be treated before, the FPV bloc and its allies did not give a quorum to deliberate. Although their strategy was disrupted and divided by this political fight, the Federation vigorously called on its supporters to not make this situation helpful to the opposition.

Finally, a special session to discuss the drafts was called. On May 4, 2010, the House of Representatives approved the law. The session started at 2:30 p.m. and lasted over twelve hours without interruptions. In a remarkable day for Congress, there were 240 interventions and the final vote ended with 126 in favor of the same-sex marriage, 114 against it, and only 4 abstentions. It was a very civilized debate in which respect and tolerance marked the debate and deliberations.

After this accomplishment, the Federation started to lobby the senators in order to persuade them to vote for the law. The Senate presents different features from the House of Representatives. There are fewer people (72), and thus it is easier to get in touch with them personally. In addition, they are more visible and known. In the Senate it is more common to find prominent political figures. These characteristics make it easier to make them socially accountable. In fact, the constituency identifies more easily with its senators and that is not true about its representatives in the House, where there are 257 people. Moreover, the Senate is far more conservative than the House. Senators represent the local states' constituencies that are much more traditional and religious than the constituency of the City of Buenos Aires and its surroundings.

At the same time, the opponents of the civil law modification intensified their activism and demonstrations against the law proposal. The Catholic Church had some severe statements against the LGBT community and the people who support its struggle. The strategy of the LGBT movement incorporated a new language at this point. With the support of a good part of the media, artists, and progressive intellectuals, they started to name the law: "Egalitarian Marriage Law." This proved to be a smart strategy that increased the positive impact of the issue in the society. Therefore, the pressure on the senators was even bigger.

In this scenario, the general legislation commission chaired by Senator Liliana Negre de Alonso (Federal Peronist Party)[25] and one of the most prominent opponents to the marriage draft law decided upon the House of Representatives' report of the majority. In the commission, that report did not reach enough votes and it became the report of the minority. In addition, the commission signed a Senate report of the majority proposing a civil union law. This draft did not include the right of adoption and prohibited assisted fertilization techniques. In all fairness, Senator Negre de Alonso was thorough. She not only called on the main figures in this topic in the city of Buenos Aires, but also went with other members of the Senate to several provinces and opened the debate to the different voices: experts, academics, social key players, and activists.

The floor session was set for July 14, 2010. A few days before that date, the archbishop of Buenos Aires sent a public letter in which he considered among other statements that the same-sex marriage law was a "pretension to destroy God's plan." The night before the Senate's session there was a huge demonstration called by the Catholic and Evangelic churches in favor of heterosexual marriage.

That Senate deliberation was opened by Senator Negre de Alonso. She showed a ten-minute video that briefed one hundred hours of debate organized in nine provinces. The session lasted more than thirteen hours. The debate was closed and only a few political figures were able to be on the floor as an audience. The media and other guests were in a special room. The debate was passionate, but polite. Likewise, there were several moments of strong tension. The uncertainty of the outcomes was present until the end. It was thought that Senator José Pampuro, the provisional president of the Senate, was going to break the deadlock. The difference of the voting in favor of the law was a surprise. Finally, on July 15, 2010, the Senate passed the law with 30 votes in favor, 27 against and 3 abstentions. The new law modified several articles of the Civil Code, replacing the words "husband" and "wife" with "contracting parties," thereby recognizing the same rights to same-sex marriages.

The process started with the use of courts in order to push the political agenda of Congress. Then lobbying passed the law within two months— a remarkable achievement in terms of speed. Finally, President Cristina Fernandez de Kirchner promulgated the law on July 21, 2010. The president signed the law in a moving ceremony. Activists of the LGBT community, human rights groups, artists, the author of the project, political figures that support the project, among others attended the ceremony. President Fernandez de Kirchner said, "I am proud to say that today we are a society more equal than last week."

After that great accomplishment, the activists were elated, but they have not been resting. They followed up on the enforcement of the law, understanding that that task is important. A long list of new same-sex marriages started to take place on July 30, 2010. The first couple got married that day at 7:45 a.m. in Santiago del Estero. Later, Alejendro Vanelli and Ernesto Larresse, who had presented the second *amparo* three years earlier, celebrated their marriage in the City of Buenos Aires, after

34 years of living together. On July 31, Martín Peretti Scioli and Oscar Eduardo Marvich, who had brought the third *amparo*, also got married in Santa Fe. On the same date, two Chileans celebrated their marriage in Mendoza, where they had been living for fourteen years. They had been together as a couple for twenty-two years. Two women married in Rio Gallegos, Santa Cruz, among a significant number of other couples. Almost six months after the law was passed, about one thousand couples had been married across the country. The majority of the marriages were celebrated in the province of Buenos Aires, or the City of Buenos Aires. However, it is important to mention that marriages have been celebrated in all the provinces, cities, and towns of Argentina. All of this happened in a remarkable environment of respect from all the Argentine society. This would have been unthinkable only a few years ago.

Activists know that this is only the beginning. They have mentioned that it is essential to have a solution for the LGBT's sons and daughters born before the enactment of Law 26,618, in order to be entitled to the same rights regarding to the recognition of their parents and/or mothers as their personal and family identity. The activists also have looked closely at the regulation of the law in order to assure the fulfillment of the National Constitution that guarantees to foreigners the same civil rights as its own citizens. For activists, this issue is extremely relevant for same-sex couples that are not entitled to marriage in their countries of origin may opt to marry in Argentina. Similarly, the organizations lobbied for the Law on Gender Identity and Health. On November 30, 2011, the House of Representatives passed the law proposal presented by the Federation and some legislators. It was backed by 167 legislators while 17 voted against and another 7 lawmakers abstained. Finally, in May 2012, the Senate passed the law with an overwhelming majority: 55 votes in favor, none against, and one abstention. The new legislation gives priority to "internal and individual experience of gender as each person feels," which may or may not correspond with the sex assigned at birth.

FINAL THOUGHTS ABOUT LGBT MOBILIZATION

By observing the experience of the LGBT social mobilization in Argentina, which included lobbying, demonstrations, and particularly the legal cases brought to the courts, several factors compelled them to focus their strategy on the use of courts. In the past, legal strategies were not at the core of the LGBT mobilization. Some small legal changes were occasionally accomplished in conjunction with other stronger organizations doing some lobbying. They offered some free legal advice for particular cases, but not strategically. The only successful strategic case was the request for the official authorization of the legal entity status for CHA. I say "successful" strategic case because the court decision may not have produced the result that was sought, and thus did not create a favorable precedent, but it did place the issue on the public agenda. This was a single isolated case because of the lack of two important factors. They did not have the powerful legal tools and arguments given to the movement by the 1994 constitutional reform. Second, there was not a strong social mobilization support structure behind those actions. Indeed, at that time the CHA was reconsidering its role due to a low level of participation. As was seen later and with better results, the ALITT had a different experience in achieving its legal authorization at the Supreme Court. However, it was also a one-time isolated case disconnected from a broader strategy.

Many factors compelled the LGBT movement to turn to courts as part of its strategic efforts to achieve their policy objectives. They realized the cultural, social, and political changes that a series of legal reforms could bring. The consequences of passing the civil union law expanded to new aspects that were not initially foreseen, exceeded the benefits expected, and went beyond the borders of the City of Buenos Aires. Those circumstances revolutionized the approach of how some organizations had been working, changing their emphasis toward litigation strategies to achieve social, political, and legal reforms. In this fashion, they have also acknowledged that their legal mobilization could count upon strong legal arguments and tools established in the set of constitutional reforms consecrated in 1994.

At that time, the conditions to start a well-planned litigation strategy were there, and the social and political climate was more encouraging. The LGBT community did have more legal tools on which to rely based on the reformed Constitution of 1994 and some new Supreme Court rulings. Also, the LGBT movement managed to develop a strong support structure for social mobilization.

Before the LGBT Federation prepared the ground, various organizations existed but they clearly were not as successful. The support structure for legal mobilization that the LGBT Federation carefully developed helps explain the enactment of the marriage law. Some features of the social mobilization confirm this conclusion. First, it is an organization that has encouraged the agreement and the union of forces of all the LGBT groups throughout the country. Second, this is an organization formed by smaller groups, which has contained them and given them a direction, and a sense of purpose. Therefore, it is an organization that truly represents the claims of the LGBT community, and has included people actually affected. Third, most Federation members have an activist background and are well trained for activist initiatives. Indeed, the organization did not need to hire legal advice because the lawyers who took the cases are active members of the group. Fourth, the Federation developed an experience and expertise in litigation needed for later success improving their *amparos* among other tactics and learned from its own practices. Fifth, although the Federation did not have a substantial budget, they wisely took advantage of the INADI and its resources as a springboard to reach its objectives.

The agreement on the strategy between the two most important groups of the LGBT movement developed once the Federation's strategy started to show some chances of success. In the end, the organizations stuck together and it worked. This movement clearly showed a capability to organize themselves, even under challenging circumstances. Through a wise use of its own resources and a well-planned strategy, the LGBT movement gained access to the judicial system. The strategy of the legal cases worked very well at comparatively low costs. The arguments introduced in court, even those in cases that turned out to be unsuccessful, helped to place the organization's issues on the public agenda, highlighting the specific rights at the core of the struggle. However, some conservative legal voices questioned some aspects of the legal process: the forum shopping and the validity of the court decisions. The LGBT lawyers strategically selected the jurisdiction in an effective use of forum shopping. The key players of the Federation were dedicated to preparing the cases full time, training the parties, and looking for the most opportune moment and the "right" judges to present the cases. In addition, they followed up on court decisions and knew the importance of the media in each of those actions.

In addition, the work of political leaders was coordinated with the forces and strategies of the social movement. The legislators knew how to manage the agenda and cooperate with them despite their different political backgrounds. They agreed that there was a common goal to achieve and left out political differences. Representative Vilma Ibarra took advantage of being the president of the General Legislation Commission to set the issue on the agenda, joining forces with the representatives that had presented initiatives to modify the marriage law before (Di Polina, Sburguer). In general, during the whole process, the politicians and the LGBT social mobilization worked as a cohesive bloc.

These efforts affected the media. Indeed, there was widespread media coverage of this issue, usually appearing on the front pages and in prime-time news shows. In the last years, the main TV channels[26] broadcast at prime time their most popular program, which involved a gay couple in the story. In general, media coverage was positive and supportive of the initiative of the LGBT movement.

On the other hand, opponents contributed to the success of the LGBT mobilization in several ways. First, the lawsuits brought by them were generally poorly reasoned and without legal grounds from a substantive law perspective, and from a procedural standpoint, because third parties who were not part of the cases presented them. Second, opponents delayed their activism against the same-sex marriage proposal. They underestimated both the power of the LGBT social mobilization and the intensity of public opinion. In this way, Argentine society showed its high level of secularism. Third, the aggressive discourse of the extreme right wing turned away the "undecided." There were many people who had initial reservations about same-sex marriage, but they did not agree with the violence of some opponent's statements. This made them more sympathetic to the LGBT cause. In the process, conservative groups became more skilled at communicating their ideas in more positive and less hostile ways.

With regard to public discourse and public relations, both sides learned from their experiences. In the case of the LGBT mobilization, they used the slogan "the same name, the same rights." Nevertheless, when the media communicated on the LGBT struggle, they often called it "gay marriage." After the House of Representatives passed the law, the Federation insisted upon a new label: "egalitarian marriage." This was a different message and it produced successful results.

The issue involving the adoption of children proved to be just as controversial. Instead of avoiding the debate, the LGBT organization addressed it squarely. They explained that the actual law allows single LGBT persons to adopt children. Thus, the egalitarian marriage law would improve and equalize the situation between adoptions by heterosexual couples and LGBT partners giving to those children the same rights of the others. They focused the debate on expanding children's rights, not discriminating against them.

The strategy of the use of courts by the LGBT movement undoubtedly had an impact on the other branches of government. Congress certainly felt the pressure of the social mobilization and the legal arguments of the court decisions addressing the fundamental law: the Constitution. Moreover, the social mobilization joined forces with the progressive political parties (Socialist and other minor parties), and found the backing of the ruling party and the executive. The executive showed its support through the INADI: first by the chief of staff, later through ministers, and eventually the president herself expressed her commitment to this struggle.

It is worth highlighting the fact that all the parties gave their legislators freedom to vote their consciences on this issue, liberating them from party discipline. This issue proved to be important for Argentine democracy. The egalitarian marriage issue was beyond the normal political "quarrels" and resulted in an informed discussion of substantial content throughout the political debate. Citizens, journalists, politicians, academics, and artists expressed their opinions in favor or against, but the whole society discussed this important issue. It was a topic that transcended political parties.

This chapter shows that social mobilization support structure contributed to those outcomes, and courts played an important role in conjunction with traditional political mobilization. Argentine private law (civil law) was constitutionalized, and the *amparo* became more ordinary. This facilitated access to justice and the equal recognition of rights to all citizens, especially disadvantaged citizens. Thus when causes are being advanced in court by groups that enjoy considerable social mobilization support structures, they are more likely to achieve their desired objectives.

NOTES

1. Charles R. Epp, The Rights Revolution: Lawyers, Activists, and Supreme Courts in Comparative Perspective, (Chicago: University of Chicago Press, 1998).
2. The *amparo* has created the possibility of bringing legal actions when either an act or omission injures, restricts, alters, or threatens the rights and guarantees recognized by the Constitution, a treaty or a law, and also to defend new rights with collective impact.
3. CELS, *La lucha por el derecho: Litigio estratégico y derechos humanos* (Buenos Aires: Siglo Veintiuno, 2008), 19.
4. Catalina Smulovitz, "Petitioning and Creating Rights: Judicialization in Argentina," in *The Judicialization of Politics in Latin America*, ed. Rachel Sieder et al. (Palgrave Macmillan, 2005).
5. Gretchen Helmke, *Courts Under Constraints: Judges, Generals, and Presidents in Argentina* (Cambridge MA: Cambridge University Press, 2005), 45.
6. María Rachid (president of the LGBT Federation and former president of LA FULANA), Personal interview, February 10, 2011.
7. See Patricio Lennard, "La Lucha Continua,"*Diario Pagina 12*, June 26, 2009. Available at: http://www.pagina12.com.ar/diario/suplementos/soy/1-831-2009-06-26.html (accessed March, 8 2011), and Marcelo Manuel Benitez, "Nestor Perlongher: Un militante del deseo," Available at: http://www.elortiba.org/perlongher.html (accessed March 8, 2011).
8. Pedro Sottile (Coordinator of the CHA Legal Area), Personal interview, February 5, 2011) and http://www.cha.org.ar (accessed March 8, 2011)
9. *La Fulana* is a lesbian rights association.
10. CSJN-Fallos: 314: 1531.
11. On December 18, 2006, law 26,183 reduced the number of the justices to five. At the moment, there are still seven justices.
12. Roberto Gargarella,"Después del diluvio. El perfeccionismo conservador en la nueva jurisprudencia de la Corte Suprema (1990–1997),"*Desarrollo Económico*38, no. 149 (Apr.–Jun., 1998): 439–456.
13. See Mary Bernstein and Anna-MaríaMarshall ,"The Challenge of Law," in Bernstein, Marshall, and Barclay, *Queer Mobilization: LGBT Activists Confront the Law* (New York: NYU Press, 2009), 7.
14. CSJN - R. 90. XLIV. Recurso de hecho. Rachid, María de la Cruz y otro c/ Registro Nacional de Estado Civil y Capacidad de las Personas s/ medidas precautorias, 8/24/2010.
15. See "Reclamopor el matrimonio gay: importanteavancedelamparopresentadopor la pareja de Rosario," *AG Magazine*, September 12, 2008, http://agmagazine.com.ar/index.php?IdNot=2920.
16. María Rachid. Personal interview, February, 10 2011.
17. Marc Galanter, "Why the 'Haves' Come Out Ahead? Speculations on the Limits of Legal Change," *Law & Society Review* 9, (1974): 95–160.
18. Freyre Alejandro C/ GCBA S/*Amparo* (Art. 14 CCABA), Exp 34292 / 0
19. Bernath Damien Ariel y otros C/GCBA S/*Amparo* (Art. 14 CCABA), Exp 36117/0.
20. Norma Edith Castillo y otros C/GCBA S/*Amparo* (Art. 14 CCABA).
21. Martín Canevaro y otro C/GCBA S/*Amparo* (Art. 14 CCABA), Exp 36410/0.
22. Freyre Alejandro C/ GCBA S/*Amparo* (Art. 14 CCABA), Exp 34292 / 0

23. From the legal point of view, this legal action was highly questioned because the person who promoted it was not part of the relationship. He was a third party whose rights or interests were not being infringed.

24. The FPV is a Peronist Party coalition.

25. This is a dissident Peronist bloc that broke with the Peronist Party.

26. *Canal 13* and *Telefe*.

NINE

The Battle for Marriage Equality in Mexico, 2001–2011

Genaro Lozano

Over the past decade, Mexican LGBT (lesbian-gay-bisexual-transgender) activists have been able to successfully advance some of the main issues on their agenda both at the federal and local level. In 2006, Mexico City enacted civil unions for same-sex couples without social security rights, while the local congress of the northern state of Coahuila enacted a more comprehensive same-sex civil union legislation in early 2007. In December 2009, Mexico City's Assembly approved same-sex marriages with full parenting rights, and debated gender identity legislation in 2008. Furthermore, the federal government has taken important steps to fight discrimination and to consolidate a more open and tolerant society. Among those significant measures, Article 1 of the Constitution was reformed in 2001 to include an explicit prohibition on discrimination based on "preferences," and it was reviewed in 2011 to include the word "sexual." Moreover, the Mexican Congress passed a Federal Law to Prevent and Eliminate Discrimination in 2003, which became the first national anti-discrimination law in Latin America. As a result of this law, the National Council for Preventing Discrimination (*Consejo Nacional para Prevenir la Discriminación*) was created in 2004 at the federal level.

Moreover, during the 2006 midterm elections, a record of thirty-eight openly LGBT candidates ran for office supported by five different political parties. Currently, there are two openly lesbian legislators at the Federal Congress, while an openly gay man holds a public office in the state of Nuevo Leon. For all these reasons, it could be argued that Mexico is

151

currently experiencing a queer revolution, by an ongoing political inclusion of LGBT people and legal changes to advance their interests.

In this chapter, I will explore how Mexican LGBT activists were able to advance the legal recognition of same-sex couples first in the form of civil unions through formal institutions—local congresses and at the Federal Congress in the period from 2000 to 2007—and then in same-sex marriages with full parenting rights in 2009. I will argue that this success has taken place under an umbrella of many factors, broadly categorized as social, economic, and political changes, that Mexico has experienced in the past two decades. Indeed, since the elections of 2000, the country transitioned from a one-party hegemony to a more democratic regime. I will argue that the transition to an electoral democracy had an important effect on the discussion of LGBT issues by taking them beyond what I will henceforth call the "small inner circle of debate" (LGBT and feminist activists) to what I will call a "larger outside circle" (formal and traditional political actors, such as presidential candidates, other political leaders, political parties, and mass media, among other actors).

Mexico is a federal country with thirty-one states and the Federal District of Mexico City. This chapter will only focus on two cases, Mexico City and the state of Coahuila, where LGBT issues were materialized in the adoption of civil unions for same-sex couples. However, a countertrend is also starting to take place. The state of Yucatan reformed its constitution in 2009 in order to define marriage as "a union between a man and a woman," while the local congress of Baja California also reformed its constitution precluding the possibility of legally recognizing a same-sex couple in this state. In addition, President Felipe Calderón, a social conservative, asked Mexico's Supreme Court to review the constitutionality of the Mexico City's new marriage law, while the Catholic Church applauded the President's decision. In a historic 9-2 vote, the Supreme Court voted against the president's action, declaring that same-sex marriages in Mexico City do not violate the Federal Constitution, possibly opening the road for similar initiatives to be presented in other local congresses.

In Mexico City, the leftist *Partido de la Revolución Democrática* (PRD) has controlled both the office of the mayor and the Legislative Assembly since the late 1990s. Mexico City has an open system of political participation and public contestation, with a vibrant network of LGBT organizations engaged in social and political changes, and to political competition, by a fiercely conservative *Partido Acción Nacional* (PAN). In contrast, the northern state of Coahuila remains one of the strong *Partido Revolucionario Institucional* (PRI) bastions, and this party controls both the governor's office and the local legislature. In the state, LGBT organizations are practically nonexistent, and there is less political competition. Each case followed a different process for achieving legislation that recognizes same-sex civil unions and marriage equality.

According to information provided by Mexico's Civil Registry, over 1,371 same-sex couples have legally married since the law came into effect in March 2010,[1] while less than 900 same-sex couples have formalized their relationship with a *Sociedad de Convivencia* since this civil unions law came into effect in 2007. In addition, according to information provided by the Civil Registry of the state of Coahuila, only 290 couples had formed a civil union in Coahuila by August 2011, four years after the *Pactos Civiles de Solidaridad* came into effect in that Northern Mexican State. In total, at least 2,500 same-sex couples have become the first generation of LGBT people to legalize their relationships in two localities of Mexico since 2007.

This LGBT "revolution" took place in a country where popular and folk culture has long praised biological determinism and traditional gender roles, as Angeles Mastretta beautifully portrayed in the fictional life of Emilia Sauri in her novel *Lovesick*, or as Jorge Negrete, one of Mexico's golden age singers and actors from the 1940s, loudly sings in "*Ay Jalisco no terajes,*" one of Mexico's "alternative" national anthems, which portrays a display of a machista society:

> Ay Jalisco, Jalisco, Jalisco
> tus hombres son machos
> y son cumplidores
> Valientes y ariscos y sostenedores
> noadmitenrivales en cosas de amores.

Hence, same-sex marriages and civil unions came literally "out of the closet" in a country that celebrates a traditional view of masculinity, where men are usually taught to be the breadwinners of their households while women continue to be the principal caretakers at home. Gay and lesbian couples are more frequently and publicly challenging the traditional stereotypes of family arrangements in Mexico. Gays, lesbians, bisexuals, transsexuals, and transgenders are defying homophobia by increasing their visibility and participation, year after year, in gay pride parades in Mexico City and other cities.[2] Mexican gay and lesbian politicians struggle to gain political spaces and legislative achievements, while daily battling in a country where effeminate men and *machorras* women are constantly harassed. The legal recognition of same-sex couples is now a reality in a country where the sexist "Epistle of Melchor Ocampo," written in 1859, is still read as customary words after a civil marriage ceremony for opposite-sex couples.[3]

Regarding homophobic attitudes, a national poll conducted in 2010 by CONAPRED revealed that over 70 percent of the participants believe LGBT rights are not respected in Mexico, while 67.3 percent of the respondents in Mexico City believe gay couples should not be able to adopt children, and over 62 percent of the participants, also in Mexico City, believed lesbian couples should not be able to adopt either.[4] However, in the years following the approval *Sociedades de Convivencia*, public opinion has become more tolerant of sexual diversity. In fact, in March 2007, a poll conducted by *Consulta Mitosky*, one of Mexico's leading polling centers, revealed that 53.5 percent of the participants said they would not live in the same house with a gay man, while 51.7 percent said they would not share a house with a lesbian. In contrast, CONAPRED asked the same questions in 2010, and the results were that 43.7 percent would not live in the same house with a gay man, while 44.1 percent would not share a house with a lesbian. These results show a significant favorable change in a period of three years.[5]

During the period from 2001 to 2007, when *Sociedades de Convivencia* was first introduced at Mexico City's local assembly and the year it came into effect, LGBT activists dealt with a society divided on the issue of LGBT rights. According to Mitofsky's poll in 2007, 47.3 percent of the participants do not agree with the phrase: "same-sex couples should have the same legal rights as a heterosexual couples," while only 45.7 percent of the interviewers believe the opposite. The same survey shows that 58.3 percent of the respondents do not agree that same-sex couples should be able to legally marry.[6] However, the 2010 CONAPRED's study revealed that a majority of inhabitants of Mexico City supported marriage equality.

During the past decade, LGBT activists were also able to court five different political parties with relative success. In Mexico City, a reluctant PRD timidly cosponsored *Sociedades de Convivencia* in 2001, and then delayed its passage for 5 years, but a more progressive faction within the PRD, led by Mayor Marcelo Ebrard, enthusiastically and strongly supported marriage equality by 2009. Other major parties, like the PRI, have ambiguously supported LGBT rights. In the state of Coahuila, PRI vigorously supported *Pactos Civiles de Solidaridad* in 2007, while in the state of Nuevo Leon, Mariano Plata, an openly gay politician, was able to win a seat in the city of Monterrey's Council supported by PRI. However, Mexico's older party has also supported banning same-sex marriages in the states of Baja California and Yucatán in 2008 and 2011, showing a party that has not been coherent on LGBT rights.

What has not changed between 2007 and 2010 is a relatively weak, scarcely funded, and divided LGBT movement in Mexico. In fact, as will be discussed later in this chapter, Enoé Uranga, who made history by presenting the first initiative in Mexico aimed at publicly recognizing same-sex civil unions in 2001, would fiercely oppose marriage equality in 2009.

As noted by Mario Pecheny, all over the world LGBT political activists have framed some of their public goals in a way that helps them to "redefine their subordinate status . . . in the name of rights. These rights are part of the struggle to make issues of sexual and intimate relationships part of a broader demand for full and equal citizenship."[7] Along these lines, Mexico has made major strides in discussing LGBT issues and in providing some legal rights to LGBT people and to LGBT couples. Arguably, during the battle for same-sex civil unions, Mexico moved toward a cultural transformation of its society. After all, despite President Vicente Fox's (2000–2006) conservative and Catholic background, he never promised to defend the "sanctity of marriage," as George W. Bush did so effectively in the United States. Moreover, the ruling conservative PAN, unlike the Republican Party in the United States, did not tried to aggressively exploit the issue of gay rights as a tool for mobilizing conservative and religious voters during the battle for same-sex civil unions.

However, a different behavior occurred with President Felipe Calderón (in office since 2006), when both Calderón and his party fought back more aggressively after the marriage equality law was approved in December 21, 2009. In February 2010, he was on an official visit in Japan, and when asked by a reporter about his opinion about same-sex marriages, President Calderón, a lawyer by training, falsely declared that "the Mexican Constitution explicitly and exclusively recognizes marriages between a man and a woman."[8] Moreover, he and his party sent five constitutional controversies to Mexico's Supreme Court to review the constitutionality of Mexico City's same-sex marriage law. Calderón asked Mexico's attorney general to send one of those constitutional controversies, while the states of Jalisco, Baja California, Guanajuato, Tlaxcala, and Morelos, also in control by the PAN both at the executive and legislative levels, sent separate controversies to Mexico's Supreme Court. All five controversies were dismissed by the Supreme Court in late February 2010, and same-sex marriages in Mexico City were declared constitutional and therefore valid in the entire country.

In addition, during this period, the issue of sexual diversity left the inner circle of discussion of LGBT activists to become a topic of discussion and debate among the outside circle of activism. Since 2000, all major political forces have taken a public stance on the LGBT agenda. Today PAN, PRI, and PRD, the three major political forces nationwide, have made public their views on sexual minorities and their rights. PAN has traditionally been opposed to expanding rights for LGBT people. PRI has not advanced a uniform agenda. Similarly, PRD has advanced a progressive leftist agenda, but this has induced a confrontation among the different factions within this party. As Representative David Razú states, "the fight for marriage equality revealed the different perceptions among political parties regarding LGBT rights in Mexico in a deeper way than *Sociedades de Convivencia* did in 2005."[9]

A BATTLE FOR EQUALITY LED BY A STRAIGHT ALLY AGAINST A LESBIAN ACTIVIST

The battle for Mexico's City first same-sex civil unions law was led by a group of lesbian activists led by Claudia Hinojosa, Estela Suárez, Alejandra Rojas, and Rosalba Carrasco, all of them longtime feminist activists, researchers, and community organizers, who closely worked with Enoé Uranga, an openly lesbian legislator at Mexico City's Assembly, in the initial drafting of *Sociedades de Convivencia*. Uranga introduced the initiative on April 24, 2001 and would be the driving force pushing for its approval, but she would leave her legislative seat in 2003 without seeing her initiative approved by the Assembly; however, she initiated a cultural battle regarding LGBT rights in Mexico that paved the way for marriage equality in 2009.

In fact, as noted earlier, in 2007, just a year after *Sociedades de Convivencia* was approved, public opinion regarding same-sex civil unions and marriage was not favorable. Perhaps that is one of the reasons why Mayor López Obrador did not support same-sex civil unions during his tenure, and why he even tried to call for a referendum on this issue in 2005. *Sociedades de Convivencia* would be approved once Andrés Manuel López Obrador left his post as Mexico City's mayor to run for president in 2006. However, the midterm elections of 2009 opened the possibility for LGBT activists to run for office under the main sponsorship of *Partido Social demócrata* (PSD), which grouped a few politicians from a progressive left that promoted LGBT rights under its electoral platform. David Razú was the only one who gained a legislative seat at Mexico City's local assembly in September 2009. Razú brought his party platform to the assembly, and upon taking office as representative he promised LGBT organizations that he would present a marriage equality bill during his first year in the assembly: "To me it was clear that we had a compromise with a progressive agenda with LGBT organizations, and that one of my main goals as legislator would be to negotiate with the PRD to push for a new law recognizing same-sex marriages in the City."[10]

Unlike Enoé Uranga, David Razú was not a long-standing activist. In fact, Razú is a straight married man with two children who would later become the main ally and supporter of marriage equality for the LGBT movement. This caused a few divisions within the LGBT movement when Razú made his same-sex marriage announcement. According to many activists who attended the first meetings for discussing the introduction of the bill with Razú, Enoé Uranga, who in 2009 gained a seat in Mexico's Federal Congress, thought that introducing a same-sex marriage bill in the local assembly of Mexico City was not a good option. According to Razú, Uranga was invited to join the initial meetings, held in early October 2009, but she never showed up. Despite Uranga's negative reaction, Razú introduced the marriage bill on November 24, 2009, with the support of fifty-two LGBT organizations, and with forty-two out of sixty-six representatives promising to vote in favor of it.

Lol Kin Castañeda, a feminist-lesbian activist, was Razú's main ally within the LGBT movement. Castañeda and her partner Judith Vázquez, a scholar on religions and sexual diversity, formed a group called *Sociedad Unida en la Defensa del Matrimonio entre Parejas del Mismo Sexo*, created as an umbrella organization to support the marriage bill. They helped Razú to organize two forums on LGBT rights and same-sex marriage in the local assembly in early November, a few days before presenting the initiative, and a second one after presenting the initiative. Some organizations participated in the first forum and after presenting the initiative up to 180 organizations and human rights NGO's signed a public letter asking the Legislative Assembly to approve the bill.

Castañeda and Razú were members of PSD during the 2009 mid-term elections. Castañeda ran for a seat at the assembly but only got a few thousands votes. Castañeda met Razú while he was president of PDS in its Mexico City chapter. According to Castañeda, "When Razú finally got a legislative seat at the Assembly, he called me and Judith for a private meeting in early September in which he asked us our opinion on introducing a marriage bill. I offered [to] him to call LGBT organizations to support the bill, and started planning on how to build a strategy for winning this debate, and which framing would be the more adequate for presenting the initiative to public opinion."

As mentioned earlier, the initiative for liberalizing marriage in Mexico City was presented on November 24 with forty-two legislators promising to give their vote to approve it. However, a few weeks later, on December 12, Edith Ruiz and Julio Moreno, two legislators from PRD, presented a motion asking her fellow legislators to approve the marriage bill but without parenting rights for LGBT couples. Ruiz and Moreno argued that they wanted to prevent LGBT couples and their offspring to be harassed by public opinion. These legislators argued that they were worried about boys and girls being bullied for having two moms or two dads. This was a setback for the discussion of the marriage bill. According to Razú and Castañeda, this was perhaps the bill's major challenge. None of them wanted to approve marriage equality with a ban on adoption, but Razú and other legislators like Maricela Contreras were confident that the bill would be approved without a ban. The legal team of the Office of the Mayor of Mexico City, led by lawyer Leticia Bonifaz, believed that if the initiative were to be approved with that ban, the ban would be unconstitutional and therefore it would never take effect. However, the bill was preapproved on that day, including the adoption ban, and sent to the Assembly floor for a vote later in the month.

The adoption ban induced a viral reaction by Enoé Uranga, who immediately initiated a public media campaign against the marriage bill, and its supporters. Uranga also privately talked and sent email alerts to

LGBT activists asking them to denounce this "fraud" to LGBT people by the PRD. Publicly Uranga attacked Razú and Lol Kin Castañeda for what she considered as "political opportunism" and for "knowing that the supporters of the marriage bill were working against LGBT families." All through December, Uranga continued her public campaign against the bill. In different newspaper and TV interviews, she claimed that "the political conditions for a successful passage of a same-sex marriage bill in Mexico City are not present, and introducing it is an irresponsible act that would provoke a counterwave in other States, inducing homophobia and constitutional amendments blocking same-sex marriages, and therefore making this bill a setback for the LGBT movement in the end."[11] Uranga was referring to a conservative reaction seen after Mexico City passed a bill liberalizing abortion in 2007. Up to eighteen states approved severe laws criminalizing women for ending their pregnancies following Mexico City's decision to decriminalize abortion.

Uranga's reluctance to support Razú's bill and her further statements against the marriage bill provoked an initial division within the LGBT movement while the bill was being discussed in the Assembly by legislators. Many activists who had closely worked with Uranga during the discussion of *Sociedades de Convivencia* were initially reluctant to support Razú. According to Lol Kin Castañeda, "many long-time activists initially followed Uranga in not supporting the bill. This was really disappointing because very respected names within the LGBT movement in Mexico, like Tito Vasconcelos, Luis Perelman, Mario Arteaga, Francisco Lagunes, and Oscar Sánchez, were listening to Uranga and did not initially support our efforts. All of them were respected activists with some influence and therefore this was a problem. Uranga was telling them that this marriage agenda will not pass and that this was not the time, but what she was really saying is that it was her who wanted to lead this and was furious that it was not her leading the marriage bill efforts but another group of people."[12]

Unsurprisingly, opposition to same-sex marriages also came from the conservative PAN party both at the local assembly and at the Federal Congress. Many legislators sided with religious leaders, such as Cardinal Norberto Rivera, in condemning this "attack against the institution of marriage and traditional Catholic values." Representatives from PAN even declared they were now in favor of modifying the *Sociedades de Convivencia* law for including social benefits for same-sex couples, but were against reforming Mexico City's Civil Code for allowing same-sex marriages, which they considered a right exclusively for heterosexual couples.

Representatives Carlo Pizano, Mariana Gomez del Campo, and Fernando Rodriguez were the PAN's main speakers against the same-sex marriage bill. During the legislative debates, those representatives argued that "marriage is an institution created for protecting the union between a man and a woman and their offspring," linking marriage with reproduction as two inseparable words. PRD legislators supporting the bill, such as Maricela Contreras, a long time feminist legislator who was president of the Gender Equality Committee at the assembly, argued against linking marriages to reproduction, and reminded PAN legislators that some heterosexual couples who are not able to have children are still allowed to marry anywhere in Mexico.

The proposed adoption ban also allowed PAN legislators to criticize the bill. Mariana Gómez del Campo, who was the minority leader at the Assembly, argued that the best interest of the child was to have a home with one father and one mother and that the same-sex marriage bill would deny children of this right. Other PAN legislators at the assembly argued similarly against the marriage bill,[13] even claiming that there were scientific studies proving that children raised by same-sex couples have psychological problems. However, they never introduced a single study as evidence. In addition, Gomez del Campo asked Cesar Nava, the national president of PAN, to fund a public consultation in which PAN asked citizens of Mexico City if they approved same-sex marriages and adoption rights for LGBT people. Gómez del Campo also announced that if the marriage bill were to be approved by the PRD at the Legislative Assembly she would look for twenty-two legislators to promote an action of unconstitutionality at the Supreme Court of Justice.

The Catholic Church also launched attacks on the marriage bill. Cardinal Norberto Rivera, one of Mexico's most influential religious leaders, used his Sunday sermons at Mexico City's Cathedral—located at the Zocalo, just in front of the local assembly in Mexico City's most famous public square—to criticize PRD legislators for "attacking the sacrosanct institution of marriage." Similar statements came from Guadalajara's Cardinal Juan Sandoval Iñiguez, who strongly condemned the marriage bill in Mexico City. Cardinal Sandoval would in fact be the Catholic Church's most visible opponent to the marriage bill during its legislative discussion and after its approval.

Additionally, a group called *Uno + Una = a Matrimonio* (One Man + One Woman = Marriage) started visiting the local assembly to protest the marriage bill. It was never clear who was behind *Uno + Una*. The group launched a website, a Facebook page, and a Twitter account in early December in which they shared some videos from some U.S. conservative organizations, such as The National Organization for Marriage, and a few documents arguing against LGBT parenting.[14] This group was the only organization publicly rallying against marriage equality in Mexico City. Other groups, like ProVida (Mexico's most influential antiabortion NGO), were not present as they were during the period of the *Sociedades de Convivencia* discussion.

The Legislative Assembly finally set December 21, 2009, as the day for voting on the reform to Article 146 of Mexico City's Civil Code, which would allow same-sex couples to legally marry. On that day, several LGBT organizations were present in the Assembly, asking PRD legislators not to change their vote, and to approve the bill without the adoption ban. At the Assembly, PRD had thirty-four legislators; PAN, fifteen; PRI, eight; PT, five; PVEM, three; and PANAL, one, for a total of sixty-six legislators. As mentioned earlier, when it was first presented, all thirty-four PRD legislators, as well as all five PT legislators and three legislators from PRI, promised to vote in favor. The bill needed at least thirty-four votes to be approved, and for Razú and LGBT activists it was critical for its passage that all legislators from PRD voted in favor plus legislators from other political forces.

Lol Kin Castañeda stated, "We wanted to show that the bill was not only supported by a majority of public opinion in Mexico City but also by different political forces besides PRD." Even if the PRD had a majority of legislators and all of them had promised to vote in favor of the bill, activists were present that day to lobby some legislators from PRI to vote in favor and to make sure PRD and PT legislators did not change their vote and also dismiss the adoption ban. PVEM is a party that is closely linked to the PRI, and LGBT activists did not get its support either. PANAL is an ally of the PAN at the federal Congress, but its only representative at the Assembly had promised to vote in favor of the bill as well. That day the vote was divided into two parts. First, legislators had to vote to approve the reform to the Civil Code allowing same-sex marriages, and, second, to vote to keep or withdraw the adoption ban. The final votes where 39 votes in favor of reforming Article 146 of Mexico City's Civil Code allowing same-sex marriages, 20 against it and 5 abstentions. Same-sex marriages were to be legal in the City starting in March 2010. As for the adoption ban, legislator Maricela Contreras asked the Assembly floor to vote to modify the adoption ban on Article 391 of the City's Civil Code. The final vote was: 31 in favor of withdrawing the adoption ban; 22 in favor of keeping the adoption prohibition to same-sex couples; and 9 abstentions. Therefore, Mexico City approved same-sex marriages with full parenting rights on that afternoon before Christmas, but the battle for equality would not stop there.

Immediately after the bill was approved, Mariana Gómez del Campo, the leader of PAN at the Assembly, announced she would seek twenty-two signatures from her fellow legislators to send an action of unconstitutionality against the law to Mexico's Supreme Court. Gómez del Campo had the support of César Nava, the national leader of PAN. Together they would finance a public consultation in Mexico City in the Spring of 2010, and look for the twenty-two signatures needed to send the action of unconstitutionality to the Supreme Court. Gómez del Campo would not be able to get the necessary signatures, opening a new front, this time directly from President Felipe Calderón.

On January 27., 2010, Mexico's attorney general announced that the Department of Justice would challenge the constitutionality of Mexico City's marriage law reform at the Supreme Court. Attorney General Arturo Chávez declared that they believed the law was not legal and that it was not in the best interest of Mexican children. The Supreme Court accepted the Department of Justice's action of unconstitutionality[15] and set summer 2010 for a discussion. Following the Department of Justice's constitutional challenge, the states of Jalisco, Baja California, Guanajuato, Morelos, and Queretaro also sent five different constitutional controversies to the Supreme Court arguing that Mexico City's marriage law would force them to recognize same-sex marriages in their jurisdictions.

A SPRING MARRIAGE AND A COURT BATTLE.

On March 11, 2010, Marcelo Ebrard, mayor of Mexico City, opened the historic *Palacio del Ayuntamiento* (City Hall) for a special occasion. Ebrard would become guest of honor of Mexico's first four same-sex marriages, just a few days after the *Ley Razú* came into effect in Mexico City. Two lesbian couples and two gay male couples[16] were the first to tie the knot in the country, and a fifth lesbian couple would be also married that day. The ceremony was only twenty minutes long, but it would mark a sharp contrast between two leftists leaders in Mexico: unlike Andrés Manuel López Obrador, former mayor of Mexico City, Marcelo Ebrard would personally embrace the public recognition of same-sex couples as a celebration of his progressive agenda in Mexico City, and he would put this issue at the forefront of his presidential campaign agenda in 2011, which he would eventually lose in an internal primary to López Obrador.

Despite the celebration, the Supreme Court was preparing itself for a discussion of the constitutional challenge of Mexico City's same-sex marriage law introduced by the Department of Justice. Legislator David Razú joined Ebrard's legal team and with a group of lawyers from *Centro de Investigación y Docencia Económica* (CIDE), a prestigious public academic institution, which prepared the arguments to defend the constitutionality of the marriage reform against the Federal Department of Justice. In addition, Ombudsgay, a human rights advocacy organization, prepared an *amicus curiae* brief[17] to defend Mexico City's marriage reform as well.

From March to August 2010, opposition to marriage reform and to LGBT parenting grew from legislators from PAN and the Catholic Church. In Guadalajara, Cardinal Juan Sandoval constantly appeared on national media asking the judges of the Supreme Court to declare unconstitutional same-sex marriages and to protect Mexican families. However, LGBT activists started a new strategy as well. Members of *Sociedad Unida* constantly visited the Supreme Court bringing a portfolio of scientific studies that dealt with gay parenting and arguments supporting same-sex marriages. According to Lol Kin Castañeda, "to us it was clear that the legislative battle was over, and that now there was a new open front. We had to lobby the Supreme Court judges, to learn about how to do it, and to rely on the legal team that was working on behalf of the constitutionality of same-sex marriages. We learned a lot as a movement in those days."[18]

In addition, some organizations, like *Sociedad Unida* and *Codise A.C.*, started organizing a communal wedding in Mexico City with couples from different states. This was a strategy aimed at opening judicial battles in other states that did not want to recognize same-sex marriages performed in Mexico City. On March 21, 2010, twenty-nine couples from states like Jalisco, Colima, Nayarit, Nuevo León, Hidalgo, Querétaro travel to Mexico City to formalize their relationships with a communal wedding. Activists from Mexico City had prepared in advance and helped the couples to ask for marriage licenses from the City in early March. Luis Guzmán and Genaro Martínez traveled from Guadalajara, Jalisco, to Mexico City, partly financed by *Codise A.C.*, to get married in that communal wedding. After the celebration, they spent the weekend in the city for their honeymoon and traveled back to Guadalajara to request social security rights. Guzmán went to the *Instituto Mexicano del Seguro Social* (IMSS) to ask for the incorporation of his husband into the system, but was denied those benefits. On April 7, 2010, Guzmán would be the first same-sex couple to sue IMSS for not granting social security to his husband. Other same-sex couples would follow suit. According to Guzmán, "Genaro and I had been together for over 8 years now, marriage was really something we never had thought of, but since it became legal in Mexico City we decided we wanted to do it, especially because I felt I wanted to give Genaro the benefits other straight married colleagues give to their spouses. So we got help from *Codise* and decided to get married in Mexico City, and fight for our rights with other activists and people."[19]

On August 16, the Supreme Court finally discussed same-sex marriages and gay parenting in Mexico City. Groups of activists gathered outside the building that hosts the Supreme Court while inside others gained access to a the session. After a heated discussion, nine judges declared same-sex marriages and adoption by same-sex couples constitutional while only two judges voted against this decision. The Supreme Court also ruled that just like heterosexual marriages held in Mexico City, any same-sex marriage would have to be recognized by other states as valid. The Supreme Court was therefore redefining not only marriage and adoption laws, but also redefining the concept of family in Mexico, opening the possibility that other jurisdictions of Mexico could join Mexico City and legislate to reform local civil codes to liberalize civil marriages.

A day after the Supreme Court decision, Cardinal Juan Sandoval declared that the Supreme Court should be renamed "The Supreme Court of Disappointment," and that the judges of Mexico's Higher Justice Tribunal "were corrupted and bought by the Legislative Assembly of Mexico City and by Mayor Marcelo Ebrard." The cardinal's accusations would open an old debate in Mexico: the separation of church and state. Mayor Ebrard announced that his legal team would sue the cardinal for his declaration, while President Calderón declared he did not agree with the Court's decision but promised that he would respect it.

The Court's decision ended a legal battle for the recognition of same-sex couples in Mexico. However, as of March 2012 same-sex couples who got married in Mexico City have not been able to enjoy social security rights granted to heterosexual couples. Public health institutions like IMSS and *Instituto del Seguro Social al Servicio de los Trabajadores del Estado* (ISSSTE) have denied same-sex married couples recognition of their marriages and have not allowed legally married same-sex couples social security rights. However, LGBT activists throughout all of Mexico have opened judicial battles, taking the LGBT movement in Mexico to a new front and new challenges in the years to come.

CONCLUSION

LGBT rights are now literally out of the closet in Mexican politics. Throughout the country's history, there had never been such a strong will among Mexican politicians to debate LGBT rights. These debates are undoubtedly historical achievements of leaders who saw in the strengthening of electoral democracy in Mexico, in public contestation, and in party competition a perfect combination for opening an opportunity in advancing LGBT rights.

As seen in this chapter, in Mexico City a leftist mayor and a legislative assembly controlled by the same political party were not sufficient conditions to advance in the full recognition of same-sex couples. Nor was it sufficient that Mexico City had a vigorous participation of LGBT organizations, which were supported by an intellectual elite, and mainstream mass media. Advancing LGBT rights was more complicated in Mexico City, a subnational jurisdiction that was more democratic, more open to political contestation and public participation. Ironically, advancing LGBT rights was easier in Coahuila, where politics are still conducted in a more closed, and clientelistic manner, and where a strong network of LGBT organizations was absent. In Coahuila, it was enough to have a political party controlling the political process in the local executive, and legislative branches in order to achieve a rapid, and secure passage of the initiative. Ideology itself cannot be the main variable to explain how this was possible since the PRD, the same party that was ambiguously supporting the passage of *Sociedad de Convivencia* in Mexico City, voted against the passage of *Pacto Civil de Solidaridad* in Coahuila, and then the same party strongly supported same-sex marriages and LGBT adoptions in 2009.

Today, the political climate is now more respectful of sexual orientation. In fact, this is also shown by the fact that for the first time in Mexico's history two of the main candidates to the presidency accepted to have a meeting with a group of LGBT activists, journalists and scholars to discuss their position on LGBT rights. In the summer and fall of 2011, Alberto Tavira, a Mexican journalist, called the presidential candidates and invited them to present their electoral proposals regarding LGBT rights to a small group of people. Josefina Vázquez Mota and Santiago Creel, from PAN; Enrique Peña Nieto and Manlio Fabio Beltrones, from PRI; and Marcelo Ebrard, from PRD, accepted the invitation. All of them were still facing internal primaries from their parties in order to win the nomination. The only candidates that did not accept the invitation were Andrés Manuel López Obrador, from PRD, and Enrique Cordero, from PAN. During those meetings, Ebrard showed full support for LGBT rights. Ebrard promised that if he won his party's nomination and then the presidential election, he would be a president committed to advance same-sex marriages in the country and to fully support LGBT rights. Ebrard reminded all the participants that he had a clear record of supporting LGBT rights in Mexico City. In early 2012, Ebrard lost his party nomination to López Obrador.

As for PAN, Josefina Vázquez Mota, who would become the first woman to win the PAN primary to be a presidential candidate, regretted her party's position on LGBT rights, and promised that if she won the election she would never ask the Department of Justice to write an action of unconstitutionality to challenge a state that decided to advance same-sex marriages. Vázquez Mota also reminded the participants that while she was a federal legislator, she voted in favor of reforming Article 1 of the Mexican Constitution to protect "sexual preferences" against discrimination. Finally, Enrique Peña Nieto, who won the PRI presidential primary (and eventually the general election), also promised that he would respect any state that approved same-sex marriages if elected president. The PRI candidate also promised that he would not interfere with the advancement of LGBT rights in the country. However, he declared that he was not in favor of same-sex couples adopting children, but asked the participants in the meetings to send him information and studies to know about gay parenting.[20]

Undoubtedly, Mexico still has a long journey to guarantee full equality of all its citizens, but the same-sex marriage debate that was opened by Mexico City has profoundly changed the political scenario in the country for years to come, revitalizing a LGBT movement and forcing all major political actors to take a clear position regarding public recognition of same-sex couples. Mexico has fully immersed itself in what seems to be a global trend in ending discrimination and in fully incorporating LGBT people to a more democratic society. As of March 2012, there are different initiatives that aim at public recognition of same-sex couples being debated at local congresses, like Jalisco, Querétaro, Guerrero, and Nuevo León, while a gender identity law has also passed in Mexico City. In the years to come, and after the presidential election of 2012, Mexico will continue to have these debates with public opinion that has moved more in favor of LGBT rights, and with political actors less resistant to support LGBT issues, but also with two states that have passed constitutional amendments banning same-sex marriages. The battles of the following years are clear, and it will require a civil society that is prepared to face old and new challenges.

NOTES

1. Of which 755 are gay couples and 616 are lesbian couples. See (in Spanish) http://www.milenio.com/cdb/doc/noticias2011/0c19fac61a5c196509a8f507beae4ccd.

2. In 2011, over 250,000 people participated in the 37th Annual Gay Pride Parade in Reforma Avenue, Mexico City's most notorious street. Gay pride parades were also celebrated in the cities of Guadalajara, Veracruz, and, for the first time, in Monterrey and Guadalajara.

3. The Epistle praises the legal union between a man and a woman as the only moral means to found a family and "conserve the species." The Epistle also asks women to vow not to "exasperate their husbands," and to treat them with the reverence due to the person who supports and defends them. In 2006, Congress asked judges to stop reading the Epistle, but the practice is still being exercised throughout the country.

4. *Encuesta Nacional de Discriminaci ón* 2010, ENADIS. Full study available at http://www.conapred.org.mx/redes/userfiles/files/Enadis-2010-DS-Accss-001.pdf.

5. The complete results of the 2007 Mitofsky poll can be accessed in Spanish in the following link: http://www.consulta.com.mx/interiores/99_pdfs/12_mexicanos_pdf/NA20070201_HomosexualidadMx.pdf, while the complete results of the 2010 CONAPRED poll can be accessed at: http://www.conapred.org.mx/redes/userfiles/files/Enadis-2010-DS-Accss-001.pdf.

6. Consuta Mitofsky. *Mitos y Preconcepciones sobre la Homosexualidad. ConsultaNacional en Viviendas.*January, 2007. México, D.F: 12.

7. Mario Pecheny, "Sociability, Secrets, and Identities: Key Issues in Sexual Politics in Latin America," in *The Politics of Sexuality in Latin America: A Reader on Lesbian, Gay, Bisexual, and Transgender Rights,* Javier Corrales and Mario Pecheny, eds. (Pittsburgh: University of Pittsburgh Press, 2010), 102–121: 102.

8. See the report at http://mexico.cnn.com/entretenimiento/2010/02/02/la-constitucion-solo-reconoce-bodas-entre-hombres-y-mujeres-calderon.

9. Conversation with David Razú in Mexico City, March 2012.

10. Interview with David Razú in Mexico City, March 2012.

11. The author contacted Uranga in different occasions in March 2012 for an interview for this chapter, but the interview was never possible. For one of Uranga's interviews on TV, see http://youtu.be/Wtgveh-DGyM.

12. Interview with Lol Kin Castañeda in Mexico City, March 2012.

13. To see some of the arguments against same-sex marriages used by different members of the PAN see: http://www.fundacionpreciado.org.mx/biencomun/bc182/Bc182.pdf.

14. To see the *Uno + Una* Facebook page, visit: http://www.facebook.com/unomasuna. To see some of the videos they used, see: http://www.youtube.com/watch?feature=player_embedded&v=uznqSiQmqHo. Their website is not online anymore.

15. To access the Department of Justice action of unconstitutionality, see: http://www.scribd.com/doc/29879091/Accion-de-inconstitucionalidad-de-la-PGR-vs-matrimonio-entre-personas-del-mismo-sexo-Mexico.

16. Lol Kin Castañeda and Judith Vázquez; Ema Villanueva and Janice Alva, accompanied by their daugher; Jaime López Vela and David González; Temístocles Villanueva and Daniel Ramos were the first four couples to be legally married in that ceremony. Jesusa Rodríguez and Liliana Felipe were married a few hours after.

17. To access Ombudsgay amicus curiae, see: http://www.scribd.com/doc/39957802/AMICUS-CURIAE-DE-OMBUDSGAY-A-FAVOR-DE-MATRIMONIO-GAY-EN-DF.

18. Interview with Lol Kin Castañeda in Mexico City, March 2012.

19. Interview with Luis Guzmán in March 2012. As of March 2012, Luis has not been able to register his husband to IMSS, Mexico's biggest public health system because the trial has not ended.

20. The author was present in the discussions held with Josefina Vázquez Mota and with Enrique Peña Nieto in 2011 in Mexico City.

Index

activists: in Chile, 17; in Paraguay, 17. *See also* LGBT movements; *specific activists*

Adler, Emanuel, 4

adoption: by Civil Partnership, 94; LGBT movement on, 147; in Uruguay, 94, 106, 109n38

Affirmative Union, 64

age, 44

agenda. *See* government agenda

AHMNP. *See Asociación Hombres y Mujeres Nuevos de Panamá*

ALITT. *See Asociación Luchapor la Identidad Travesti-Transexual*

American Convention of Human Rights, 8, 9

American Public Opinion Project (LAPOP), 42

Americas, same-sex marriage across, 56

amparo: description of, 13, 20n39, 59, 148n2; same-sex marriage relating to, 137–140

Argentina: ALITT, 135; *amparo* in, 13, 20n39, 59, 137–140, 148n2; Buenos Aires, 3, 6, 12, 132; Catholic Church in, 14, 59; civil union law in, 3, 6, 12–13, 133–134; constitution in, 131; cultural changes in, 12; Egalitarian Marriage Law, 142–144; egalitarian marriage reform in, 140–144; FALGBT, 13; family in, 137, 141; FPV in, 30; human rights in, 10; judicialization in, 58–60; lawsuits in, 135, 138; LGBT mobilization and organization, 132–134; LGBT mobilization strategy, 134–140, 144, 146; LGBT movements in, 30; LGBT rights in, 132; national civil union law in, 13; national same-sex

marriage law in, 3; Our World Group, 132; party affiliation in, 136; public opinion in, 35; reform in, 131; religion in, 59; same-sex marriage law in, 13–14, 34, 36, 58–60, 137–144; same-sex policies in, 11–13; subnational civil unions in, 12–13. *See also Comunidad Homosexual Argentina*

Asociación Hombres y Mujeres Nuevos de Panamá (AHMNP): on discrimination, 83; formation of, 81; initiatives of, 82; mission of, 81; on public policy, 82; representation of, 82

Asociación Luchapor la Identidad Travesti-Transexual (ALITT), 135

atheist beliefs, 42

Augsburger, Silvia, 140–141

autonomy model: in Colombia, 119–122; description of, 119; on equality, 121; gender relating to, 120; weaknesses of, 120–122

Babb, Florence, 25

Bachelet, Michelle, 30

Batllism tradition, 104

Belgium, 6

bill writing, 93–95

Bolivia, 10

Brazil: civil union law in, 15; cohabitation rights in, 15; human rights in, 10; judicialization in, 60–61; LGBT movements in, 30; PT in, 30; same-sex marriage in, 60–61; STF in, 60–61

Broad Front. *See Frente Amplio*

Buenos Aires: civil union law in, 3, 6, 12; Our World Group, 132

Burstein, Paul, 75

About the Contributors

Maria Gracia Andía is professor of law at Universidad de San Andrés in Argentina. She is an associate researcher at the Center for the Implementation of Public Policies Promoting Equity and Growth (CIPPEC) and a member of the Institute of Social Sciences Methodology at the National Academy of Moral and Political Sciences in Argentina. She has advised local governments, legislators, and international organizations on legal and institutional issues. She received a law degree from Universidad de Mendoza in Argentina, and was a visiting researcher at Columbia University in New York City. She holds a PhD in law, policy, and society from Northeastern University in Boston, Massachusetts.

Daniel Bonilla is the Distinguished Leitner Center Visiting Professor at Fordham Law School and is Associate Professor and Co-director of the Public Interest Law Group at University of the Andes, Bogotá, Colombia. He graduated with a law degree from Universidad of the Andes and earned his master's and doctorate in law at Yale University.

Margarita Corral is a doctoral candidate in Political Science in the Department of Political Science at Vanderbilt University. She works as a research assistant for the Latin American Public Opinion Project (LAPOP). Margarita holds an MS in Latin American studies from the University of Salamanca. Her interests are political representation in Latin America, democratization, and public opinion.

Germán Lodola is assistant professor of political science at Universidad Torcuato Di Tella, associate researcher at the National Council of Scientific and Technical Research (CONICET), and holds a PhD from the University of Pittsburgh. He is the author of numerous articles on comparative political economy, subnational politics, and social protests in Latin America. He has also published, with Mitchell Seligson, a book-length analysis of public opinion attitudes in Argentina.

Genaro Lozano is a doctoral candidate in political science at The New School for Social Research, teaches at the Instituto Tecnológico Autónomo de México, and is managing editor of *Foreign Affairs Latinoamerica*.

175

Adriana Piatti-Crocker is associate professor at the University of Illinois Springfield and is a comparative politics scholar on Latin America and gender and politics. Piatti-Crocker edited a book on diffusion of gender quotas in Latin America and coedited *Same-Sex Marriage in the Americas: Policy Innovation for Same-Sex Relationships*. She has published several articles and case studies on gender quotas in Argentina, Latin America, and Afghanistan, and more recently has focused on veil bans in Turkey and Western Europe.

Jason Pierceson is associate professor of political science and legal studies at the University of Illinois Springfield. His research interests include public law, political theory, and the politics of sexuality. He is the author or coauthor of several books on same-sex marriage, including *Same-Sex Marriage in the Americas: Policy Innovation for Same-Sex Relationships* and *Courts, Liberalism and Rights: Gay Law and Politics in the United States and Canada*.

Shawn Schulenberg is assistant professor and director of graduate studies in the department of political science at Marshall University. His research centers around issues of sexuality and politics in Latin America, where he has written extensively on lesbian/gay/bisexual/transgender (LGBT) movements in Argentina, Brazil, and Panama. He is coeditor of and contributor to *Same-Sex Marriage in the Americas: Policy Innovation for Same-Sex Relationships*, and has also published in the *Journal of Human Rights*.

Diego Sempol is a doctoral candidate in social sciences at Universidad Nacional de General Sarmiento and Instituto de Desarrollo Económico y Social (UNGS-IDES). He is also assistant professor and researcher at the Institute of Political Science, School of Social Sciences, University of the Republic of Uruguay, and member of the National System of Researchers.